Holocaust Literature of
the Second Generation

Holocaust Literature of the Second Generation

Marita Grimwood

palgrave
macmillan

HOLOCAUST LITERATURE OF THE SECOND GENERATION
Copyright © Marita Grimwood, 2007.

First published in 2007 by
PALGRAVE MACMILLAN™
175 Fifth Avenue, New York, N.Y. 10010 and
Houndmills, Basingstoke, Hampshire, England RG21 6XS.
Companies and representatives throughout the world.

PALGRAVE MACMILLAN is the global academic imprint of the Palgrave Macmillan division of St. Martin's Press, LLC and of Palgrave Macmillan Ltd.
Macmillan® is a registered trademark in the United States, United Kingdom and other countries. Palgrave is a registered trademark in the European Union and other countries.

ISBN-13: 978-1-4039-7980-3
ISBN-10: 1-4039-7980-4

Library of Congress Cataloging-in-Publication Data
Grimwood, Marita.
  Holocaust literature of the second generation / by Marita Grimwood.
     p. cm.
  Includes bibliographical references and index.
  ISBN 1-4039-7980-4 (alk. paper)
  1. Holocaust, Jewish (1939–1945), in literature. 2. Children of Holocaust survivors, Writings of—History and criticism. 3. Holocaust, Jewish (1939–1945)—Psychological aspects. 4. Holocaust, Jewish (1939–1945)—Influence. 5. Holocaust survivors—Biography—History and criticism. 6. Children of Holocaust survivors—Biography—History and criticism. I. Title.
  PN56.H55G75 2007
  809'.93358—dc22

                                    2007061158

A catalogue record of the book is available from the British Library.

Design by Scribe Inc.

First edition: July 2007

10 9 8 7 6 5 4 3 2 1

Printed in the United States of America.

For Jonathan and for Jacob

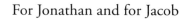

Table of Contents

Acknowledgments

Most of the work on this book was conducted in the School of English Literature, Language, and Linguistics at Newcastle University. It would not have been written without the guidance and encouragement of Linda Anderson and John Beck. Other colleagues assisted and supported me in the course of this project: I owe particular thanks to Anne Whitehead.

Thanks are due to Sue Vice, as well as to Nicola King and an anonymous reader at Palgrave Macmillan for their thoughtful and constructive comments on the manuscript.

I am grateful for grants from the former Arts and Humanities Research Board and the University of Newcastle, which enabled this book to be written.

Part of Chapter 5 and short sections of the introduction appeared as "Postmemorial Positions: Reading and Writing After the Holocaust in Anne Michaels' *Fugitive Pieces*" in *Canadian Jewish Studies / Etudes Juives Canadiennes* 11. I am grateful to the editors of that periodical for allowing that material to be reprinted here.

Thanks to my colleagues at conferences and elsewhere whose enthusiasm and discussions have contributed to the development of this project. A number of people in Durham deserve a mention for their friendship and support. Particular thanks to members of the quiz team, past and present.

My family has been a constant source of support: thanks to Roy, Joan and Sally, and to the late W. J. le Vaul-Grimwood.

Roy, Joan, Jim, and Gwyn helped generously with childcare in the final stages of manuscript preparation. Grateful thanks, too, to Jacob Matthew Grimwood-Long for his enthusiastic acceptance of these arrangements.

Finally, a very big thank you to Jonathan Long.

INTRODUCTION

Holocaust Writing of the Second Generation

If one were to pinpoint the moment that children of Holocaust survivors, the "second generation," found widespread visibility in the United States, it would be the 1979 publication of Helen Epstein's *Children of the Holocaust: Conversations with Sons and Daughters of Survivors.* Still in print nearly thirty years later, this groundbreaking collection of interviews and autobiographical reflections by the author brings the experiences of children of survivors out of the realm of clinical professionals and into the public domain. Epstein's book explores how her parents' experiences affected her and also uncovers the perspectives of other children of survivors. As the first book of its kind, it also sets out to inform the general public about the experiences of survivors in the aftermath of the war, and to survey, often critically, the clinical studies that were made of them and their children.

From this point on, the output of fictional and autobiographical texts by children of survivors burgeoned. It is an indication of this massive surge in literary production that Alan L. Berger published the first survey of second-generation texts in 1997. *Children of Job: American Second-Generation Witnesses to the Holocaust* discusses a range of novels, short stories, documentaries and docudramas. It looks at the work of writers including Thomas Friedmann, Barbara Finkelstein, Art Spiegelman, Melvin Jules Bukiet, Thane Rosenbaum, Carol Ascher, Julie Salamon, and Lev Raphael and serves as an indication of just how many second-generation texts had found their way into print by the late 1990s. Berger's survey represents the first real attempt at second-generation canon formation.

This process continued the following year with Efraim Sicher's edited collection *Breaking Crystal: Writing and Memory After Auschwitz* (1998). Sicher's book is an edited collection of critical essays from both Israel and the Diaspora. Unlike Berger, who focuses exclusively on children of survivors, Sicher starts with "the broadest possible view of the 'second generation,' following George Steiner's self-definition as 'a kind of survivor.'" (Steiner writes as a postwar Jew, but not a child of survivors.) For Sicher, this approach makes sense as "the phenomenon of the Holocaust is a nagging absence in the personal history of those who were not there and a 'trace' in public memory."[1] In the twenty-first century, two anthologies have served to update and continue the process of canon formation. Alan and Naomi Berger's *Second Generation Voices: Reflections by Children of Holocaust Survivors and Perpetrators* (2001) has thematically grouped contributions by writers, clinicians, and others with a strong interest in the second generation as children of either survivors or perpetrators. Melvin Jules Bukiet's *Nothing Makes You Free* (2002) is subtitled *Writing by Descendants of Jewish Holocaust Survivors*, thereby limiting the book's scope to survivor families whilst encompassing a broader range of family relationships than the term "second generation" has most often been taken to imply.

It is also notable that, with the exception of Berger's *Children of Job*, these works do not limit themselves to considering texts of a given nationality. Second-generation writing is by its nature an international field. While not wishing to elide the cultural specificities of immigrant experiences and memorial traditions, it is clear that in this case drawing rigid boundaries between national literatures is both arbitrary and limiting. Owing to the nature of postwar migration, even pinning a given writer down to a single country can be difficult. Thus, while most of the texts discussed at length in this volume were produced in the United States, I have frequently drawn on material from elsewhere.

Throughout the 1980s and 1990s and up to the time of writing, there has been a steady academic interest in the second generation, whether defined in its narrow or broader sense. However, the study of Holocaust memory has tended to concern itself overwhelmingly with public and mass manifestations of cultural memory, many of which have become canonical in this discourse. Notably, museums including the United States Holocaust Memorial Museum, memorials, stage and film adaptations of Anne Frank's *Diary of a Young Girl*, Spielberg's film *Schindler's List*, Claude Lanzmann's *Shoah*, and Holocaust memory's commodification in all of these forms have become touchstones in discussions of how the Holocaust is represented and remembered. These discussions have often been fascinating and highly productive.[2]

Second-generation writing, however, and what it has to say about the Holocaust's continued impact at the level of the individual, has been less closely examined. With the exception of Art Spiegelman's *Maus* books, which have become canonical in both literary and cultural studies of Holocaust memory, the vast body of works by the second generation has remained marginal to debates. On one level, this is symptomatic of a gendered field of study, where studies of public and mass culture by male academics have come to occupy a central place.[3] Yet even in this context, the impact of second-generation experience demands urgent examination. The scale of the familial dimension to North American Holocaust memory has escaped extensive analysis despite the tendency of writers of all kinds—historians, novelists, anthologists—to devote space to declaring a personal connection to their Holocaust-related subject matter. A search of library shelves suggests that, among those writers of fiction and nonfiction whose subject is the Holocaust, more have a personal connection to it than not. Many articles and book chapters have been written about particular second-generation texts, often by academics who themselves share a second-generation identity. Yet rarely have these studies been brought together to interrogate key issues and wider questions.

In addressing this imbalance, this book addresses writing that, I argue, does not *represent* the Holocaust so much as respond to its ongoing effects in the present. The works discussed here are by writers who make no claim to firsthand experience of that period. Instead, it is the very absence of this experience that is often an uncanny presence in their writing. And it is the *literary* manifestations of this presence, the representation of historical events' continuing aftereffects, that form the focus of this book.

My concern is with writers whose subject is a pressing, often familial link or concern with the Holocaust. In line with Sicher, I take a broad view of the second generation, in which the exact nature of this link varies from writer to writer. Some have parents who were in concentration camps, while others are painfully aware of the fate of more distant family members who failed to escape. For others again, it is a more general sense of how the events of the Holocaust have shaped the consciousness of later generations and communities that forms the focus of their work. Many are children or grandchildren of survivors, while still others have grown up in close proximity to survivors.

Many of the earliest of these writers are also second-generation immigrants, being the first of their families to be born in the new country, and as such, they share the dual cultural perspective common to many second-generation immigrant communities. Thus, this book uses the term "second generation" as a point of departure, finding exploring the boundaries of the term to be a more fruitful approach to literary studies than focusing narrowly within it—a standpoint I will explore later in this chapter. However, my discussions will at times inevitably be affected by the pre-existing emphasis on children of survivors.

My work stands at the intersection of two discourses. The first of these, which has encompassed discussions of Holocaust representation as well as the Holocaust's legacy of trauma, is a psychoanalytic and psychiatric discourse growing out of clinical trauma studies. The second discourse is rooted in criticism of literature, art, and film, and is consequently concerned with the creative output of the second generation and others on the subject of the Holocaust. With Marianne Hirsch's concept of "postmemory" at its heart, this discourse, as much as its clinically based counterpart, is concerned with describing the nature of second-generation memory.

I will begin by addressing some questions of terminology. I will then go on to discuss some features which are particularly significant in writing that thematize the intergenerational dimension of Holocaust memory. Finally, I will engage in close textual readings of autobiographies and novels from different (sub)genres. Chapter 1 looks at Helen Epstein's *Children of the Holocaust: Conversations with Sons and Daughters of Survivors* as documentary memoir. Chapter 2 discusses Louise Kehoe's family memoir *In This Dark House*. Chapter 3 examines Art Spiegelman's *Maus: A Survivor's Tale* as a graphic auto/biography, with particular attention to the relationship between the visual and the written aspects of the text, and how this reflects the author's relationship with his father. Chapter 4 considers Joseph Skibell's *A Blessing on the Moon* as a fantasy novel, which draws on fairy tales and other sources to imagine the author's murdered great-grandfather haunting a fantastic Polish landscape. Finally, Chapter 5 addresses the issues raised by Anne Michaels's use of highly aestheticized prose in her poetic novel *Fugitive Pieces*. The texts under consideration become less directly representational toward the end of the book, and their authors' relationships to the Holocaust less proximate.

Defining Survivors and the Second Generation

As I have already implied, what sounds like a narrow and well-defined field is rife with complications, and the difficulties in delimiting it begin with the term "survivor." In her book *The War After*, Anne Karpf summarizes the essentials of the debate surrounding this word. Is it appropriate, she asks, that "a refugee from Nazi Germany be bracketed with a Holocaust survivor?"[4] Both groups were victims of the same historical events, yet it may be argued that "Hitler's Final Solution was unprecedented, and living in a concentration camp or in hiding, being daily exposed to the dangers of death was an incomparable experience."[5] She notes that even survivors' support agencies fail to agree on a simple definition, as "one [. . .] includes in its target group any Jew who emigrated from Germany after 1933, while membership of the Holocaust Survivors' Centre in London is open to anyone who came to Britain after Kristallnacht in 1938."[6] Nor is it easy to make a psychological distinction:

Similar psychological effects—survivor guilt, feelings of helplessness—have been detected in those who left Nazi occupied countries between 1935 and 1939 as in those who remained. They shared the experience of losing their homeland and mother tongue, but living under total terror, it's been suggested, was particular to survivors.[7]

Of course, it is important to acknowledge the wide variation in people's experiences. However, such discussions can, as Karpf highlights, carry "an unpleasant whiff of competition for victimhood."[8] The "hierarchy of suffering," and policing of victim "status" implicit in this debate are certainly uncomfortable. Yet one need look no further than the now notorious case of Binjamin Wilkomirski to know that (Holocaust) victimhood in the late twentieth or early twenty-first century carries a certain desirability, and to understand why the matter of definition is so important.[9] Partly as a result, academic debate on the subject of defining "the survivor" continues energetically.[10]

This debate, just like the traumas or memories associated with the Holocaust, has been passed to the next generation in a new form. If definitions of survivorhood are contested, then definitions of the second generation will inevitably be contested as well. Consider the following passage, taken from Melvin Jules Bukiet's editorial introduction to *Nothing Makes You Free: Writings by Descendants of Jewish Holocaust Survivors*. In the first place, he writes, the term "second generation" has become outdated as further generations have appeared. In addition,

a thornier question has to do with one's date of birth. Imagine a writer born on May 7, 1945, the day before World War II officially ended in Europe. Not that so many women were pregnant in the winter of 1944, but imagine one. Is that hypothetical child a survivor or a child of survivors? Strictly speaking, he or she would be both, but the essence of this book is to explore the inherited rather than the experienced. (26–27)

Exploring the inherited is my concern too, but the "thorny questions" do not end there. Children whose parents sent them to safety abroad, and then became Nazi victims themselves, may be plausibly defined as either refugees or survivors depending on the criteria being used, such as the date of their leaving Europe. Yet in terms of their relationship to the war years, and how they might choose to write about that time, such children might conceivably have more in common with the group known as children of survivors.

In the case of defining survivors, anxiety centers on the fact that one term may cover a range of vastly differing experiences, as even having been "in the camps" does not denote a single kind of experience or "degree" of traumatization. With the second generation, the opposite may be seen as a "problem" in the quest for a clear definition. For young children, loss of, or separation from, their parents is commonly their greatest fear. The precise political circumstances of its happening, assuming children are not witnesses to violence, may in many cases be irrelevant, suggesting that here a difference of terminology (survivor or refugee) can mask similarity of experience. The term "children of victims" might be more appropriate. After all, it is not only those who died that were victims, and the use of the term in Holocaust studies as opposed to "survivor" brings with it a raft of implicit assumptions. Distinguishing clearly between "victim" and "survivor" is questionable in circumstances where death and survival were such matters of chance, and where the fates of close family members could differ so widely. Surviving after great suffering, and in the knowledge of the suffering and deaths of others in your family, is one kind of Holocaust victimhood. Lawrence Langer posits "survival" and "atrocity" as better terms than "life" and "death" with which to think about the Holocaust, as the former two terms are more concerned with the past than the future. He also points out that any discourse which celebrates survivors in an uplifting manner implies an opposing discourse for those who were not so lucky.[11]

From a literary perspective, however, what matters most is not whether the nature of the traumas experienced fit particular historical or psychological categories, but whether and how the experience is written. For the purposes of this book, choosing to concentrate only on writers who fulfill a particular variant of the criteria described above seems arbitrary and unproductive. As I have mentioned, Alan L. Berger has already published a thorough survey of the field of American second-generation fiction and film and it is not my intention to reiterate all or part of his project. Instead, I have chosen to compile a corpus of texts in which writers born after the Holocaust actively explore fictional or autobiographical family relationships to it. Therefore, while I dismissed works by Kindertransport children, child survivors, and child refugees from my inquiries, by making chronological distance from the event the key criterion, I was able to choose from works by their descendants, as well as from the children of those who survived the camps. Thus, Helen Epstein and Art Spiegelman are the children of camp survivors. Louise Kehoe writes that her grandparents died in Auschwitz, though it would perhaps be simplistic to call her father a refugee. Moving to more distant connections, Joseph Skibell is the grandson of one who "escaped."[12] Finally, Anne Michaels' father and his family left the border of Poland and Russia in 1931, when he was thirteen, although Michaels, born in 1958, cites growing up amongst European immigrants in post-war Toronto as the key to her interest in the subject.[13] Of course, there are still further, unavoidable problems inherent in making such a selection. In the introduction to his edited collection, Melvin Jules Bukiet wonders the following: "Is it possible that there is a Second Generation Wilkomirski in the table of contents? Yes."[14] In this sense, a writer like Anne Michaels who insists carefully that her novel is not autobiographical, is also removing herself in advance from debates that hinge on questions of definitions and "authenticity," and is consequently far less potentially problematic than—say—Bukiet, whose second-generation identity is at the forefront of his own presentation of his work.[15] My gauge of these writers' "authenticity" or value for my own project is, therefore, based partly on textual evidence, and partly on their own declared family circumstances and motivations for writing.

The Intergenerational Transmission of Trauma

What *are* these writers' connections with the past? Are such connections simply forged through imaginative investment and/or cultural conditioning, or might some of them be victims of a kind of secondary trauma? Post Traumatic Stress Disorder (PTSD) has been defined as

> a response, sometimes delayed, to an overwhelming event or events, which takes the form of repeated, intrusive hallucinations, dreams, thoughts or behaviors stemming from the event, along with numbing that may have begun during or after the experience, and possibly also increased arousal to (and avoidance of) stimuli recalling the event. This simple definition belies a very peculiar fact: the pathology cannot be defined either by the event itself—which may or may not be catastrophic, and may not traumatize everyone equally— nor can it be defined in terms of a *distortion* of the event, achieving its haunting power as a result of distorting personal significances attached to it. The pathology consists, rather, solely in the *structure of its experience* or reception: the event is not assimilated or experienced fully at the time, but only belatedly, in its repeated *possession* of the one who experiences it.[16]

The key points about trauma, as theorist Cathy Caruth describes it here, are the inability of the traumatized person to *experience* it except in its belated manifestations (such as nightmares and flashbacks), and trauma's very unlocatability in a particular event. Furthermore, the American Psychiatric Association's "category A" definition of PTSD is "a response to an event 'outside the range of usual human experience'"—a formulation that comes with its own problems.[17] The recovery of trauma victims is marked by their ability to narrate what has hitherto been an unmediated return, resisting further conceptualization. Yet in bearing witness to the event and being cured of the traumatic symptom, that event must be "transformed. . . into a narrative memory that allows the story to be verbalized and communicated, to be integrated into one's own, and others', knowledge of the past," even though the resulting narrative will necessarily alter the event's remembered nature.[18] Its undecidability points to both a difficulty and an openness when it comes to determining whether the children, and other descendants, of Holocaust survivors can be said to be traumatized. If they are, what is the nature of that trauma?

The term "intergenerational transmission of trauma" has at least two meanings that run concurrently through contemporary academic discourse. Ruth Leys, in her pointed critique of Caruth's reading of *Moses and Monotheism*, which she undertakes in *Trauma: A Genealogy*, bases her definition of the term on an article by Walter Benn Michaels in which he discusses the cultural construction of historical trauma (particularly the Holocaust for Jews) as a component of national identity.[19] "In racial antiessentialism," Michaels writes, "the effort to imagine an identity that will connect people through history is replaced by the effort to imagine a history that will give people an identity."[20] This "transmission" is cultural in nature, and individual experience in the present seems to have little to do with it. On the other hand, there is a concept of intergenerational transmission that, if not always construed biologically, is nonetheless familial in nature, whereby, for example, a parent or grandparent has experienced a trauma firsthand. It is primarily this interpretation of the term that I shall explore here. Children growing up with relatives who have direct experience of, say, the Holocaust might themselves present symptoms which are in some way symptoms of trauma. The recent proliferation of autobiographical and fictional works by the children of Holocaust survivors suggests that, in Alan L. Berger's words, these children "[have inherited] the Holocaust as an irreducible part of their Jewish self-identity" despite the fact that they were born after it occurred, a formulation which could be read as encompassing both of the above definitions of "intergenerational transmission."[21] In their works, children of survivors tend to address the issue of growing up with the profound sense that their parents' experiences are inescapable and somehow their own.

In "Parting Words: Trauma, Silence and Survival," Cathy Caruth asks, "What is the nature of a life that continues beyond trauma?" (11). For the child of survivors, the bearer of a life born out of such continuation, the question is pertinent. Reflecting Carolyn Steedman's assertion in her own intergenerational family memoir *Landscape for a Good Woman* that "children are always episodes in someone else's narrative," the child of survivors stands as her parents' assertion of life in direct opposition to their experiences of death.[22] That this opposition is either consciously or unconsciously performative as well as symbolic is implicit in the exceptionally high birth rate among survivors almost immediately after their liberation: many of their children, such as the Canadian writer J. J. Steinfeld, were born in Displaced Persons camps[23] where, according to Alan Berger, "the birth rate. . . was the highest of any Jewish community in the world."[24]

Such statistics confirm the status of children of survivors as part of their parents' reintegration into everyday life; yet as Dina Wardi in particular has argued, children may at the same time be explicitly conceived and conceived of as memorials to people from the past, "not perceived as separate individuals but as symbols of everything the parents had lost in the course of their lives."[25] Her central thesis is that a particular child is designated the family's "memorial candle," and that there is a special parental investment in that child's relationship to the past. Often, children born in 1946, "around the time of the most traumatic period in the lives of their mothers and fathers" are the "memorial candles." Such children are frequently given multiple family names, representing more than one beloved family member who had died. Wardi continues as follows:

> Other factors often influenced this choice, among them physical resemblance to specific objects that had perished and the child's being of the same sex as an important figure that had perished. According to Heller (1982), the survivors tended to choose girls more often than boys for the role of "memorial candles," perhaps because the *halacha* prescribes that it is the mother's religion rather than the father's that determines the religion of the child, and so a daughter with the role of "memorial" candle can serve as a factor preserving the family Jewishness as well. But this is not the only reason—another reason is that in Jewish families the role of taking care of emotional problems within the family is generally a feminine role.[26]

This may go some way towards explaining why such a high proportion of contemporary Jewish family memoirists are women. Wardi reports that "when the inner life of each family member and the interpersonal interactions between them are joined together and interwoven within the ego, a synthesis of feelings and internalized representations of the totality of family representations is created." This may extend to a complete undifferentiation of ego within the family.[27] Furthermore, she reports that "some of the survivors still do not believe that they have really remained alive" and this is transmitted to the children.[28] In the "memorialization" process, children may thus be encouraged to identify not only with dead family members, but with living ones who would appear to illustrate Caruth's point that "the trauma is not only the repetition of the missed encounter with death, but the missed encounter with one's own survival."[29]

Yet despite possible attempts to orient them towards the past, children are irrefutable evidence of their parents' ungrasped and ungraspable survival, showing that they have not merely survived beyond trauma but have carried it, or part of it, into a new life. This in turn has further implications. As Caruth speculates,

> described in terms of a possession by the past that is not entirely one's own, trauma already describes the individual experience as something that exceeds itself, that brings within individual experience as its most intense sense of isolation the very breaking of individual knowledge and mastery of events. This notion of trauma also acknowledges that perhaps it is not possible for the witnessing of the trauma to occur within the individual at all, that it may only be in future generations that "cure" or at least witnessing can take place.[30]

According to this understanding of trauma, the child of survivors' role vis-à-vis her parents may (once more) be not merely *symbolic* of continuation, regeneration, or memory and mourning, but *instrumental* in the traumatic process itself. James Herzog states that "experience with. . . survivor-parents lends strong presumptive evidence to the notion that unbound, unintegrated, and unshared trauma is most likely to overflow. The very acts of caretaking, as well as the affective climate, then become the medium for the message."[31] The child may thus become a site of the parents' psychopathological excess: in the context of the lack of ego-differentiation described by Wardi, the parents may see their children as extensions of themselves; and as such they become spaces for the working-through or the witnessing of their trauma. Children of survivors, in the light of such theories, are rendered passively subject to their parents' pathologies: secondhand symptoms, Wardi, Caruth and Herzog imply, may be an inevitable result of firsthand trauma.

In keeping with the work of Wardi and others, Rowland-Klein and Dunlop's work formulates transmission of trauma as explicitly dependent on "an object relations framework which emphasizes the interactional relationship between parent and child."[32] They cite a number of earlier studies in support of their thesis, proposing that

> survivor parents enter a process of self-healing and unconsciously use their children as a means of psychic recovery through a means of projective identification, whereby the parent splits off the unwanted part of the self, which is then projected into the child, and internalized in it. The child then starts to think, feel and act in accordance with the projection.[33]

Consequently, "there is pervasive anxiety despite few objective dangers in their present lives."[34] The children are psychologically prepared for a life filled with dangers that they will never, in reality, have to face. Many children of survivors find themselves mentally equipped to face extreme situations even though they have no external reason to suppose that such events will ever occur; they are protecting bodies that are not their own. Living in anticipation of trauma, their lives function as a repetition of their parents' encounter with death, even as the children's very lives serve to move beyond such an encounter.

In the light of such theories of inherited trauma, it is tempting to consider the fact that many children of survivors use their "autobiographies" to tell their parents' stories alongside, or intertwined with, their own as evidence of blurred ego boundaries. The extensive use of this autobiographical strategy in second-generation writing leads to the question of how far narrative structures might be replicating psychological structures.[35] In keeping with Caruth's statement above, which posits later generations as participants in the process of "working-through" the original trauma, Esther Faye argues

> that we should not confine our understanding of this second generation's storytelling to the notion of "representation," be that artistic or literary, with its implication of necessary failure to give meaning to the memory-traces left by the Shoah. For within the "fictions" of representation produced in the oral and written testimonies of the second generation, a kernel of "real" and unassimilated "deep memory" sometimes makes its appearance.[36]

Citing a clinical example of a young woman whose feelings about her mother's experiences are displaced onto a strict veganism and empathy with animals, Faye argues that the second generation can be subject to traumatic symptoms. Just as survivors necessarily lived their traumas indirectly, unable to assimilate the experience at the time, so their children, rather than merely (re-) representing their parents' lives in their psychological and literary responses, are dealing with a part of this trauma that, although occurring before their lifetime and therefore doubly indirect, is nonetheless trauma itself rather than simple representation.[37]

Perhaps most suggestive of all in this area of thought is the concept, developed by Nicolas Abraham and Maria Torok, of the transgenerational phantom: a passing on of "family secrets" of which neither parent nor child is consciously aware. Abraham and Torok's theory is at the opposite extreme to the "transmission" of identity politics described by Walter Benn Michaels. It is a pathological, psychoanalytic perspective on transmission, whereby children may, unknown to themselves, be carriers of "a secret buried alive in the father's unconscious."[38] For this reason, it cannot *simply* be part of wider questions of identity politics. The phantom manifests itself in actions of the child by "obstructing [his or her] perception of words as implicitly referring to their unconscious portion" and "referring to the unspeakable." Abraham gives the following example:

> At best, phantom words of this kind can be invested with libido and determine the choice of hobbies, leisure activities, or professional pursuits. One carrier of a phantom became a nature lover on weekends, acting out the fate of his mother's beloved. The loved one had been denounced by the grandmother (an unspeakable and secret fact) and, having been sent to "break rocks" [*casser les cailloux* = do forced labour—*Trans*.], he later died in the gas chamber. What does our man do on weekends? A lover of geology, he "breaks rocks," catches butterflies, and proceeds to kill them in a can of cyanide.[39]

Like the trauma symptom, the words "breaking rocks" both "point to a gap [and] refer to the unspeakable." Where a child is aware that the parent is a Holocaust survivor, such a mechanism could apply to a particular aspect of that parent's experience, such as a shameful act of collaboration, or a mother's being forced into prostitution. The necessity of repression lies in the child's "horror of transgression," which "is compounded by the risk of undermining the fictitious yet necessary integrity of the parental figure in question": the phantom is the result of maintaining a family romance at all costs.[40] In the case of a child who is not aware of the Holocaust's relevance to his or her family history, the existence of such a psychic mechanism might go some way to explain the sense of relief felt by adults learning of their Jewishness for the first time,[41] and the phenomenon reported by Barbara Kessel whereby a number of her interviewees had apparently converted to Judaism before unexpectedly discovering their Jewish ancestry.[42]

As Helen Epstein and others have argued, however, the *over*-pathologization of the second generation is a tendency that needs to be resisted.[43] Schaverien, too, warns both against the dangers of therapists treating all second- and third-generation clients as "members of a damaged group" and of allowing a necessary sensitivity to their clients' family traumas to cause them to attribute all their problems to the Holocaust.[44] Likewise, I do not wish to attribute trauma to all the writers studied here; my project is to read theories of transmission and literary texts in a way that allows them to interrogate and shed light on each other, rather than simply to use the texts as "illustrations" of theoretical concepts. One of my reasons for adopting this approach is the particular hybrid nature of many of these writers' work, whereby the lines between the literary and the academic are repeatedly blurred. Firstly, when they work in the arenas of autobiography and fiction, whether and how thoroughly they reference their historical and clinical sources is a matter of personal preference. It can thus be hard to identify how far their writing is infiltrated and/or informed by clinical and theoretical concepts. Take, for example, the following passage from Lisa Appignanesi's memoir *Losing the Dead*:

> The psychological tropes, the ways of confronting and filtering experience, which structured [my parents'] lives grew largely out of [the] war and subsequent immigration. I suspect they passed these patterns on to my brother and me, as surely as they passed on their genes and with as little choosing. Understanding this transgenerational haunting is part of the journey—and perhaps in a century where migration, forced or chosen, is the norm, it is its most common part. Memory, like history, is uncontrollable. It manifests itself in unruly ways. It cascades through the generations in a series of misplaced fears, mysterious wounds, odd habits. The child inhabits the texture of these fears and habits, without knowing they are memory.
>
> The journey is not a pleasure cruise, with its stopping points already marked out in good, linear fashion. In a sense it is more like an archaeological excavation. The objects sought for, alluded to in story, even documented in the formality of "survivor interviews" or archives, may or may not be there, or they may be so written over by tales and memory and the passage of history, that one can only guess from the traces at their original shape and use.[45]

In this passage, Appignanesi uses and elaborates on Abraham's term "transgenerational haunting". She also draws on the Freudian models of excavation and—in her reference to "traces" and "psychological tropes"—*Nachträglichkeit*. These are all concepts that could be gleaned from the first chapter of a critical work such as Nicola King's *Memory, Narrative, Identity* (11–15). Theories of memory are incorporated into the text poetically, in service to Appignanesi's perspective as a second-generation family memoirist and as an established fiction and nonfiction writer. It is perfectly normal for creative writers to research the subject of their books, but such close interplay between texts does call into question the value of making a clear distinction between criticism or theory as a methodological tool of study, and text as its object. The distinction is even more questionable in the light of the fact that, increasingly, the division is being blurred from the other side, too, with critic Nancy K. Miller having written a family memoir (*Bequest and Betrayal*) that incorporates critical responses to other texts such as *Maus*. A range of writers make use of dedications, photographs, prefaces, and opening chapters to explain or "confess" their relationship to their Holocaust subject matter. Such signaling of personal investment in a topic can be useful for the reader, but it may also serve to establish the writer's credentials, or his or her "right" to write on an emotive topic.[46]

Family Romances

The trauma for which many members of the second generation seek recognition is only their own, if it is theirs at all, through its belonging to an other. Enlisted against their will in their parents' healing process, they may come to resent the expectations placed upon them. In "Family Romances," Freud discusses the common fantasy in which children imagine that they have been taken from their "real," socially superior family to live with the one they currently know as theirs, and which they are beginning to question and reject as they grow up and form their own distinct identity.[47] Yet, Freud insists as follows, such fantasies are not as hostile as they appear:

> If we examine in detail the commonest of these imaginative romances, the replacement of both parents or of the father alone by grander people, we find that these new and aristocratic parents are equipped with attributes that are derived entirely from real recollections of the actual and humble ones; so that in fact the child is not getting rid of his father but exalting him. Indeed the whole effort at replacing the real father by a superior one is only an expression of the child's longing for the happy, vanished days when his father seemed to him the noblest and strongest of men and his mother the dearest and loveliest of women.[48]

Children of survivors who write often express their consciousness of the relationality of their trauma in terms of a kind of post-Holocaust family romance in which, unlike Freud's original conception, the idealized family is not by definition wealthy or of higher social standing, but psychologically healthy. Typically, where mental illness is mentioned, survivor-parents are portrayed as any combination of depressive, obsessive, neurotic, or suicidal, and their children's lives seem to echo and distort this.[49] Nadine Fresco, for example, suggests that anorexia in some members of the second generation stems from an unconscious wish on their part to look like emaciated survivors.[50]

These writers' family romances are thus on one level explicitly, and perhaps consciously, post-Freudian, constructing stories of misfortune in a literary discourse rooted in psychoanalysis. Such autobiographies frequently make explicit the difference between the parents "before" and "after" their Holocaust experiences by interspersing the texts with fictionalized episodes of the parents' lives before their child's birth. These texts often emphasize that the parents owed their survival to any combination of youth, good looks, education, and competence—attributes that were subsequently modified in physical or cultural terms, first by trauma and then in the process of emigration.[51] The pre-trauma parent in the post-Holocaust family romance represents the very ideal of beauty, talent, and "normality," attributes that the child now believes she cannot attain due to her parents' conspicuous difference from other parents in terms of accent, behavior, or taste. The parents in the present may alienate the child with their dislocation in the world with which the child is familiar. Yet, at the same time—and particularly in the light of impaired ego differentiation—the parents serve to reinforce the child's awareness of her own difference and perhaps her unsatisfactory social acceptability in the present environment. Under pressure from within the family to support the parents, and not to cause them pain, the child resolves her conflict by reviving the pre-Holocaust family. In the traditional Freudian account of the family romance, the child understands there to be two families—the idealized, aristocratic "original" family, and the imperfect family in the present that fails to fulfill her fantasies—while the analyst understands there to be only one. The literary post-Holocaust family romance differs in the child's awareness of the "two" families being one, yet this does not prevent the need for their coexistence in her mind, nor does it mean she is aware of the elements of fantasy in her perception of the younger family. Indeed, as I have already shown, it is impossible to tell how much a critical awareness of recent thinking on memory and identity informs children of survivors' creative writing. The numerous thematic and semantic intersections between fictional, autobiographical, critical, and clinical writing on the topic and the slipperiness of these generic boundaries can give the *impression* of a coherent body of thought that transcends genre and represents a psychological and experiential truth shared by all children of survivors. This is not the case—a fact that Gary Weissman notes, with reference to another writer, "may surprise readers, since our understanding of the second generation is largely shaped by second-generation writers who are actively engaged in addressing the Holocaust, and who appear to describe a burden and a mindset shared by *all* children of survivors."[52] For example, Nadine Fresco, writing as both a child of survivors and the interviewer of other children of survivors, writes the following:

> born after the war, because of the war, sometimes to replace a child who died in the war, the Jews I am speaking of here feel their existence as a sort of exile, not from a place of the present or future, but from a time, now gone forever, which would have been that of identity itself.[53]

The Jews she is speaking of are a subgroup of children of survivors, and this short quotation reflects the quest for "authenticity" that is apparent in many of their writings. The identity from which these children of survivors are exiled is, as we have seen, their own identity as individuals independent from their parents, but possibly also their identity as Jews: many parents hid their Judaism from their children, led by their experiences to equate it with persecution rather than a rich and viable cultural identity.[54] The far-reaching effects of anti-semitism in determining survivors' and their contemporaries' attitudes toward their Jewishness are attested by a number of writers.[55] Fresco notes as follows that the child of survivors' identity is often further shadowed by that of a phantom pre-Holocaust child, idealized alongside the young, pre-Holocaust parents:

> What can be done with that frustration, that jealousy at being unable, like those dead children, to remain an unchanging object of love. The amputated are left only with phantom pains, but who can say that the pain felt in a hand that one no longer has is not pain. These latter-day Jews are like people who have had a hand amputated that they never had. It is a phantom pain, in which amnesia takes the place of memory.[56]

Freud's family romance depends on the growing child's sense of being slighted by the parents, often as a symptom of her resentment at having to share them with siblings. In contrast to this, and with the post-Holocaust child's identity being bound up with that of her parents, the lost pre-Holocaust siblings possess a stable status and identity, often symbolized by their frozen presence in photographs and also, as Fresco suggests, in their position as constant, beloved objects of mourning. As Artie, the protagonist of *Maus II* puts it, "The photo never threw tantrums or got in any kind of trouble. . . . It was an ideal kid and I was a pain in the ass. I couldn't compete. . . . It's spooky, having sibling rivalry with a snapshot!"[57] Despite being part of the same family, they cannot be siblings in any meaningful way, as they have never been simultaneously alive.[58] Particularly in cases where the dead children are half brothers and half sisters from a parent's first marriage, the second-generation child's existence is predicated on the same history that led to the earlier children's deaths. To the "replacement" children of survivors, these phantom children are paradoxically missing, not in their rightful place, and nonexistent, in the sense of never having existed. One variant that Freud reports in the family romance occurs when "the hero and author returns to legitimacy himself while his brothers and sisters are eliminated by being bastardized."[59] Over-identification with the parents and their experience of loss, coupled with her inability to "compete" with the idealized, dead child, makes such a romance eminently desirable to the "replacement" child, if unthinkable on a conscious level. Hamida Bosmajian notes that, in *Maus*, Artie's dead brother's legitimacy is called into question discreetly and obliquely in one of the father and son's exchanges during which Vladek (the father) diverts Artie from discussing Richieu's premature birth.[60] Seeing themselves as inadequate substitutes for the children who came before them, it is, in a sense, these beloved children's identities from which their "replacements" have been exiled and which they later strive, through family romances, to restore.

These family romances take many literary forms. Helen Epstein re-creates her "ideal" family by seeking out other children of survivors who feel similarly troubled. Helen Fremont, through publishing her family's story as *After Long Silence*, discovers members of her extended family she never knew existed, and who (unlike her mother) are prepared to accept her female partner. Louise Kehoe establishes a Jewish identity for herself, counter to her father's attempts to lose it. Joseph Skibell attempts a fantastic fictional re-creation of his murdered ancestors. Anne Michaels portrays in fiction the breakdown of one such Holocaust family romance. Many writers travel to the European countries their families left to attempt to establish a personal link with their families' traumatic history.

The question of the relationality of trauma, of whether and how one generation's spoken or unspoken past is linked to the past of a subsequent generation, is one of distance and ownership: how close are these writers to their families' pasts and what "rights" do they have over them? Henri Raczymow writes that what he feels compelled to articulate as a writer is the "positive nothing" of his Jewish identity.[61] Torn between the "double bind" of the prohibition of writing and an urgent need to write, he sees writing as ultimately inevitable, for, as he states, "as any psychoanalyst will tell you, the time comes when you have to speak of what is troubling you."[62] In "Moses and Monotheism," Freud gives a widely quoted illustration of the latency inherent in trauma. He envisages a train crash, in which an apparently uninjured passenger develops "in the course of the next few weeks. . . a number of severe psychical and motor symptoms, which can only be traced to his shock or whatever else it was."[63] This lends a new suggestiveness to Raczymow's description of the position of Jews living in postwar France and "the feeling all of [them] have, deep down, of having missed a train. You know which train."[64] Whilst the image of the train is significant in a special way for Raczymow—and in any writing about the Holocaust—it is hard to resist drawing this image together with Freud's illustration. The survivor, unable to comprehend his own survival, is the "unscathed" train crash victim susceptible nonetheless to belated symptoms. For Caruth,

what is truly striking about the accident victim's experience of the event, and what in fact constitutes the central enigma revealed by Freud's example [of the train crash], is not so much the period of forgetting that occurs after the accident, but rather the fact that the victim of the crash was never fully conscious during the accident itself. . . . The experience of trauma, the fact of latency, would thus seem to consist, not in the forgetting of a reality that can hence never be fully known, but in an inherent latency within the experience itself.[65]

For the child of survivors, there is a belated latency: not merely that of trauma, but also that of physical absence and/or non-being at the time of the trauma. And again, for those whose parents did not, like Raczymow's, remain in Europe, there may be a profounder dislocation still. While Raczymow can describe the Jewish quarter of his Paris childhood as "a simulacrum of *Yiddishkeit* [Jewishness]" or "a *Yiddishkeit* shot through with holes, with missing links: the names of the dead," the world of the American second generation, if they are exposed to *Yiddishkeit* at all, has undergone a geographical and cultural transformation that makes it harder to see *what* has been shot through with holes.[66] If Raczymow feels he has missed a train, perhaps those among the American second generation need to search harder to find what they have missed, or whether they can be said to have missed anything at all, no matter how much some of them may feel they have.

George Steiner considers it a "personal" perspective when he writes the following:

> If I am often out of touch with my own generation, if that which haunts me and controls my habits of feeling strikes many of those I should be intimate and working with in my present world as remotely sinister and artificial, it is because the black mystery of what happened in Europe is to me indivisible from my own identity.[67]

His suggestive use of words—"out of touch with my own generation," "haunts," "indivisible from my own identity"—reflects back to much thinking in trauma theory, psychoanalysis, and autobiographical theory that I have mentioned. Yet he does not consider himself a survivor although, given that his family arrived in America in 1940, he would be defined as such in some quarters.[68] The problem faced by Steiner and other Jews born "afterwards" is that of being able to justify feelings that, by nature of their very distance from the individual, seem inauthentic, or in Steiner's words, "sinister and artificial." Like Fresco's "exile from identity," Spiegelman's "sibling rivalry," and Raczymow's "memory shot through with holes," Steiner is affected by a traumatic history that seems imbued with an authenticity or reality he feels he cannot claim for his own life.

However, forces of identity politics may work against self-censorship. As Barbara Kessel writes,

> reclamation of. . .Jewish heritage mirrors a growing trend in American society: the desire of people to investigate and discover who they are. The search may

be religious, ethnic, racial, or sexual identity, but in all cases the searcher is looking to develop or confirm personal identity within a larger (and presumably welcoming) community.[69]

As Kessel implies, this trend has been in important respects a positive one, and it undoubtedly forms a large component of the receptive cultural climate into which second-generation and related texts are received. The fact that many children of survivors write about traumatic childhoods of one kind or another should not completely cover over the alternative, or simultaneous, specter of the desirability of victim status in the present climate. As Alain Finkielkraut writes,

> the Judaism I had received was the most beautiful present a post-genocidal child could imagine. I inherited a suffering to which I had not been subjected, for without having to endure oppression, the identity of the victim was mine. I could savor an exceptional destiny while remaining completely at ease.[70]

This identity, Finkielkraut's critique argues, has sometimes been taken to permit Jews born after the Holocaust to luxuriate in—"savor"—the idea of suffering. Such an identity might provide a superficially appealing alternative to the sense of moral or existential inferiority that is a recurrent theme in second generation texts, including *Maus* and *Fugitive Pieces*. This is a different kind of family romance, and one that a number of writers from the second generation and beyond seem—critically or otherwise—to recognize.

Burial and Disinterment

In Felman and Laub's book *Testimony: Crises of Witnessing in Literature, Psychoanalysis, and History*, Felman asks the following question:

> What would it mean. . .for the witness to reopen his own grave—to testify precisely from inside the very cemetery which is not yet closed? And what would it mean, alternatively, to bear witness from inside the witness's *empty* grave— empty both because the witness in effect did not die, but only died unto himself, and because the witness who did die was, consequent to his mass burial, dug up from his grave and burned to ashes—because the dead witness did not even leave behind a corpse or a dead body?[71]

In the entanglement of life and death, burial and unburial, and closure and reopening expressed in this passage, Felman draws on a network of images that Holocaust literature seemingly cannot escape. The return from the dead is, like the family romance, a powerful image in post-Holocaust writing: the survivor's difference and authority is based on the return from his encounter with death, which ties him as a signifier to death and the grave. He is at once a symbol of hope in the face of death, and a problematic rebuke to too much hope: according to Hanna Yablonka, the voice of ghetto fighters "was practically the only one to be heard in Israel" in the two year period before its establishment as a state.[72] Gilead Morahg attributes the four decade absence of the Holocaust as a theme in Israeli literature to the fact that it was the antithesis of Zionist ideology and self-perception.[73] Yablonka also attests to a stereotypical opposition of the active ghetto fighters to the millions of submissive victims.[74] The Israeli idea of the survivor was too redolent of death to be compatable with the triumphant emergence of the new state.

Post-Holocaust literature has often figured the survivor as having returned from the dead, or indeed the mass grave itself, and unable to return fully to life. Such works question what it means to survive and how survivorhood may sometimes be incomplete, or less than the simple continuation of life after the threat of death. In Isaac Bashevis Singer's *Enemies: A Love Story*, Tamara returns virtually from the grave—she miraculously escaped death at a mass execution—but it is her husband, Herman, whose life is overwritten by hers. Her return threatens to unmask his existence, which he has kept concealed from official records. Having survived the war in hiding, he knows the potentially fatal consequences of the identity into which his wife's presence will reinsert him and flees it, deserting not only Tamara but a second wife and a mistress. The conflicting roles of these three women themselves reflect his fear of fixed identity. Herman's disappearance allows two of them to be involved in one another's lives in a way that would have been unthinkable in his presence.

In Philip Roth's *The Ghost Writer*, Nathan Zuckerman fantasizes that Anne Frank has actually survived, but that she decides not to reveal her true identity, as the story of her death has become more important than that of her life could ever be. In *Briar Rose*, Jane Yolen retells the Sleeping Beauty story as a Holocaust tale in which a girl is resuscitated after being lifted—apparently lifeless—from a mass grave. Although she survives, her real name is lost. Saul Bellow's Mr. Sammler, in *Mr. Sammler's Planet*, both escapes from a grave, and survives by hiding in a tomb. Joseph Skibell uses this image of the survivor in a ghost story structure that interrogates the ambiguous nature of survival in *A Blessing on the Moon*, and in Anne Michaels' *Fugitive Pieces*, Jakob escapes and then buries himself to hide from the Nazis who murdered his family; on emerging, he is rescued and carried to safety.

In historical terms, perhaps this preoccupation with burial alive should not be surprising: surviving the Holocaust was often a matter of seeming not to exist, whether by hiding or "passing" as a non-Jew outside the camps, maintaining anonymity within them, or fortuitously escaping death and fleeing a mass murder site after dark. Shoshana Felman writes, "as illustrated by the Nazis' own perception of the 'operation' of the gas vans, the Nazi project is essentially a project of containment: the gas van is designed primarily as a death container—as a moving grave and as the enforced confinement of a burial alive."[75] The Holocaust, in Felman's reading, brings burial alive into the new terminology and technology of mass extermination.

Some of the characters in the literary works I have mentioned have suppressed their identities so successfully that reclaiming them is a problem: in many of these texts, society fails to bear witness to the experience of survival and the survivors can only renew life as different people—or, in the imagery of Skibell and Michaels, be "reborn." In Roth's and Singer's works, re-establishment of the survivor's original identity can only occur at the expense of another's identity.

This burial of identity, or lack of witnessing, is also the burial of stories. Peter Brooks remarks that "burial alive has a rich literary career" and goes on to suggest that this "may point to a specifically literary obsession with the buried utterance: the word, the tale, entombed without listener."[76] The use of the image to describe the situation of the survivor therefore inserts the survivor's traumatic return into a continuous literary tradition, covering over the real historical nature of the trauma. As George Steiner has observed in relation to another literary image,

> the camp embodies, often down to minutiae, the images and chronicles of Hell in European art and thought from the twelfth to the eighteenth centuries. It is these representations which gave to the deranged horrors of Belsen a kind of "expected logic."[77]

Entombment before death may well "be a nightmare responding to our most primitive fears," but what does it mean for such a nightmare to become reality?[78] What does it mean for this massive trauma to pass so effortlessly into literary tradition? Balzac's story *Le Colonel Chabert* acts as a powerful analogy to the position of the survivor. As Brooks asks in relation to Chabert, an escapee from a mass grave on a Napoleonic battlefield, "what does it mean to look *like* a man dug up from the grave. . .when literally you *are* thus dug up?" Brooks explains that there is

> some problem of collapsed metaphor, a metaphor unaware that its tenor and its vehicle have become identical, that it has lost the tension of displacement inherent to metaphor, ceased to function as that active "transaction between contexts."[79]

This collapse of metaphor describes what is at work in recent Holocaust literature's usage of the burial alive: it is at once metaphor and reality, our "worst nightmare" and that nightmare come true. Perhaps this suggests that when asked to confront such extreme events, all we can do is revert to literary figures, which are the closest approximation most people's experience can offer. In doing so, we refuse—abuse?—the transaction that metaphor demands, placing fresh limitations on our understanding. Dan Bar-On observes that "the thought and language structures are so fragile that they easily collapse when we try to create a bridge between memories or feelings and the present reality (including that of the listener). How can one 'translate' such experiences into ordinary language?"[80] We seem to need the metaphor of returning from the grave to express survivorhood in general. Thus, when a return from the grave has *actually* occurred, we need to undo the literary convention in order to reclaim the linguistic space needed to express the event.

Autobiographical works by children of survivors often reveal at the beginning or the end that the parent has died, stating or implying that this death was the very motivation to tell the story. The writing of the story thus becomes an act of disinterment, where the "disinterred" story comes to stand for the parent.[81] For most Jewish children, such a disinterment of stories, a "discovering and inventing of facts," seems enough, yet whose story is it? Children of survivors' stories, even where they are seemingly based on or in history, can never be the same as those of the parents whose lives they so painstakingly research and rewrite. Equally, the stories of Balzac's Colonel Chabert and Skibell's Chaim Skibelski become, through the absence or noncooperation of crucial witnesses who could restore their property and identities—such as Chabert's wife and the Poles who occupied Chaim's home, respectively—stories of characters who, in surviving, remain tied to the past, unable to perform the crucial act of departure into the future. These characters are at once survivors of historical events and those who come after these events. As Caruth writes,

> appearing against the background of this operation of the Charter [i.e. a legal, historical command to forget], Chabert's return before the law can thus be understood as the return of memory against the very action of the legal attempt to forget.[82]

Chabert returns from an official, physical death at a site of official history, a battlefield, to find that "the repetition of the trauma. . .takes the form, not of a physical or mental, but of a social and a legal death."[83] His effective disinterment has occurred at the wrong moment in history for the restoration of his war-hero identity to be fully achieved. As Victoria Aarons writes of American

Jewish post-Holocaust writers, "when we subordinate our own lives to a perception of the importance of a historical symbol or event—when, in other words, history becomes an emblem, an icon by which to measure our value—we lose our individual identities in the very struggle to form them."[84]

Children of survivors themselves mark a "return" in the form of a new generation, yet, like Chabert's return, they may feel that theirs is incomplete and overwhelmed by a moment in history that will never be truly theirs in the way that their self-identities demand. The temptation may be for parents to see their children as a total renewal, failing to recognize them as "an episode in [their own] narrative." The thirty-year-old Helen Epstein writes at the end of *Children of the Holocaust* that *now* "[her] mother. . .has learned that her children cannot always be happy, healthy and free of pain."[85] This expectation of total life, in the knowledge that their parents returned almost from death, can be a psychological burden to children in addition to their possibly urgent desire to know about the past. The continuity of generations that is normally celebrated in families—the passing on of names, the child's resemblance to elder relatives—may, in post-Holocaust families, become a reason for mourning. Names are bequeathed as memorials; inherited features may serve to remind parents not only of those who died, but perhaps also how those features were in themselves treacherous.

The child of survivors is thus herself a disinterment. She represents the continuation of a story that her parents might wish would remain buried: the story of their trauma, their near death, and perhaps even their Jewishness.[86] In establishing her own selfhood, the child needs to find a story of her own, even if it has to include that of her parents. In the process of writing the stories that she wishes to be her parents' stories, the child belatedly bears witness to the older generation's experiences refracted through her own. Memoirs by children of survivors are acts of narrative that incorporate the rupture of trauma, into the story of a new life. In this the child's life follows Caruth's conclusion that "the theory of trauma does not limit itself to a theoretical formulation of the centrality of death in culture, but constitutes—in Freud's, and our own, historical experience of modernity—an act of parting that itself creates and passes on a different history of survival."[87]

Postmemory

The child, grandchild, or other descendant of survivors, in other words, is not simply subject to (grand-)parents' wishes and pathologies, although several autobiographers suggest that this position is one they have worked hard to avoid.[88] To consider the works of children and other descendants of survivors who write about that experience is to acknowledge the operation of a creative activity which defies the passive image suggested by some of the clinical findings discussed above. Marianne Hirsch has coined the term "postmemory" to describe not only the relationship of children of survivors to their parents' experiences but also their mode of representing those experiences. Taking pains to clarify that her use of the prefix "post-" is not meant to signal a movement *past* or *beyond* memory, she explains that

> postmemory is distinguished from memory by generational distance and from history by deep personal connection. Postmemory is a very powerful and very particular form of memory precisely because its connection to its object or source is mediated not through recollection but through an imaginative investment and creation.[89]

She does not make clear, however, whether such "investment" is a matter of artistic choice or family history. She goes on to say that postmemory

> characterizes the experience of those who grow up dominated by narratives that preceded their birth, whose own belated stories are evacuated by the stories of the previous generation shaped by traumatic events that can be neither understood nor recreated. I have developed this notion in relation to children of Holocaust survivors, but I believe it may usefully describe other second-generation memories of cultural or collective traumatic events and experiences.[90]

Hirsch implies here that "second-generation memories" are clearly situated within the family framework that she uses to discuss photography, and which the title of her book, *Family Frames*, would seem to suggest. Narrative, memory and—implicitly—biology unite to form postmemorial identities. The child's personality finds itself "dominated," or buried, by the parents' experiences, so that identity becomes not simply a matter of asserting the self's independence, but of a constant dialogue between pasts that alternately cover over one another. As it does for Colonel Chabert's identity, the past threatens to bury the child of survivors' present identity that demands to be lived. Just as the establishment of Chabert's legal identity would require the annulment of that of his wife (for she would lose the title and status gained through her new marriage), the Holocaust survivor's and his child's stories serve to partially bury each other, rendering parent and child unable to fully bear witness to one another. "Relational auto/biography," whereby the child of survivors writes her parent's life story both within and alongside her own, echoes the structure of family memory, dependent on and yet different from that of previous generations, and it has consequently proved a popular mode of writing.[91]

Elsewhere, however, Hirsch's formulation seems less precise. The following presents another of her definitions of postmemory, which has quite different implications from the first:

> postmemory is not an identity position, but a space of remembrance, more broadly available through cultural and public, and not merely individual and personal, acts of remembrance, identification, and projection. It is a question of adopting the traumatic experiences—and thus also the memories—of others as one's own, or, more precisely, as experiences one might oneself have had, and of inscribing them into one's own life story. It is a question of conceiving oneself as multiply interconnected with others of the same, of previous, and of subsequent generations, of the same and of other—proximate or distant—cultures and subcultures. It is a question, more specifically, of an *ethical* relation to the oppressed or persecuted other for which postmemory can serve as a model: as I can "remember" my parents' memories, I can also "remember" the suffering of others, of the boy who lived in the same town in the ghetto while I was vacationing, of the children who were my age and who were deported. These lines of relation and identification need to be theorized more closely, however: how the familial and intergenerational identification with my parents can extend to the identification among children of different generations and circumstances and also perhaps to other, less proximate groups. And how, more important, identification can resist appropriation and incorporation, resist annihilating the distance between self and other, the otherness of the other.[92]

This account of postmemory is so all-encompassing that it is hard to conceive of it as a modification of Hirsch's previous definition, which suggested that the term pertained strictly to children of survivors.[93] Now, it is not only potentially "cultural and public," but postmemory can also be "adopted" as a position—a crucial difference from the earlier definition that posited the bearer of postmemory as passively "dominated" and "shaped" by the unknown past. Introducing this element of choice brings the concept closer to Ruth Leys' and Walter Benn Michaels' more culturally based accounts of "intergenerational transmission," which I discussed earlier. The element of choice also introduces an ethical dimension to the position: it now has to do with locating a form of identification that relates primarily to the "oppressed and persecuted" and respects otherness. Hirsch mentions "familial and intergenerational identification," but only as something that can "extend" beyond the family.

However, I would suggest that examination of the literature of the second generation, and other descendants of survivors, reveals that the contradictions in Hirsch's two formulations may be employed more fruitfully than is at first apparent. The ways in which children, and other descendants of survivors, represent their experiences in literature are most productively described as a matrix of what I have termed "postmemorial positions." This more complex model could account for, rather than elide, both conscious and unconscious "intergenerational transmission." It could also ask the question of what is transmitted: is it the parent's trauma or the parent's memory? Or does the transmission of knowledge, or the behavior of the traumatized parent, actually traumatize the child in turn? On another level, the theoretical acknowledgment of such a matrix of postmemorial positions has the potential to free up the critical discourse from a sense of needing to ring-fence definitions of survivors and "the second generation," acknowledging that while the experience of a child of a refugee (for example) may not be historically equivalent to that of a child of survivors, these experiences and the texts that emerge from them may at times be usefully considered together.

Postmemory thus needs to be understood as an umbrella term that encompasses a number of sub-positions. This book, in its discussion of a range of autobiographical and fictional texts, aims to contribute to the more detailed theorization of these. Although my approach leans towards Hirsch's first, narrower definition of postmemory, which relates it specifically to children of survivors, I would resist a strictly biological interpretation. For example, in interviews, Anne Michaels attributes her interest in the Holocaust to growing up in Toronto surrounded by survivors and their offspring—to living in something approaching the kind of *milieu de mémoire* that Pierre Nora suggests no longer exists.[94]

Working through the Present

As this chapter so far has implied, the texts I have chosen form a coherent corpus for a number of reasons. Firstly, as I have stated, they explore a family relationship to the Holocaust from the point of view of someone born "after." Helen Epstein attempts to understand her own family dynamics, and personal choices, through a process of interviewing others from the second generation; while Louise Kehoe finds that an unacknowledged link to the Holocaust is behind her own family's troubles. Art Spiegelman frames his "biography" of his father with a portrayal of his own relationship to his parents and their traumatic pasts. Joseph Skibell responds to a family silence with a fictional re-creation of his murdered great-grandfather; and Anne Michaels explores the loss experienced by a fictional child survivor, as well as a child of survivor who turns to him as a father substitute.

Secondly, I believe these texts constitute attempts at a literary "working-through" of the Holocaust. For Dominick LaCapra, following Laplanche and Pontalis, working-through should not be construed in straightforward opposition to acting-out. Nor should it, in the manner implied by Freud that LaCapra finds problematic, be construed as a normative process that constructs its opposite state(s) as pathology. Rather, it is worth "relating it to ethical and political considerations" and recognizing that "it is bound up with the role of distinctions that are not pure binary oppositions but marked by varying and contestable degrees of strength or weakness."[95] My argument is not that my chosen texts offer a definitive example of how the Holocaust has been, or should be, represented from any particular standpoint. Instead, I argue that they all represent serious attempts to engage with questions of history, memory, and representation in relation to the Holocaust. Helen Epstein's *Children of the Holocaust* investigates her own responses alongside those of other children of survivors. While I highlight some issues in the structuring of her interviews, she acknowledges that some of her interviewees' comments are so distant from her own experience as to make her feel uncomfortable.[96] Throughout the book, Epstein is willing to acknowledge life as a child of survivors to be an ambivalent experience. Equally, some critics have felt uncomfortable with Anne Michaels' finely-wrought poetic prose, which they feel to be inappropriate for the subject matter. Even so, within the framework of this prose, she reflects on her literary undertaking with a high degree of sophistication. Louise Kehoe gives an account of her own process of discovering and working through a hidden past. This process exposes her father's cruel behavior as an elaborate acting-out of this same secret history. In his novel, Joseph Skibell comes to terms with his family's silence, attempting to construct the past in a way that communicates something to him, and using fantasy to mark out a clear distance between his own text and the reality of his great-grandparents' lives.

In this context, I would like to posit second-generation writer Thane Rosenbaum's novel *Second Hand Smoke* as one that fails to engage with precisely these kinds of issues.[97] The novel tells the story of Duncan Katz, a child of survivors who works as a state war crimes investigator. The opening paragraph of Rosenbaum's prologue as follows is revealing:

> He was a child of trauma. Not of love, or happiness, or exceptional wealth. Just trauma. And nightmare, too. Wouldn't want to leave that out. As a young man he seemed to have come equipped with all the right credentials: primed for loss, consigned to his fate. But what kind of career exploits such talents? And who would want such a job?[98]

This child of survivors has none of the complexity revealed in many other accounts of the second generation. There are no positive or individual qualities to complement or problematize the effects of the Holocaust on Katz's life;

despite being "second hand," they, of all his experiences, have the primary influence on him.

The anger that led Katz to war crime investigation in the first place gradually takes over his life, and he is finally fired when it emerges that he has resorted to "unethical" means to obtain evidence against a notorious war criminal (Katz visits the man with a hidden tape recorder, posing as a neo-Nazi fan of his). In addition to losing his job, his wife leaves him, taking their daughter with her. After his mother's death, Katz learns he has a brother in Poland, and the rest of the novel explores the relationship between the two men. Unlike the angry, self-destructive Duncan, Isaac works as a yoga instructor and as the caretaker of a Jewish cemetery in Poland. The contrast between the two brothers is drawn out, and the solution to Duncan's problems is finally addressed, in a scene in which they visit the part of the Auschwitz camp that has not been turned into a museum. There, they are trapped by neo-Nazis who shave their heads, dress them in striped suits and lock them in one of the old barracks. Duncan discovers how inadequate his anger is for dealing with this situation compared with his brother's self-possessed serenity, and then, in a rather conventional narrative twist, we discover that these neo-Nazis were inside Duncan's head and that he and Isaac have not been imprisoned at all.

Unlike the descendants of survivors in the texts I have chosen to discuss, Rosenbaum's characters Duncan Katz and Adam Posner (from Rosenbaum's book of linked stories, *Elijah Visible*) are repeatedly reinserted into their parents' Holocaust narratives and do not move forward into their own. Only when he has achieved total identification with his parents can Katz move beyond their experiences. Michelle A. Friedman argues that rather than remembrance, "much contemporary American Holocaust memory-work seems propelled by a different force: mythologization," which "responds to the longing for 'total' understanding and a totalizing narrative and successfully transforms the past into something familiar and functional."[99] On the other hand, she argues that artists such as "[Art] Spiegelman and [Deb] Filler. . .illustrate how the labor of remembrance can be seen as a struggle to sustain the tension between past and present."[100] Aharon Appelfeld seems to make a similar point when he writes the following:

> When I refer to literature, I do not include all those fantasies about the Holocaust, those commercial productions, perverted stories, and sensational and scandalous writings which have inundated us since the end of the Second World War. Literature with a true voice and a face one can trust is very scarce. The number of such works could be counted by a child.[101]

There is a limit to how far writing that mythologizes, or sets out with primarily commercial goals, is "about" the Holocaust as history. Often, writers draw on the Holocaust as a topic to lend weight to what is essentially unoriginal or otherwise poor quality writing.[102] I have chosen texts that I believe are "about" the Holocaust and are part of a process of remembering rather than mythologizing (although I would not wish to claim that the two processes can be totally separated). I understand this to mean that they deal with the writer's present, rather than just their families' and communities' pasts, following Dominick LaCapra's formulation that "memory. . . points to problems that are still alive" in history.[103]

This is one of the reasons why I have not restricted the corpus of texts in this book to either autobiographical or fictional works. Both genres are capable of asking and addressing important questions about the historical material that inspired them. The texts I have chosen are linked by their historical/psychological theme, and this book's concern is to explore the *range* of ways in which this theme has been represented. Thus, these texts have been partly selected for their variety. Like Sara Horowitz, I am interested in fiction's capacity for "thinking about the Holocaust."[104] Neither of the novels to which this book devotes a chapter attempt to disguise their own fictionality. Rather, Skibell's and Michaels' works are characterized in different ways by a self-aware "literariness" that makes it clear to the reader that they are not attempting to rewrite history. Yet despite this, both novelists, who have publicly expressed their sense of family or community connection to the Holocaust, use ideas of autobiography and family history to create their fictions. Both use first person narratives to create what might be called fictional autobiographies. Conversely, the autobiographical texts to which I devote the first three chapters are as "constructed" as fictional narratives, and their manners of figuring the relationship of one generation's past to another's present are as varied. This book's bibliography is full of works that draw on a mixture of imagination, personal recollection, family interviews, and historical research. Thus, given the thematic subject of this book, examining both fiction and autobiography permits a consideration of a process of exchange between the two genres.

Giving a new emphasis to present-day family links to the Holocaust may help to explain why, as David Brauner contends, the term "postwar. . . has become increasingly pertinent" with passing time.[105] Whether this will continue, as new generations that have never met their survivor (great-)grandparents arise, is unclear, though Tim Cole believes it will.[106] Even if it does, the character of its demise may be no less interesting than that of its rise. As Ellen S. Fine observes, all of us who live in the shadow of the Holocaust are heirs to the memory of the past. Yet, as Levinas affirms, at each moment in time, this memory evolves and is newly interpreted. The memory of the second generation is at present being created and constructed through a language of its own, and it will then be transmitted to generations to come.[107]

The Holocaust remains a profoundly personal matter for many people who were not there. Precisely what it is that is being constructed and transmitted as its influence passes down the generations is what this book is about to explore.

CHAPTER 1

The Documentary Memoir:
Helen Epstein's *Children of the Holocaust*: Conversations with Sons and Daughters of Survivors

Introduction: Relational Biography and the Second Generation

The period since the end of the 1970s has seen a proliferation of autobiographical texts dealing with the experience of North American children of survivors, the "second generation." In one sense this was only to be expected, as this time coincides with the coming of age of the post-war children of those who fled Europe. In another, however, it may be noted that relatively few of these writers were already established as authors of full-length books, although many of them have professional connections to other areas of the media and creative arts.[1] The fact that many of these children of survivors were branching out into new territory by writing memoirs suggests that there is a particular motivation for the second generation to write about their experiences. By far the most famous of these texts is Art Spiegelman's graphic autobiography *Maus*, the cartoonist's first book-length work, which receives detailed treatment in chapter 3. However, most of these memoirs are written by women, and I have reflected this in my choice of texts for discussion in the next two chapters.

To a large extent, these second-generation memoirs form a coherent body of writing with shared generic and thematic features. Most are characteristic of a theoretical model of autobiography that Nancy K. Miller describes as having mainly been developed in the context of women's autobiographical writing.[2] According to this model, women tend to write autobiographies that configure the writer's identity in relation to others. Meanwhile, male autobiographers, seen as writing in the tradition of Augustine and Rousseau, work to the notion of a fully separate and unified self—a concept that theorists of autobiography have called into question in recent decades. In *Auto/biographical Discourses*, however, Laura Marcus writes that "recounting one's own life almost inevitably entails writing the life of an other or others; writing the life of another must surely entail the biographer's identifications with his or her subject, whether these are made explicit or not."[3] Where such a process *is* more explicit, such as in Spiegelman's *Maus* books, Philip Roth's *Patrimony*, and Carolyn Steedman's *Landscape for a Good Woman*, Paul John Eakin uses the term "relational biography." He goes on to describe it as follows: "one important variety. . . takes the form of the family memoir, in which the lives of other family members are rendered as either equal in importance to or more important than the life of the reporting self."[4]

The distinction inscribed in the theoretical model I have described, and which Marcus and Eakin suggest to be an over-simplification, represents a critical recasting of longer-standing debates about genre. For example, Marcus identifies "the question of what constitutes autobiography proper, in opposition to popular 'confessional' literature or memoir" as one of the more enduring features of the history of autobiographical criticism. The most common grounds for such a distinction, she says, have traditionally been that autobiography is "the evocation of a life as a totality [while] memoirs. . . offer only an anecdotal depiction of people and events." She also points out that the memoir/autobiography distinction is sometimes applied to the question of the author's *intention* rather than the literary form.[5] Thus, while concerns around this topic are "ostensibly formal and generic," the discourse implies "a typological distinction between those human beings who are capable of self-reflection and those who are not." Such a distinction is, according to Marcus, "still current, often correlated with class and cultural capital."[6] Drawing on Georg Misch's *Geschichte der Autobiographie*, in which Misch defines memoir as inherently passive and reactive compared to autobiography's "active" project of self-definition, Marcus critiques the wider political implications of such a dual classification. Autobiography, she writes,

> becomes a statement about the individual's power, not so much, or not only, to act upon the world, but to assert the centrality of self by viewing the world as an "emanation" from the self. The writers of memoirs, conversely, efface themselves within the histories they observe and record. It is no accident that women have tended to write "memoirs" rather than "autobiographies," and that the memoir-form has been consistently belittled in autobiographical criticism.[7]

The (sub-)genre of "memoirs," according to this assessment, is marginalized due to the powerlessness of the writers. If it is also true that these writers "efface themselves" in their work, then their social or cultural marginalization is replicated both within and by their texts. Second-generation autobiographical texts are usually classified by publishers as "memoirs," and I will return to the question of genre later in this chapter. Like Marcus, I query the political assumptions behind the memoir/autobiography distinction. I subsequently go on to ask how a close reading of second-generation memoirs can further inform these theoretical considerations.

While the past events and present conflicts that lead children of survivors to write may be beyond their own control, autobiographical texts often seem to represent the writers' attempts to define a coherent identity within their families on their own terms. In this way, the authors may achieve a centrality through authorship that the familial hegemony of their parents' experiences has denied them. The "memoir" or "relational biography" as employed by second-generation writers allows parental experiences to retain prominence in the writers' lives while offering the generic flexibility to accommodate the authors' "own" stories. These texts thus foreground two processes: identity construction within the text, and the very act of writing for publication. Thus at the level of the production and dissemination of the text, and—through an implicit analogy with the writers' actual lived experience—in the text itself, these works attempt to destabilize the dominance of parental narratives in the writers' lives. In doing so, I argue, they call into question the theoretical accounts of memoir that I have just described. In addition, they serve to create and maintain a particular public understanding of "the second-generation experience."

Helen Epstein: The First of the "Second Generation"

Sketching out a "brief history" of the American second generation in his book on writing by children of survivors, Alan L. Berger credits two books with drawing to the American public's notice "the existence of second-generation witnesses as a distinct group having a particular purchase on the meaning of Jewish identity after Auschwitz." The first of these, an edited collection entitled *Living after the Holocaust*, is described as "a rich collection of fiction, poetry, conversations, and scholarly studies."[8] The second is Helen Epstein's *Children of the Holocaust*.

Published in 1979—the year after Art Spiegelman began work on *Maus*—*Children of the Holocaust: Conversations with Sons and Daughters of Survivors* is the first book of its kind and thus had a significant impact on future writers, and on the second-generation community.[9] Yet it also differs significantly from subsequent second-generation autobiographical works. Ostensibly a series of interviews, a form that reflects Epstein's journalistic background, the book interweaves the author's own story, and those of her parents, with those of her second-generation interviewees. In so doing, it falls between fully interview-based works—such as Dan Bar-On's *Legacy of Silence*, which deals with children of Nazi perpetrators—and most second-generation memoirs, which tend to focus on the author and his or her parents. Despite the space it gives to children of survivors beyond the author's immediate family, *Children of the Holocaust* has a structuring narrative that keeps the author-interviewer's own story in play throughout.[10] My reading of this text, which is concerned with what an autobiographical text does when it tells the story of more than one person, takes the operation of this narrative as its primary focus.

According to Paul John Eakin in *How Our Lives Become Stories*, "in the memoir as traditionally defined. . . the story of the self, the "I," is subordinated to the story of some other for whom the self serves as privileged witness."[11] He modifies this definition with regard to his own chosen corpus of texts, which includes Spiegelman's *Maus* books. In Eakin's corpus,

> the story of the self is not ancillary to the story of the other, although its primacy may be partly concealed by the fact that it is constructed through the story told of and by someone else. Because identity is conceived as relational in these cases, these narratives defy the boundaries we try to establish between genres, for they are autobiographies that offer not only the autobiography of the self but the biography and the autobiography of the other.[12]

Therefore, he claims, "once we begin to entertain a notion of autobiography in which the focus is, paradoxically, on someone else's story, the hitherto neglected class of narratives we often call memoirs will emerge in quite a new and revealing light."[13] According to Eakin's argument, the traditional view that Marcus describes, whereby the memoirist, or relational autobiographer, "effaces" herself in the text, may be rather more complex. Referring to Carolyn Steedman's widely-quoted remark in *Landscape for a Good Woman*, that "children are always episodes in someone else's narrative," Eakin considers that children who author their parents' stories can "become self-determining and more: they make someone else into 'episodes' in their own narratives."[14] Children of survivors often report feeling overshadowed by events experienced by their parents. And in Epstein's text in particular, which explores the relationship of the writer/narrator to her interviewees as well as to her parents, a complex pattern of intra-textual power relations is at work.

Paradoxically, Epstein presents the starting point for her "relational" autobiography as the sense of isolation arising from her position as a child of survivors. She sees this in quasi-pathological terms, describing her feelings about the war and her parents' experiences of the Holocaust as an "iron box" inside her as follows:

> For years it lay in an iron box buried so deep inside me that I was never sure just what it was. I knew I carried slippery, combustible things more secret than sex and more dangerous than any shadow or ghost. Ghosts had shape and name. What lay inside my iron box had none. Whatever lived inside me was so potent that words crumbled before they could describe.[15]

While she knows members of her extended family, particularly her grandparents, only through photographs, the iron box grants these people a physical space commensurate with their psychological importance in the narrator's life as follows:

> Sometimes I felt my iron box contained a tomb. . . . My grandmother Helena sat in one corner on a chair like a throne. Her brown hair was swept up above her ears and she looked stern although my father always said she had never hurt a soul. My grandfather Maximillian stood beside her, erect and tall like a military man. My grandfather Emil paced back and forth, arguing with himself in German, and my grandmother Josephine stood dreaming in a corner, dressed in shawls. (11)

In order to provide these relatives with the "tomb" that they lack, Epstein elaborates on the photographs that are their only real memorial space. Their figurative position inside herself, "entombed" and thus "fortified" and "inaccessible" (13), suggests her sense that the absence of her grandparents is balanced by an awareness of their continuity in herself. However, she also situates her living parents in a similar place as follows: "The iron box contained a special room for my mother and father, warm and moist as a greenhouse. They lived there inside me, rare and separate from other beings" (12). This iron box is not so much a place of memory—she never knew her grandparents—as one containing that "rare and separate" dimension to her parents' life experiences that cannot be played out in the Epstein family's relationships: their traumatic pasts. "I needed company to look inside [the box]," Epstein writes, "other voices to confirm that those things I carried inside me were real, that I had not made them up. My parents could not help me with this; *they were part of it*" (13; emphasis added). Her parents' being "part of" this problem precludes them from being the "company" she needs. In describing cases such as Epstein's, where a figure close to the autobiographer is "the other" in relation to whom the author's life is written, Eakin uses the term "proximate other." "In these cases," he writes, "it is difficult not only to determine the boundaries of the other's privacy but indeed to delimit the very otherness of the other's identity."[16]

As I explored in the previous chapter, Epstein's image of the iron box reflects clinical work on children of survivors that has used a number of different models to account for the child's overidentification with the parents. Dani Rowland-Klein and Rosemary Dunlop explore J. S. Kestenberg's idea of children of survivors' "transposition" into a dual existence in both past and present as a result of such identification.[17] As Aaron Hass summarizes,

> a mistrust of outsiders which permeates some survivor homes may also have interfered with the creation of boundaries between parent and child. From many different quarters, a pattern has emerged of problematic psychological and physical separation from survivor parents.[18]

Epstein's image of her parents within the iron box, inside herself yet distinct and inaccessible, evokes an auto/biographical space that suggests stories within stories. Yet unlike the "transgenerational phantom" of Abraham and Torok's work, Epstein's "iron box" is part of her *conscious* existence whose evolution she has monitored—although unconscious mechanisms may lie behind it. According to Nanette C. Auerhahn and Dori Laub's findings, "massive trauma. . . shapes the internal representation of reality of several generations, becoming an unconscious organizing principle passed on by parents and internalized by their children."[19] Consequently, they continue,

> Children of survivors can become chained to parents' versions of reality, which may become the matrix within which normal developmental conflict takes place. These children are less immediately constrained from giving expression to their parents' conflicted themes; their distance from the experience itself, as well as the compelling quality of their heritage, can make them inevitable spokesmen for it.[20]

In such cases, the question of what constitutes "autobiographical" experience is no longer straightforward. In Auerhahn and Laub's formulation, the tension between being "chained" to one's parents' experiences while being simultaneously "less constrained" in giving voice to them than they are themselves hints at such a difficulty: second generation autobiographers are caught between an overshadowing yet unexperienced history and the possibility of representing that history.

As a result of the feelings she describes about her "iron box," Epstein writes, "I set out to find a group of people who, like me, were possessed by a history they had never lived. I wanted to ask them questions, so that I could reach the most elusive part of myself" (14). Her project thus explores relationships with two distinct kinds of "others": her parents, whose history "possesses" her, yet is also "entombed" within her; and her interviewees, in whom she hopes to find a peer group.

Children of the Holocaust foregrounds how Epstein comes to gain the trust of her interviewees. Key to the author's representation of this process is Deborah Schwartz,[21] a former state beauty queen, who is wary of her prospective interviewer. "In the first rush of excitement," writes Epstein, "we had agreed that I would stay with her in Toronto. Then came a cooler, more distanced telephone call. Perhaps it would be better if I found a hotel or made other arrangements?" (20) Deborah is characterized by Epstein as a publicity-seeker, for much is made of her past as a beauty queen. She is used to press attention, and not only to granting interviews but to using them as a forum for her own agenda: she consciously sets out to use her platform as a beauty queen to raise awareness of her parents' wartime experiences. Yet she is evidently unhappy about talking to Epstein alone. When Epstein arrives to interview her, she discovers that Deborah has also invited her younger brother and two friends who are themselves children of survivors. Deborah's defense tactics prove successful as one of her friends, Eli Rubinstein, is the first to begin talking. Epstein uses his story to hint about her own background, as well as to point to the story Deborah will come to reveal. She writes the following: "Like my mother, and Deborah and Joseph's mother, Eli's mother would often drift into a memory of the war as she stood in the kitchen preparing dinner, or sat at the kitchen table afterwards" (26). Eli's story also begins to illustrate the process by which Deborah's trust is gained. For example, after he tells the group about his parents' view of education, Epstein writes, "Deborah looked up at him. She had been listening attentively, more than a little surprised. Like the rest of us, she was hearing Eli describe her own family" (27). Epstein thus hints at what Deborah will tell her in the future.

Epstein characterizes the atmosphere in the room in terms that constitute the members of the group as parts of a single living organism as follows: "I had the peculiar sensation of plasma flowing through the five of us" (26). As with her parents and the image of the iron box, this image of "plasma" figures the group as closer than merely "proximate." We finally hear the rest of Deborah Schwartz's account after a further three hundred pages. By this time, we know the stories of Eli Rubinstein's younger sister, and Deborah's younger brother, as well as those of several other children of survivors. Thus, Epstein uses Schwartz's initial mistrust as a structural device, saying that a year elapsed before Schwartz was persuaded to change her mind. Schwartz's hesitancy reflects the manner in which Epstein causes her own story to unfold. Apart from the introductory chapter in which she introduces the image of the "iron box," the reader learns little of Epstein herself for some time. However, in chapter 3, in which she records her interviews with Eli Rubinstein's sister, Rochelle, Epstein concludes the following:

> Of all the children of survivors I had met, Rochelle struck the most responsive chord in me. I, too, had never been able to feel what I imagined other people felt when they spoke of the war. . . . That night, as I sat bent over my typewriter, listening to Rochelle's soft, hesitant voice coming out of my tape recorder, I began to cry. I typed with tears blurring my view of the paper on which I was transcribing her words, and I began to remember things I had never allowed myself to remember before. (45)

Rochelle's testimony is written here as being responsible for Epstein's own testimony, and this paragraph is thus immediately followed by two chapters devoted to Epstein's own family background. In Epstein's book, the telling of a like tale is a cue or precondition for self-disclosure, just as Deborah Schwartz speaks openly about her own life only after hearing others' stories. When this process is completed, Schwartz and Epstein become friends. Epstein's writing replicates the process of mistrust and questioning that she says characterized the interviews: an initial wariness of her own readers leads to their implied rehabilitation as trustworthy and sympathetic. The transformation that takes place here has the effect of identifying the author with her own subjects, as if anxious to show them that she, too, is vulnerable and suspicious of researchers' motives, and that they have not been deceived in trusting her.

This book is therefore "relational" on three levels: Epstein's relation to her parents, whose stories she includes as part of her own; the interviewees' relation to Epstein; and finally, Epstein's relation to her readers, which is significant in this work in which the author is so clearly the writer and reader of other people's stories. It seems fitting that the first popular memoir about being a child of survivors, a subject that is inherently relational from the beginning, should thus offer such a complicated take on the question of autobiography.

Thus, in her efforts to combat her uncomfortable sense of uniqueness and isolation, Epstein positions herself at the opposite extreme: her own life story becomes a template for the other lives she writes. The particular mode of relational biography she favours therefore threatens to become prescriptive. Even concluding her tale about Tomas, the Czech son of a survivor who had an incestuous relationship with his sister, Epstein muses, "what had happened between them, I came to think, was less the result of physical attraction, or circumstances, or a desire to take revenge, but of a desire to heal. . . It was, I thought, a form of restitution" (279). Epstein attempts to understand Tomas's experience by playing down the taboo at its center so she can overlay it with her own: her quest for "healing" leads to a group meeting; his leads to incest. In this instance, the disparity of experience is especially dramatic, but it serves to illustrate the process that I have already shown is at work elsewhere in the book.

Her structuring of the book, reflecting as it does her reliance on the stories of others to legitimize hers, is therefore a process of normalization. It takes a selective approach whereby, despite the image (quoted earlier) of the tearful author transcribing (or symbolically "crying") Rochelle's recorded words helplessly onto the paper, she is really firmly in control. Her task is one of selecting her subjects' similarities to herself, or of selecting the manner in which they can be made to resemble her. It seems a particularly persuasive instance of Eakin's assertion that "the telling of the story of the other offers these oral historians a measure of self-determination, for the other's story, the other's life, is possessed—indeed created—by the recording self."[22]

Put another way, Epstein's reading and writing of other people's stories, and her writing of her own story, seek to validate her experiences by defining children of survivors as a group. Laura Browder argues that, in what she calls "ethnic autobiographies," there exists between the reader and writer an "implied contract" that the memoirist's story is that "of a people" and thus "must often conform to his or her audience's stereotypes about that ethnicity."[23] Such autobiographies are not concerned with individual uniqueness and autonomy. In these cases, the narrative "value" of an individual's life is dependant on its typification of the ethnic group's experience. This does not equate to "effacement," the word used by Marcus to describe the memoirist's position—as opposed to that of the autobiographer—in his or her text. Rather, the ethnic autobiography may be understood as a quest for a voice by the disempowered that will only succeed while the autobiographer is understood to be typical of the collective experience they are attempting to describe, establishing it as "typical" of the second generation. For survivors in the secularized Jewish community of her childhood, Epstein notes that

> the Holocaust had become a touchstone of their identities as Jews and it became a touchstone for their children as well. The trouble was that while it conferred an identity, it provided no structure, no clue to a way of life. (260)

With an event at the core of their identities that provoked a religious awe without a guiding religious doctrine to go with it, Epstein has turned her attention to second-generation *autobiographical* identities. Epstein writes herself into an autobiographical identity that depends on the experiences of her contemporaries for its cultural value.[24] In attempting to define such an identity, however, she risks delimiting and oversimplifying the "second generation" in a way she appears to wish to resist when she writes that "children of survivors. . . had all grown up in situations of great complexity, acutely aware of how our parents were driven by an impetus toward life as well as death" (203).[25] Given her acknowledgment of the difficulties of psychiatry in accounting for survivors' post-traumatic symptoms, it may be assumed that she is keen to avoid similar problems in descriptions of her own generation. Yet despite her declared intention of finding others like herself, nowhere does she signal her awareness of the dangers of her book's "normalizing" potential.

From the 1960s, the idea of the Holocaust as a source of Jewish identity developed in an unprecedented manner, partly, as Peter Novick argues, due to conscious attempts by Jewish leaders to foster a sense of Jewishness in relation to the Holocaust in a generation of young people who seemed uninterested in other aspects of Jewish culture.[26] If "ownership" of the Holocaust was something available to all Jews, then even the question of children of survivors finding a particular identity grounded in the war years was perhaps more questionable than Epstein's comments above suggest. As I observed in the introduction, this new centrality of the Holocaust to Jewish identity more generally occurred around the same time that the first children of survivors were reaching adulthood. It is thus easy to see that the pathological view of the second generation that finds indirect expression in Epstein's metaphor of the iron box was valuable, or even necessary, to attempts to establish both their own and public understanding of issues specific to them. She herself resists viewing it in pathological terms as follows:

> As I talked to more and more of my contemporaries, I began to feel that they were all carrying around a version of my iron box, the contents of which they had left unexamined and untouched, for fear it might explode. It also became clear to me that our parents' wartime experiences had not given rise to a handful of clinically categorized symptoms but to a particular world view. (220)

Although the iron box is presented here as an *alternative* to the clinical view of the second generation, this paragraph forms part of the conclusion to her (largely uncritical) overview of clinical literature. I have already discussed the resonances of Epstein's image with certain aspects of psychiatric and psychoanalytic discourse, and it recurs here in clear contradiction to her own argument. Here and elsewhere, her book seems to reflect primarily what she portrays as her own psychological need for a peer group. The vast majority of North American memoirs written by children or grandchildren of survivors in the English language are by authors who lack, or who have lacked in the past, a strong religious or cultural Jewish affiliation. It is tempting to read their relationship to the Holocaust as a substitute for such affiliation in a climate where minority status is celebrated and the threat of violent or discriminatory anti-Semitism has lessened.[27] Undoubtedly, the fact of the recent or imminent deaths of many of the "first generation" also figures significantly in any attempt to explain the large numbers of autobiographical texts currently being written by children of survivors.[28] Possibly due to this latter reason, for many of the writers engaged in addressing such issues, redefinition of personal history and ethnicity often seems to mean redefining family, as Epstein tries to do, figuratively at least, in her search for a "community" of people like herself. Certainly, many of them posit Jewish ethnicity or Holocaust-based identity as a personal solution and/or narrative resolution. As such, they—with Epstein as their forerunner—are engaged apparently unintentionally, and possibly owing to the centrality of the Holocaust to contemporary Jewish identity more generally, in creating the stereotype of the child of survivors whose life is dominated by the Holocaust. It would therefore seem that the relational memoir in Epstein's hands works less to "efface" or "fragment" her own identity than to reinforce it and, through the stories of others, build up a coherent self in a way that has previously eluded her.[29]

In her final paragraph, Epstein literalizes the idea of the "family" of children of survivors she mentioned at the beginning as follows:

> My brothers, like many other children of survivors, have lately begun for the first time to ask my mother questions about our grandparents, the relatives we never knew, and exactly where and how our parents survived the war. Like Al Singerman, who at the age of thirty-one, has begun to talk to his father, like Ruth Alexander and Tom Reed, my brothers are often astonished at what they hear—and filled with pride. (345)

Epstein is no longer looking for a family among strangers, but for echoes of the strangers she has met, such as Ruth Alexander and Tom Reed, within her own family. The point at which her brothers begin to fit her normative template of children of survivors is that at which she chooses to end her narrative. This reinforces the sense of a normalizing agenda underlying her project: until her brothers are affected by the Holocaust, they are not really "family" in the sense she wants. She makes her need to find kindred spirits clear, as we have seen, but we should reflect on the fact that Epstein's brothers do not appear to be particularly concerned by this aspect of their lives.[30] As I mentioned in the introduction, there are certainly others like them, and like the musician Aviva in *Children of the Holocaust*, whose very lack of interest renders them of only marginal interest to Epstein's investigations.[31]

Intergenerational Conversations

To return to the terms of my opening discussion of memoir and relational autobiography, in the course of Epstein's account, "proximity" and "otherness" have implicitly been reassessed. There are two important, intertwined strands to this process: Epstein's relationship with her parents, and her developing role as interviewer/witness. In her final chapter, Epstein describes how she came to apply her professional role as interviewer to her parents when she worked for an oral history project as follows:

> The taped interviews I conducted with my mother and father were useful because, for the first time in my life, I heard their histories from start to finish in clear chronology instead of in bits and pieces. I now had a reliable source to refer to, a stable, unchanging record of my family history. (334)

This "reliable," "stable," and "unchanging" record of her family history is externalized in her tape recorder. Yet it is in approaching her parents' experiences in this manner that she begins to work through her relationship with the past. After these interviews, she reads more testimonies as follows:

> The numbness I felt when I heard my own parents' stories disappeared when I read the accounts of others. I could take those in more readily. For the first time, I saw my parents' lives in the context of others. I could put them in perspective and measure them against a community. I had never known any family to place them in. Those survivors I had never met, whose lives I read about in transcript after transcript became a substitute for family. It was then that I realized I had to talk to their children. (336)

By further externalizing her parents' stories, seeing them as part of a constellation of similar histories that is not family-specific, Epstein is able to confront the past in a way that brings her emotions fully into play, rather than remaining "numb." It is through this parallel, much like the one I infer from her view of psychiatric accounts of the two generations, that she sees a value in contextualizing her own experiences, too. As she sits at her first group meeting for children of survivors, it is no longer the similarities between those gathered there that strike her, but rather the differences. "We ourselves," she writes, "were strikingly different people, people who would not have met under ordinary circumstances" (340). While the survivors whose testimonies she has read are "a substitute for family," the nuances of her narrative begin to suggest a new distance from them. Instead, following her father's death, her relationship with her mother altered: "the silence between us had been broken, the constraint that had muted our conversation was gone" (344). Epstein notes that this alteration is detectable on both sides: "My mother, in turn, has learned that her children cannot always be happy, healthy and free of pain. She worries less" (345). In other words, a proper two-way *conversation* has been established. The word "conversation" also implies a clearly separate subjectivity from that of Epstein's mother, whose grief apparently threatened to overwhelm the author during her childhood. This conversation has replaced the sealed inaccessibility of the tomb, where those who died without proper rituals of mourning were "stored" but unreachable. As Epstein talks to her mother, she herself becomes one of the children of survivors mentioned in the book's subtitle, and no longer the interviewer. Ironically but also fittingly, the opening of this dialogue is predicated on her father's death, as Epstein observes: "my mother seems to have inherited the vitality my father left like a legacy to us" (344). A normal funeral both ends her father's life and completes, perhaps even more than the birth of children, her mother's sense of acceptance that she and her family are free from immediate threat. Her father's choice of cremation over burial, so he could "be part of life, the water, the fresh air" (342), and the burial of his ashes "at the top of the tallest mountain in western Massachusetts" (342), provide an image that is almost the total opposite of the "iron box" with its suggestions of the tomb.

Epstein's book is her attempt at a productive fusion of the professional and the emotional, and her view of herself as a facilitator of dialogue or "conversation" is at the heart of this union. As a child, she attempted to keep dialogue going during times of stress for the family, standing outside the bathroom door, for example, "with excuses for opening a conversation, disguises for [her] need of reassurance" (59) when her mother had locked herself in. At these times, she writes,

> I listened hard. I thought I could somehow leach the pain from her by listening. It would leave her body, enter mine, and be lessened by sharing. Otherwise, I thought, it would one day kill my mother. She could kill herself easily behind the locked door. She could give herself an injection or swallow a bottleful of pills as I stood waiting outside. (60)

From childhood, Epstein has believed in the power of the exchange of words, speaking and listening, to keep unthinkable consequences of past traumas at bay. This puts particular strain on her as, she writes, "there was no way I could shout back at my father; no way I could reproach my mother"

(61). Furthermore, "in our home words ricocheted between worlds, their meaning uncertain. My parents told stories but the stories never explained" (64). Her parents' words refer to a world so different from the America of the present that their meaning is uncertain. Epstein's relationship to the past, then, is figured as a failed attempt to communicate: symbolically, this failure is what is kept in the iron box.

It is in the woods with her parents and their friends, however, that this preoccupation with words first seems to point to a vocation as a writer. Epstein explains that the state parks around New York were where her parents chose to spend their weekends in order to escape the city and its sense of confinement. These parks are informal meeting places for exiles like themselves, permitting Epstein an insight into her parents as they were in their pre-war identities, and giving her a sense that she occupies a space between worlds as follows:

> I felt as if I carried unwritten plays inside of me, whole casts of characters who were invisible and voiceless, who could only speak through me. The people at the picnic table were voiceless in America. There, in the woods, they spun stories and told jokes and formulated theories, but once back in the world of the city, their voices were stilted and halting. They could not find the right words. . . .
> I had access to both worlds. I could move back and forth, serve as courier, interpreter and spy. It was I who asked for instructions when we got lost on the back roads in the country: it was I who corrected my father's spelling and syntax when he wrote letters to the mayor of New York. (167–68)

Epstein is a cultural, but above all a linguistic, broker between her two worlds. "I did not have to gather my thoughts," she writes; "the words came into my mouth fully formed, as though I were a medium and other people were speaking through me. . . . I stumbled through the woods. . . buffeted by visions of saving, of reclaiming, of healing" (168). Epstein seems concerned with failed dialogues between parent and child, survivor and America, survivor and psychiatrist, and between children of survivors themselves. Consequently, she portrays herself at different times as interpreter, translator (as with Tomas, the Czech student in Israel) and scribe, or amanuensis, (as she listens to Rochelle's testimony or is in the woods). In these roles, she facilitates the act of conversation without being either the speaker or interlocutor.

As Epstein notes, uniting two sides of a conversation also occurred in the course of writing the book: "For nine years," she writes, "I had been writing about other people's lives, learning to extract the essence of their experience and sensibility. Now, for the first time, I wanted to apply those skills to myself" (15). Here, as I mentioned earlier, Epstein makes this seem like a natural progression, from professional to personal. Yet the following, appearing a few pages later, calls this into question:

> I did not like talking about my parents or the war, because talk meant accepting that the war had happened and, more than anything else in the world, I wished it had not. The idea that my mother and my father had been forced out of their homes and made to live like animals—worse than animals—was too shameful to admit. To tell people that my parents had been in concentration camp in a cool rational tone was a kind of denial. (19–20)

It is precisely "the essence of. . . experience and sensibility," the target of her journalism, that Epstein has been repressing with regard to her parents. Not only does reading the testimonies of others prepare her for dealing with her parents' stories, but her journalistic role as an interviewer plays out in her conversations with others what she cannot do with her parents.

Conclusion: Re-evaluating Memoir

Epstein writes that she grew up in the care of parents who "had determined not to frighten [her] with their recollections, yet. . . did not want to lie" (47). Her exposure to their stories of the past gave her a strange sense of loneliness and influenced certain life choices, such as her decision to study in Israel. Psychiatric evidence to date suggests that children of survivors are more predisposed to psychopathology if they conform to particular criteria, and Natan Kellerman's synthesis of these criteria is highly informative.[32] Epstein fulfills some of these criteria on the grounds of being the first born, being born soon after the Holocaust, her parents' suffering disturbances due to extreme mental pain, and both her parents' being survivors. Her brothers, obviously, are not the first born, nor were they born very soon after their parents' traumas.[33] Epstein was also the only one of her parents' offspring to be born in Czechoslovakia, at the *site* of their suffering, a factor that might also have influenced her relationship to her parents' pasts. Her sense of loneliness, despite knowing other children of survivors at home and school, is more comprehensible in the light of this information. Her normalization process, then, employs very specific criteria that cannot be seen as characteristic of all children of survivors. She wishes to legitimize and give credibility to what she feels is (or should be) a powerful relationship between her parents' past and her own life.

In her book's concluding remarks, Epstein says with an implicit sense of relief, "my mother. . . has learned that her children cannot always be happy, healthy and free of pain" (345). Meeting other children of survivors with similar feelings allowed her to shed some of the responsibility she had previously felt for her parents, permitting her to give more space to her own wishes. This reading of the text serves to reinforce Eakin's point that "relational autobiography" can, in breach of traditional perceptions, be the autobiography of the writer and not that of her subject. In the following quotation, Nancy K. Miller, however, proposes a deeper level of complexity:

> It is not always easy to tell where we stand in relation to each other, nor who decides. The difficulty of that deciphering, darkened further by the betrayals of dreams and the tricks of memory, should remind us of the dangers inherent in drawing the lines of identity with too much certainty. Rather than models, we would do better to imagine more perplexing figures whose intimate and violent dialogues with living and dead others perform the bedrock of self-construction itself.
>
> Still, in the end. . . perhaps autobiographers write because they need the others only readers represent.[34]

To return to the terminology of my opening quotations from Laura Marcus, Epstein neither "efface[s]" herself in the text, nor does she present herself as central and powerful by perceiving the world "as an 'emanation' of the self." Rather, she attempts to effect a move from a pathologized marginality to a normalized, "healthy" centrality; and a close examination of her text reveals the "intimate and violent dialogues" that threaten to undermine this project. All autobiographies are equally constructed in nature. In broadening the scope of what he calls "relational biography" to include all autobiographical writing, Paul John Eakin writes,

> the selves we have been may seem to us as discrete and separate as the other persons with whom we live our relational lives. This experiential truth points to the fact that our sense of continuous identity is a fiction, the primary fiction of all self-narration.[35]

In this formulation, an autobiographical text necessarily deals with different identities or selves, as the writer/subject has not remained constant and fixed. The process of identity construction that I have examined in Epstein's book is thus present in any autobiographical text. This text illustrates the problems inherent in one author's attempt to overcome a sense of marginality in her own life—like other such writers, she has been painfully conscious of herself as a mere emanation of her parents' worlds.

CHAPTER 2

The Family Memoir:
Louise Kehoe's *In This Dark House*

Introduction: Unspoken Histories

The second generation of Helen Epstein's "community" is defined by knowledge: even in instances where historical information about parental experience is limited, she and most of her interviewees share a sense of that history's implications for their parents and themselves. Given the limitations imposed by Epstein's agenda, it is clear that she does not present the whole story. Implicit in my reading of *Children of the Holocaust* is the fact that a historical or psychological consciousness of the past is not an inevitable part of second-generation experience. Through another detailed textual reading, this chapter considers the implications of the absence of information. It also aims to show that a writer concerned with her family's Holocaust past for reasons different to Epstein's can nonetheless produce a text that raises strikingly similar questions about autobiography. Between them, Epstein's *Children of the Holocaust* and Louise Kehoe's *In This Dark House* map out the territory of second-generation experience on an axis that ranges from the author having an acute and sensitive awareness of her parents' Holocaust experiences on the one hand, to being totally unaware and indeed deliberately misled about the subject on the other.

The claim that the absence of Holocaust knowledge in later generations of survivor families is a subject worthy of close attention can be substantiated from beyond the fields of literature and psychoanalysis. For example, upon Madeleine Albright's appointment as U.S. Secretary of State, a *Washington Post* article described her parents as Jewish refugees from Czechoslovakia. Albright's response, that she was unaware of her Jewish identity, was unsurprisingly met with incredulity in many quarters. Yet further investigation shows such cases to be neither incredible nor rare.[1] Art psychotherapist Joy

Schaverien noted this phenomenon when, starting in 1988, she ran workshops in London:

> Many [of those attending] were second generation survivors who had not previously identified themselves as Jewish. . . . Many who were in their forties had been brought up without awareness of the fact that one, or even in some cases both, parents were Jewish. . . . Having grown up in ignorance of the truth, for their own protection, the realization had been a shock, but also a relief, because at some level the truth is always known.[2]

Barbara Kessel, whose book *Suddenly Jewish* contains many compelling narratives on this theme, notes that "several [people whose parents kept their experiences secret] concluded that Holocaust survivors cannot discount the possibility that being Jewish might one day again be dangerous" and subsequently chose the suppression of a potentially lethal identity over the transmission of cultural and family history.[3] However, the "shock" and "relief" of Schaverien's clients indicates that total secrecy is hard to achieve. As Kessel writes,

> what do we learn about the concept of identity from those scores of people who said they were attracted to Judaism well before they discovered their Jewish ancestry? Fourteen of the individuals interviewed felt so strong a pull that they converted before they found out they had Jewish lineage.[4]

The question of "knowing" versus "not knowing" cannot be reduced to a clear either/or opposition: what is unsaid by parents may reveal as much as what is openly spoken; and equally what is remembered and forgotten by the second generation may point to an unconscious ambivalence about Holocaust knowledge.[5] In a suggestive instance of the transmission of an unspoken history, Susan Jacoby's memoir *Half-Jew* reinforces Schaverien's assertion that "the truth is always known." In the following excerpt, Jacoby expresses how she feels that on an unconscious level she must have known about her father's Jewishness:

> Until I began writing this book, I had forgotten one of the recurrent dreams of my adolescence—a nightmare in which I was a prisoner in a concentration camp. . . . Concentration camp dreams, I learned as an adult, were in no way unusual among my contemporaries—children born shortly before, during, or soon after World War II. But while I have many friends who remember similar dreams, every one of them is Jewish, brought up in a Jewish home where the murder of the six million was treated. . . as a death in the family.[6]

These instances may be seen as evidence of an unconscious process of inter-generational transmission that has been documented by clinical researchers examining survivor families.[7] Louise Kehoe's memoir *In This Dark House* describes one instance of the repression of a family's true history.

Although the events Kehoe describes take place largely in Britain, it seems particularly fitting to be writing about her book alongside American and Canadian works. David Brauner, for example, in *Post-War Jewish Fiction*, discusses Kehoe in the context of British women writers. However, the author relates these events at a time when she has relocated to the United States and has been declared Jewish there. It is only possible to speculate on whether she would have written the book (or how similar a book she *could* have written) had she remained in Britain's comparatively subdued climate of identity politics. However, very few second-generation memoirs are written from a wholly British point of view. One excellent example, Anne Karpf's *The War After*, writes as if to inform an audience completely unaware of the issues facing children of survivors: it was published in 1996, when Alan L. Berger's survey of published second-generation texts, *Children of Job*, was to come out in the United States the following year. It is also notable that other second-generation writers who live in Britain, such as Eva Hoffman and Lisa Appignanesi, have spent significant portions of their lives in Canada and the United States. In this context, Kehoe's "Anglo-American" book is interestingly placed.

Kehoe's book is subtitled "A Memoir," but it makes extensive use of novelistic techniques in ways that David Brauner characterizes as two "problems" inherent in her literary project:

> first, that [Kehoe] has to resort to speculation when attempting to account for her parents' actions before she was born and during the period when she was too young to have any personal recollection of the events described; and second, the temptation faced by any autobiographer or biographer (and this is, in fact. . . both a family memoir and an autobiography), to imbue history with a retrospective significance.[8]

Such concerns are "problems" indeed for the historian, and perhaps the biographer, but, as I discussed in the introduction, boundaries between fiction and autobiography are necessarily unclear in this field. Writers of "second-generation fiction," such as Barbara Finkelstein and Thomas Friedmann, are clearly—inevitably—drawing on their own experiences to some extent. Equally, while few memoirists completely eschew the "fictional techniques" used by Kehoe, they exhibit varying degrees of self-awareness about this issue.[9] However, like a number of second-generation autobiographies,

Kehoe's contains a prefatory note that states that "this book represents the truth as I see it, but because of the sheer complexity of the story it has been necessary to introduce occasional elements of fiction." In David Brauner's words, "she employs many of the techniques of fiction to create suspense by withholding vital information, whilst at the same time carefully embedding hints of future developments within the narrative."[10] Kehoe is not only aware of the haziness of generic boundaries, but also chooses to work with, rather than against, this awareness.

In This Dark House is the story of a childhood rendered traumatic by a tyrannical father who psychologically, and sometimes physically, abused the author and her siblings as they grew up in a tiny English hamlet. An account of the author's childhood experiences and their impact on her in adulthood takes up the majority of the book. A much shorter concluding section covers the period following her father's death. It is in this section that the reader learns of Kehoe's father's secret Jewish identity, and the guilt and self-loathing arising from his being safe in England while his parents were and deported to Auschwitz is revealed as the reason for his cruel behavior. The author then briefly reviews her life, pointing out the clues to her father's real identity that, with hindsight, seem obvious. Notably, many of the clues that she discusses at this point are not to be found in the foregoing text. A re-reading, however, shows that the text contains many further indications that she chooses not to refer back to in this way. The concluding section thus seems to be a pointed invitation to re-read the book, providing the following model for such a re-reading: it "frames" the main body of the memoir in a way that characterizes the modes of interpretation that are figured in the text itself. The gaps in the reader's knowledge, like those in the narrator's knowledge, are not the only reason for this; the book's rural setting also functions to disguise its horrific subtext, and indeed this setting changes dramatically in significance when the full story comes to light. Consider, for example, this passage, which is the opening of chapter 1:

> In the southwest of England, where the river Severn ambles gently through the undulating Cotswold countryside, the scenery is timeless and unmistakably agricultural. The landscape is latticed with natural hedgerows—prickly and impenetrable thickets of sweetbrier and hazel, hawthorn and elder—which divide field from field and farm from farm along ancient boundaries. The narrow, winding roads are used by livestock more than cars, and the few drivers who do negotiate those twists and turns do so at snail's pace, knowing that they may at any moment come upon a flock of sheep or a herd of cattle plodding sedately toward their barn at milking time.[11]

The emphasis on an archaic, remote, rural setting in a southwest England reminiscent of Laurie Lee's or Thomas Hardy's is in striking contrast to her parents' motivations for moving there, as surmised by Kehoe, which seem to have been to do with escaping an unpalatable present. However, within this rural context, Kehoe gives many coded hints of the truth behind her father's behavior, several of which become particularly clear on re-reading. One such example is her description of the farm's annual cattle roundup. Every year, farm hands drove the cows into the orchard, with liberal use of sticks, and a selection was carried out on the grounds of productivity. There was "a fretting and mounting chorus of mooing as mothers were separated from their calves" until they would be herded up the ramp into the cattle truck, where "the men encircled the hapless animals, beating and clubbing them, forcing them forward up the ramp," until the truck was "crammed to capacity" (43). This is a particularly obvious manifestation of a pattern of references that lead us to the Holocaust as the center of the family's problems. However, in the context of a rural coming-of-age narrative, this scene serves to deflect the reader's attention from a meaning that is obvious when the passage is quoted in isolation. This memoir is, in David Brauner's words, "[Kehoe's] attempt to restore the ruins of her childhood by reinstating into her own life story the facts that her father hid from her for so long, the facts that she hopes will explain, and consequently provide some consolation for, her father's brutal treatment of her and her family."[12] In order to achieve this, she overlays her childhood memories with her later knowledge of family history, in much the same way that her father's denial of his past is tempered by his references to it that reveal little in isolation, but, when taken together, suggest a strong desire to tell.

Where Epstein's quest for knowledge led her beyond her own family, Kehoe's requires her to examine her family more closely. Kehoe's father attempts to control his children's access to the past by withholding information from them and offering pictorial or written clues. These clues turn out not to be wholly truthful in themselves, as they are cryptic, incomplete, or evasive. As we shall see, however, they can easily be read as pointers to a hidden history. Yet, in her retrospective analysis, Kehoe does not always highlight this, choosing instead to draw the following conclusions from other aspects of her father's behavior, such as his use of Yiddish and Hebrew words, which has hitherto gone unmentioned:

> As I look back on my childhood with the ineffable wisdom of hindsight, I can see many examples of revealingly Jewish things he said and did. . . . Machinator that he was, though, I think he derived a sneaking pleasure from parading these things so brazenly in front of us and seeing how indifferent we were to them. Certainly it must have helped to reassure him that his identity camouflage was

still working well, that he had succeeded in diluting his Jewishness to the point of imperceptibility. (219–20)

The specifically Jewish words and phrases that were camouflaged in their multilingual household are now, Kehoe insists, obvious signs. If, as Schaverien says, "at some level the truth is always known," then Kehoe wishes here to make the following companion point: at some level, there is always a desire to reveal the truth. Or if, in Nicolas Abraham's terms, "what haunts are not the dead, but the gaps left within us by the secrets of others," Kehoe's father attempted to control and delimit those gaps in his children.[13]

Decoding the Past: Photographs, Postcards, Graves

To a large extent, the truth is revealed in this book through a complex system of pictures and framings, on which my reading centers. Rather like Epstein's device of withholding Deborah Schwartz's testimony, these pictures and postcards provide the narrative structure for Kehoe's gathering of information. Near the beginning of her memoir, Kehoe writes about her mother's photographs of her father in uniform, and of his grave in France. In a process of double framing, the picture of the father's grave is tucked into a corner of the larger picture's frame. Mama, the reader is told, chose to marry an older man because of her idolization of her own father, who was killed in the First World War, even though "she had no memory of him" (9). However, as the following excerpt reveals, this is not entirely true:

> Such was her pride in her dead father that as a child she was unshakeably convinced that the Lord's Prayer opened with the words "Our Father, who art in Heaven, Harold be Thy Name." It had come as both a shock and a disappointment to her when, having learned to read, she discovered that the official version was addressed to someone else entirely. (9)

In the absence of "real" memories, if these can be said to exist, Kehoe's mother constructed her own set of memories as a child from her sense of his continued presence. This powerful alignment of father with God in her memory is used to illuminate the family dynamics that form the subject of Kehoe's book, particularly in her mother's clear act of father-substitution as described here: "My father, almost twice her age, so accomplished, so handsome and so mesmerizingly strong-willed, must have seemed to her the personification of the father she had never had, and her devotion to him was immediate, unwavering and lifelong" (9–10). Kehoe's mother appears to have been looking for a father/God replacement against "her intuition, her conscience and her abundant common sense" (10). This hints at a truth beyond the plain tyranny of her husband. Her own needs render her an instrument of his desire to be master of his own origin, and are complicit with his aim to be more than a family patriarch. Without a wife who would "[defer] to him in all things," he could not have carried out his project of reinventing, or more precisely, of uninventing, this origin. That Mama was so ambitious and gifted, being one of the first women to study at the architectural school to which she was admitted, could only emphasize his power over her when he succeeded in "encourag[ing]" her to give up, to live with him without being married, and to abort several babies that she wanted to keep (10–11). Secondly, as a well-known Modernist architect in Britain, he could not change his name, so his children became a site for reworking and acting out his problematic identity. Unable to reinvent himself, he attempts to reinvent them, keeping everything about his past secret except for the "fact" that "Berthold Lubetkin was not his real name" (55). Knowing everything about his children's origins, he let them know nothing about himself. When we discover that in fact Berthold Lubetkin *is* his real name, his deception is revealed as a double denial that posited, for a time, his own name as a false origin. He drew attention to where the truth lay only to deflect interest by an assertion of its falseness.[14] Mama's photographs assert her father's power through absence: there is not merely a photograph of the man but of his grave as a marker both of his absence and of the fact that he once existed. Perversely and in a similar manner, Father uses his name as a marker of the fact that his identity was once known, but is not any longer.

There is a further irony to this deceit. One of the many insults to which Lubetkin subjects his children is that of "non-'betkin" (63), suggesting they are unworthy of the family name. As Kehoe writes, "Dad expected his children to mirror his beliefs, and to do so enthusiastically. Any dissent or deviation was viewed not just as a sign of intellectual degeneracy but also as a deliberate act of disloyalty toward him" (41). Sharing his name, in her father's opinion, meant sharing wholeheartedly in his identity, even when that identity was itself contrived. Indeed, his forcing his children to share his identity and ideas turned them into perpetuators of the very myths that were designed to conceal their true origins. However, even if they succeeded to some degree in repressing their own personalities in his presence, their physical identities were inescapable. Thus,

> despite the fact that Robby's nose and Dad's were identical in every respect. . .
> Dad used to comment at every opportunity about how ugly and prominent
> Robby's nose was, and how he was going to take Robby to Vienna and make

> him have plastic surgery on it to abate its intrusive presence and bring it down
> to a more acceptable shape and size. (67)

Berthold Lubetkin did not expect his children to mirror him physically in the way he expected them to do so ideologically. Kehoe speculates that the "mulish fidelity to the Soviet Union" that he imposed on his children "owed a great deal to the Soviet policy of denying the existence of a Jewish peoplehood and identity" (216). "Jewish" looks were a special problem for Lubetkin, and this preoccupation may partly explain why his son Andrew's "existence [was] studiously effaced" (25) after his childhood death; it is noted that he "was in every way [his surviving elder sister's] opposite. While she was dark, he was fair" (24).[15] He is thus not simply a dead child, but one whose looks played a part in the process of forgetting an unwelcome past.

These examples hint at the ways in which family truths may come to be "known" without ever having been knowingly shared. Such truths emerge when Father's lies and evasions come into direct collision with the truth. The intersection of the true and false identities at work in the book occurs notably at three points before the truth is established, and each of these three instances has an impact on the lives of Kehoe and her elder sister, Vicky. The first concerns Father's oversight—or perhaps, given his enthusiasm for abortions, his acute awareness—that children are as much part of the past as they are the future, and is concerned with another way in which his children's appearances tie them to his past as described in the following passage:

> Late one night I stirred from a deep sleep to find Dad sitting beside my bed,
> gently stroking my hair. He thought I was still fast asleep, of course, but I
> wasn't. There was a full moon that night, and in its light I could clearly see the
> tears which filled his eyes and trickled down his cheeks. "You look so much like
> my mother," he whispered. Then he kissed my forehead and quietly slipped
> out of the room. (57)

In a physiological return of the repressed, the author as a child has come to reflect her father's denied parentage. In a double irony, the author describes this incident she is never supposed to have witnessed as "[her] most treasured gift from him" (57). It is a gift not only of part of the past that has been denied her, but also of an insight into the love hidden behind her father's brutality. His speaking tenderly to her only when she is asleep is a powerful symbol of the lack of communication that haunts his relationship with Kehoe and her siblings well into adulthood.

The second incident is her parents' reaction to the author's cruel treatment by an anti-Semitic doctor during a visit to Bavaria. Following a bicycle accident that occurred while visiting a pen-friend, she is taken to a hospital where the doctor first questions her about her Jewish name and then proceeds to carry out procedures in a deliberately painful way, eventually requiring her to strip for a tetanus injection in her breasts (110–11). Her parents' studied indifference to this event that is felt by Kehoe to be a "violation" (112) provokes her final departure from the family home at the age of fifteen. Where the first incident revealed her father's concealed love for her, this one sees him feigning indifference.

In the last of the three events, in narrative terms if not chronologically, Kehoe's sister falls in love with a young Jewish man in Paris who wishes to marry her and, based on her name, argues that she must be Jewish, a fact of paramount importance for him. Vicky begs her mother to tell her the truth, and her mother averts the probability of her daughter's marriage by telling her a false story about her father's background (the contents of which I shall return to later). These incidents mark the points where the repressed past accidentally reveals itself: the historical and genealogical truth of the children's identities crosses over with the lived reality of their perceived identities. For the author, the incident involving the anti-Semitic doctor marks out her parents' failure to acknowledge her Jewishness as a strand of their general lack of nurture and support. It becomes the final step in her adolescent alienation from them because, without knowledge of their motives, it appears consistent with aspects of her father's earlier behavior toward her. This lends significance to the fact that one of the few details we learn about the course of her life after her father's death is that, after moving from England to Boston, she has herself pronounced officially Jewish: knowledge of Jewishness becomes symbolic of freedom from parental tyranny (225).[16]

These inadvertent revelations make little sense at the time, and indeed the story of Vicky's Jewish boyfriend is only revealed to the author after her father's death. Their hidden subtexts are not evident at the point of their occurrence. In this they differ from the system of pictures, postcards, and framings that I referred to earlier, as the circumstances of the transmission of these invites the reader's interpretation in each case. The first of two pictures that Berthold Lubetkin gives to his adult daughter is presented at the railway station, at the end of a visit he makes to her in London:

> The train had begun moving now, and I was running alongside it, shouting my good-byes to him, sending my love to Mama. "Here," he shouted back to me, throwing an envelope out of the window in my general direction before snapping the window shut and sinking gratefully into his seat. I ran after the envelope, which was now being blown along the platform in the wake of the departing train, and got my foot to it just as it was about to blow onto the track. Picking

it up, I turned to wave one last time to Dad, but the train had rounded a bend in the track and disappeared from view. (142–43)

Quite apart from the iconic significance that the Holocaust has lent to partings and departures at railway stations, there are several signs here—the desperate farewells as the writer keeps pace with the train, the near loss of the envelope on the track, the belatedness of the attempt to acknowledge receipt—that point to an enactment of the repressed Holocaust past in the author's writing. There is a clear sense of salvaging a relic from what is portrayed here as a grand and poignant—even clichéd—scene of departure, despite the author's troubled relationship with her father that she has disclosed at length. Even more strikingly, her father's chosen mode of delivery, the letter thrown from the train window, draws on his unacknowledged past: letters were thrown from the transports on their way to concentration camps, as messages to loved ones or warnings to others, where they were sometimes found and posted to their intended destinations.[17] This, as with most of the other textual clues to her father's past, goes unremarked when the "truth" is finally revealed: we are given no clue as to whether either member of the family was aware of the full extent of this resonance. Anne Whitehead has written, in reference to Etty Hillesum's similar dispatching of a postcard, that "the sending of the post card inaugurates a creative act of parting, which projects a future audience or witness and opens up a trajectory with unforeseen and unforeseeable possibilities."[18] This gesture of Lubetkin's thus constructs a present departure as a future return to an unacknowledged past. It not only enacts that past, but, as the following passage describes, the gesture contains within it an invitation to interpretation:

I opened the envelope and inside found one of the postcards Dad had just bought from the gallery shop. It was a picture by the surrealist Giorgio De Chirico, an eerie, dreamlike scene, full of foreboding, with long, ominous shadows and inexplicable juxtapositions: an empty, desolate landscape with a tall brick chimney in the distance and another one beside it belching smoke. In the foreground stood a lone, empty railway freight car. The picture was titled *The Anguish of Departure*. I turned it over and on the back, in Dad's hasty, crabbed handwriting, was the sardonic message *Come and see us again before we die*. (143)

The symbolism of this painting in the context seems so obvious to contemporary readers as to barely need analysis; is the author's dismissal of its "inexplicable juxtapositions," like her father's assertion of his name's falseness, simply drawing the reader's attention away from the obvious path of inquiry so as to suspend narrative resolution? Both the picture and its title confirm

the implications of the circumstances of its transmission. As I discussed earlier, the author suspects a secret pleasure on her father's part at being able to
make such an obvious allusion to his past yet have it go unnoticed. Her interpretation of his words as sardonic points to the possibility of a sense of loss on
his part: in performing this gesture, he still fails to communicate any warmth
toward his daughter. The title "The Anguish of Departure" may be read as an
attempt to speak through the artist's words, a last attempt at communication
and even reconciliation. Hence, the message that she reads as sardonic—
"Come and see us again before we die" —becomes profoundly moving.

The grounds for this interpretation are strengthened in the light of the
author's discovery, among her father's possessions after his death, of another
postcard, sent from Riga, which I quote here in full:

> Dearest Berthold, I got a letter yesterday from your father in Warsaw. It is the
> second letter I have had from him recently, this time dated May 19, 1940. Your
> parents are healthy. They live in the old house still, but only in the kitchen
> because the other part of the house was bombed by the Nazis and burned
> down. Your father is astonished that he has heard nothing from you. Why do
> you not write to him? If it would make it easier for you please write to me and
> I will pass news to your parents. Surely you could write to me, your own
> cousin? You do remember you have a cousin Mira, don't you? Your father asked
> me to send food—butter and cheese. These things are not available now in
> Warsaw. Loving wishes, your cousin Mira. (201)

The first postcard appears to have been a "clue" to this earlier one, which
provides a symbolic and historical symmetry to Kehoe's father's gesture. Here,
as Berthold may have felt with hindsight, the subtext is a message from his
own parents saying "Come and see us again before we die" —a subtext that
he either refused or was unable to acknowledge at the time of receipt. Later,
the knowledge of the implications of his failure to act would have given this
card the status of a final attempt at communication before Auschwitz, as if
flung from the window of a train. Yet the author can only reach this conclusion after she has made the link between the Mira who signs herself here, and
the Mira whose American telephone number is scribbled in her father's
address book. It is she who provides further details, eventually confirming
Auschwitz as Kehoe's grandparents' place of death.

Analyzing these "texts within the text" also provides a key to a reading of
Berthold's domineering and abusive behavior, which now appears to be a
long process of acting out the trauma of his failure to act and save his parents.
His cousin remembers him as a spoiled and rebellious young man:

> His pranks were the stuff of family legend. . . . Of course his parents, Mira's
> Aunt Fenya and Uncle Roman, were heavily to blame for Berthold's wilfulness
> and dilettantism: he was their only child, and they indulged him at every turn,
> never disciplining him with any conviction or consistency. (207)

In continuing this pattern of unreliable behavior by failing to help his parents, he betrays them. Thus, his attempt to domineer and prevent rebellion
in his own children can be seen as a warped self-protection instinct: his lying
about his origins masks his own perceived failure of respect or duty toward
his parents, a failure he is anxious to prevent in his own children. This self-
protection is simply the converse of a desire to save his children from themselves, and from the self-loathing he has endured for his whole adulthood.

A moment of departure is also the occasion he chooses for his second parting gift to his daughter. This time he is about to board a plane,

> But suddenly he turned back, and fumbled for a moment with the ticket enve-
> lope. "Here," he said, handing me a tiny, faded photograph of a long-haired
> little boy wearing a sailor suit and a voluminous straw hat. "I thought you
> might want this. It's me when I was four years old. Now bugger off." And he
> turned resolutely away and was swept with the tide down the tunnel to the
> plane. (176)

Once more, the text suggests that the picture was almost lost or forgotten.
His rude dismissiveness underlines the fact that he is unwilling to elaborate
on this sudden disclosure of information. However, it seems that his wish to
tell Kehoe the truth cannot be fully acknowledged either. This is confirmed
by the fact, noticed by the author when perusing the picture with a magnify-
ing glass for internal clues, that it is not a whole picture but a fragment
clipped from a larger one. Like his false claim that his name is not his own,
this picture points not to a certainty but to a larger absence. It is revealing
that the author's search is internal, looking for "textual" clues in the picture,
when the context is possibly more informative. She chooses to concentrate on
what her father has given her, retaining her father as the source of information rather than looking more widely, which would be in effect to question
his honesty. However, her mother, with her iconic photograph of her own
father's grave, has provided a model for this. Photographs have been presented from the very beginning—of both the text and of the author's life—as
sites of (over-) interpretation and (over-) investment. They are also sites of
paternal authority.

The final "text" in the book, one of the "framing" pictures, is another photograph. This picture is among several that Mira shows Kehoe, including

some that portray the author's grandparents. Kehoe's selection of this particular picture for close scrutiny in the text is revealing:

> All my life I had wondered what lay in our family's past and who Dad really
> was. Now I knew, and when Mira showed me a photograph of her father's
> grave in the Jewish cemetery in St. Petersburg, with the Star of David and the
> name LUBETKIN carved on the polished black granite headstone, it seemed
> to me that Dad could have no secrets from me any longer. That simple, stark
> inscription was as eloquent and unambiguous a statement of identity as I was
> ever likely to come across, and I could hardly take my eyes off it. (212)

The immediate resonance is with her mother's photograph of her own father's
grave, overlapping with the picture of the man himself, as if to confer a definitive authority on his life. In this newly-discovered photograph of her cousin's
father's grave, Kehoe has found the imaginary paternal origin she had been
looking for: it is not insignificant, perhaps, that this grave is not that of her
own grandfather—for whom, we presume, no grave exists—but that the origin she seeks becomes displaced on to her great uncle. This is particularly
interesting given her reliance on texts and clues provided by her father up to
this point. Additionally, unlike her mother's photograph of a grave, which
supplements that of a person, here the person is absent. Yet the author feels
that this picture is definitive, seeing the family name literally engraved in
stone along with the Star of David. Her unquestioning sense that this picture reveals her father in some respect and is an "unambiguous. . . statement
of identity" owes far more to her mother's own interpretation of fatherhood
than to her father's identity as such. While the father may be figured here as
giver of identity, the mother is equipped, and equips her daughter, with the
tools of interpretation.

Unusually for the authors of memoirs of this kind, Kehoe expresses no
desire to travel to visit the places where her family lived and died, though the
revelation does take place during the cold war period. Seeing the photographs, including that of the grave, appears not to provoke her curiosity.
Instead, dismantling her father's mythology is enough. The story he created
about his origins was a double bluff. It is an alternative traumatic myth in
which he is the son of Admiral Stepan Makarov of the imperial Russian navy:

> Admiral Makarov was a strict disciplinarian, and Dad hated him. Dad had an
> older brother who was an ensign in the navy aboard the Admiral's ship, and
> one night, as a punishment for some infraction, the Admiral made him
> stand, lashed to the mast, on deck all night in the depths of a frigid Gulf of
> Finland winter, dressed only in a thin nightshirt. Dad's brother—whom he

> adored, apparently, died of exposure as a result, and Dad never forgave his father for what he had done. That was why he shunned the name, and forbade Mama ever to mention it to any of us. (186)

In this traumatic founding myth, Kehoe's father figures his own father as the origin of his namelessness. He failed in his paternal duty, and thus forfeited the right to pass on his name to his children. He presents himself as a loyal victim of his father, when in fact Berthold Lubetkin's real or perceived deficiency in filial loyalty resulted in his failure to save his parents; his survival equates to a lack of victimhood, so that survivor guilt is entwined with his view of himself as a son. Consequently, "having hated himself to capacity, he let his bitter self-loathing spill over to taint his children, those three dark-eyed, dark-haired echoes of himself, who reminded him daily of his parents and his past" (215). The wilfully forgotten father thereby reasserts himself through the grandchildren, and, in doing so, threatens the supremacy of the myth.

One striking instance of such an intergenerational process at work is Kehoe's anorexia, which she attributes to having been co-opted into her father's "grotesque ritual of forcing Mama to eat against her will" during her final illness (172). Very early in the text, Kehoe "wonder[s] at what point [her] father stopped calling [her] mother Maggie and instead began calling her Mama, *which is the way Russian children address their mothers*" (19; emphasis added). In force-feeding his wife ("Mama"), and indeed in all of his more genuinely loving treatment of her, he is compensating for his failure to feed and care for his own mother. This overcompensation, known to Kehoe herself at the time only as bizarre and distressing behavior toward his wife on her deathbed, is reflected in her own life-threatening anorexia, causing her to mirror, unconsciously, the plight of her starving grandparents. Her only clue to a link with an earlier generation is her sense that her personal difficulties will best be resolved by an understanding of her father's unknown background (172). Her father never acknowledges her illness, "probably hoping that if he ignored the problem studiously enough it might quietly pack its bags and disappear," much as he has been aiming to achieve with his past (169).

Conclusion: The Unknown Grave

Kehoe's powerful representation of the past's simultaneous concealment and revelation in family life raises interesting questions. For Kehoe's readers, the question of whether "the truth is always known" is unanswered, but this is possibly not the crucial theme. Rather, the text suggests that the past is a formative part of one's life whether it is known or not, and the very fact of its uncertainty can shape identities even as it casts doubt upon them.

For Kehoe, like Epstein, photographs and graves are inextricably linked, and photographs of graves are the markers of mourning that have significance for Kehoe. Her emphasis on these photographs rather than the pictures of the people now buried within the graves gestures to a closed-off family past. If her father's concealment represents something like Abraham's "secret buried alive in the father's unconscious,"[19] then at the point of revelation, it is acknowledging the fact of concealment that is important, rather than the substance of what is concealed. Only later does the author decide what the uncovered secret will mean for her life.

Photographs and graves—for Epstein as well as for Kehoe—represent closure of and access to the family past in answer to questions of identity. The retrospective intergenerational link that the reader can make between Kehoe's anorexia, her grandparents' experiences, and her father's behavior toward her mother serves to "justify" or explain the problems that her father refused to acknowledge. The author's lack of critical attention to the "clues" that, as I have shown, she represents in detail, also serves to situate the revelation of her father's identity and the nature of her grandparents' deaths as totally unexpected. That is, the text is particularly and paradoxically conscious of the unconscious nature of her body's responses. In this way, she could be seen as extricating herself from any implication of failure of communication or understanding, and she consequently places her physical and mental distress beyond her own control. She thus reasserts her position as an independent agent by marking the limits of where such agency could reasonably be expected to apply. Her strong reaction to the photograph of her great-uncle's Jewish grave and her subsequent decision to have herself declared Jewish symbolize the belated grasping of an identity that reaches beyond her father; while it is also his identity, it is one she has chosen herself, and—most importantly—counter to his impositions.

This identity is also a rejection of the pre-modernist narrative suggested by her upbringing in rural England. Kehoe is not, like Anne Karpf, conscious of experiencing Jewishness alongside, and in conflict with, England and Englishness.[20] Instead, the links to Jewishness that she uncovers—the questions about her Jewish name from the doctor in Germany and her sister's boyfriend in France, the grave in Russia, Mira in New York—exert a pull away from England. For this text, Jewishness is not only an internal space whose shape and ownership remain hard to define, but also another country. The cruelty and repression of the past that are re-enacted in Kehoe's childhood turn the rural English landscape into a place from which she must escape.

In this case, as in Epstein's, relational autobiographical writing works to reclaim, redefine, and legitimize identities that have been dominated—by the Holocaust and by parents—in very different ways.

CHAPTER 3

The Graphic Memoir:
Art Spiegelman's *Maus: A Survivor's Tale*

The Graphic Novel and the Holocaust

From the publication of the first volume of *Maus: A Survivor's Tale*, in 1986, Art Spiegelman's graphic memoir, in which a cartoonist son interviews his survivor father about his experiences, has been both critically interrogated over its use of animal figures—most notoriously mice to represent Jews and cats to symbolize Germans—and praised for its creative treatment of its theme. It has sold extensively, been widely translated, and emerged as the most firmly canonized of all second-generation Holocaust narratives, despite (or possibly because of) its cartoon form.

In addition to the approximately one hundred articles that have been published on *Maus discussing the text in its own right, and particularly as a "Holocaust text,"* it has also become a key text in discussions of autobiographical theory. It is widely considered to have "transformed the status of the graphic novel" as well as the language used to describe it.[1] It is also a striking illustration of a tendency toward a deeply self-conscious subjectivity on the part of second-generation writers and artists, a tendency that only magnifies a quality of much historical and fictional "Holocaust writing" more generally. As James Young observes,

> like others in his media-savvy generation, born after—but indelibly shaped by—the Holocaust, Spiegelman does not attempt to represent events he never knew immediately, but instead portrays his necessarily hypermediated experience of the memory of events.[2]

The graphic medium of the work allows Spiegelman to lay bare many of the internal mechanisms of the second-generation relational auto/biography, raising questions about the relationship between parents' and children's stories

and autobiographical writers' relationships to their material and to the narrators of their texts. In this it provides a valuable context and framework for the
elaboration of issues that pertain to many other texts, including those that
form the subjects of earlier chapters.

The use of animal figures in *Maus* has been controversial. Different animals represent different national or ethnic groups, with mice signifying Jews,
and cats signifying Germans. In addition, pigs represent Poles, dogs (both
black and white) represent Americans, and frogs represent the French. Yet
these correspondences are not portrayed in *Maus* as straightforward and
unproblematic identities. Rather, they are sites for demonstrating the inadequacy of the crude, racially determined categories employed by the Nazis. For
example, Spiegelman shows himself and his father's second wife, Mala, discussing Artie's discomfort with the fact that his accurate depiction of his
father's stinginess conforms to the anti-Semitic stereotype of the miserly Jew.
Mala's asssertion (notably angry with Vladek rather than the stereotype) that
no one else they know, including other survivors, is like him in that respect,
undermines the stereotypes of both the Jewish miser and the saintly survivor.
Throughout *Maus* we meet other survivors, including Mala herself, Pavel the
therapist, and Vladek's neighbors in the Catskills who clearly do not share
Vladek's manias. This makes it clear that "mice" are not united by flaws or
virtues, but by a Jewishness that may be more to do with the perceptions of
others than with any cultural affiliation.[3] Furthermore, some of the Jewish
characters in wartime Poland are able to pass as Poles. This is signified in the
drawings by mice wearing pig masks, which signals once again the inadequacy of Nazi perceptions of "Jewish" characteristics. As Spiegelman himself
has written,

> my anthropomorphized mice carry trace elements of Fips' anti-semitic Jew-as-
> rat cartoons for *Der Stürmer*, but, by being particularized they are invested
> with personhoood; they stand upright and affirm their humanity. ("Little
> Orphan Annie's Eyeballs," 17)

The appropriation of the Nazi concept of Jews as vermin subverts anti-
Semitic caricature by individualizing the mice, emphasizing the ambiguity
of "Jewish" characteristics and questioning a simplistic understanding of
"racial" origin.

A further obvious objection to the use of animal figures is the potential for
suggesting a "naturalization" of the Nazis' social hierarchy. However, as critics
such as Marianne Hirsch have noted, Anja's distaste for the *real* rats that share
one of their hiding places, and Pavel the therapist's fondness for pet cats, foreground the anthropomorphized animals as representational choices (*Family*

Frames, 27). Accusations of trivialization are similarly unconvincing; as Daniel Schwarz has pointed out, unlike most cartoon mice who can "come back to life again and again, we soon realize that these mice stay dead" (289). This observation hints at the productive tension between format and theme that Spiegelman exploits to the full. Rather than being merely an effective way of dealing with difficult subject matter, the graphic format of *Maus* offers new potential for analyzing and representing the subject.

Whose Trauma? Whose Narrative?

Maus explores the relationship between Artie, the cartoonist protagonist, and his elderly survivor father, Vladek. Like Helen Epstein's parents, Vladek is prepared to talk about the past. Unlike them, however, he views his son's life as secondary or subsidiary to his own experiences. Hamida Bosmajian argues that this over-presence, or uncontainability, of the father's life story finds its most obvious image in the subtitle to the first volume, "My Father Bleeds History":

> Vladek bleeds history not only in the sense of a possibly therapeutic blood-letting of his own experiences, but in the continuous seepage of repressed and displaced memories that affected Artie every day of his childhood. (7)

It is in precisely this "seepage" that Artie's problems exist. Even though, as Bosmajian goes on to say, "No stories can cure the unhealed wounds in father and son," Artie responds by writing the story of their respective traumas and their struggle with one another.[4]

Yet Vladek's role as storyteller in Artie's life is paralleled by that of his first wife, Artie's mother Anja, who committed suicide in 1968 when her son was twenty. Her diaries of her experiences in the camps were written for Artie, but burned by Vladek before the younger man had become aware of them. For Artie, therefore, since his mother's death, the overly-present and the overly-silent versions of the survivor-parent have coexisted. Spiegelman highlights both of these influences in two very different "mini-narratives" that—significantly, as I shall explore—stand outside the main body of the text. The first falls at the beginning of *Maus I*, after the title page but before the first chapter, forming a kind of preface or epigraph. This is a two-page sequence that shows the ten-year-old Artie being abandoned by his friends, and his father responding to his sobs by saying, "If you lock them together in a room with no food for a week. . . then you could see what it is, friends!" (*I*, 5–6).[5] The first message of the book, then, is that the young Artie had to learn quickly to take his father's experiences and feelings more seriously than his own.[6] The sequence in which the more complex effect of his mother on his life is addressed is in the same volume, in a sequence entitled "Prisoner on the Hell Planet: a Case History" (*I*, 100–103). This is a cartoon that Spiegelman drew when he was much younger. He inserts it into the text of *Maus I* at the point in the narrative when his stepmother reveals that a neighbor drew her attention to it and that Vladek subsequently found and read it. This cartoon shows that Artie was expected to be the one to comfort his father in the aftermath of his mother's suicide, despite the fact that Artie had recently spent some time in a mental hospital himself. It also shows that friends and family, as well as his father, made him feel personal guilt and responsibility for his mother's death (*I*, 101). This depiction of Anja's suicide illustrates Artie's own trauma—his bereavement and his subsequent inability to grieve for his mother in the way he needs to—which acts as a counterpoint to his father's experiences of the Holocaust. His sense of entrapment by guilt and familial expectation is represented by the prisoner's garb that Artie wears for the duration of the cartoon. In the context of Anja's subsequent silence and silenc*ing* by Vladek, in his burning of her diaries, and Vladek's overriding of his son's grief with his own, we are led to understand that Artie's unresolved feelings about his mother and her death are partly due to a sense of lack of control over both lived experience and the way it is understood, or narrated, by those around him. The inclusion of this independent sequence, rather than its stylistic incorporation into the rest of *Maus*, testifies to *Artie's* trauma rather than that of his father. The "Prisoner" sequence was never intended for his father's eyes, and indeed Artie even apologizes for any hurt it may have caused him (*I*, 104). Artie says that "it appeared in an obscure underground comic book" (*I*, 99), thereby representing an alternative outburst of grief when the conventional public channels were found to be unavailable. In the final frame of the "Prisoner" sequence Artie tells his mother she has "committed the perfect crime. . . . You *murdered* me, Mommy, and you left me here to take the rap!!!" (*I*, 103). The episode is given greater force by the inclusion in the opening frame of a photograph of Artie as a child with his mother—the only photograph of either of them to appear anywhere in the two *Maus* books.[7] This implicitly acknowledges the mouse Artie as a "real" person, and his trauma, too, as real. Paul John Eakin explains the power of photography in this context thus:

> the relational autobiographer in the act of writing does indeed stand apart, studying family from a distance, and the sense of detachment, of separation, that this posture affords is doubtless one of its primary attractions. Photographs of family, however, of the individual as part of the group, remain stubbornly intact, setting up a kind of tension

between the reality of the collectively assembled bodies and the individual's story of the journey away from them told in the accompanying life story.[8]

It is possible to read the inclusion of the mother-son photograph in "Prisoner" as a form of resistance to this, as it is positioned in the context that most shockingly and dramatically refutes the illusion it presents of the family's togetherness. It also emphasizes the book's function as a narrative of the silence and absence of Artie's mother, in a kind of counterpoint to that of his father's overbearing, over-present dominance depicted at the beginning.

The frame following that of the photograph enhances the image of Artie as essentially childlike with his being shown, already in prison uniform, beside a height chart consisting of lines on a wall. He is above the five feet six inches mark, yet the chart goes down to four feet. The speech bubble in this frame reads the following: "In 1968, when I was 20, my mother killed herself. . . . She left no note" (*I*, 100). Aged twenty, he is already an adult, yet the height chart emphasizes that he is only at the beginning of his independent adult life. The fourth frame records that he was living with his parents at the time following his release from the state mental hospital, in a partial return to childhood dependence. Finally, the date of May 1968 and Artie's age of twenty situate his mother's death and his "imprisonment" at a moment in history when his generation was, collectively and symbolically at least, experiencing more freedom than ever before.[9] The precise historical moment highlights Artie's sense that part of his life has been lost forever—a part that represented a historic breaking away from the older generation, to which he is now tied by trauma. Artie thus appears to be trapped in a childlike powerlessness and banished forever from any perceived "innocence" that may have been attached to it. The timing is also related to the intentionality that Artie attributes to his mother in his words, "Congratulations!. . . You've committed the perfect crime" (*I*, 103), indicating a childish self-centered conviction that the real motive of her suicide ("she left no note!") was to cause maximum distress to her already fragile son. As well as illustrating the respective influences of Anja and Vladek on Artie's life, these two mini-narratives, set apart in different ways from the "main" text, are the only occasions in which the text overtly and explicitly becomes Artie's autobiography rather than that of his father.

The highlighting of the intergenerational discord in these two snapshots of parent-child relationships is, I believe, key to a fully meaningful reading of the *Maus* books. While they can be seen on one level as representing a battle for meaning and ownership of history, I will argue that the graphic narrative problematizes this question of genre further, with a disruption of the generational order and the power relations that such order presupposes. Eakin has pointed out that in *Maus*, along with other recently published "relational lives," "the story of the story structures the narrative we read; the stress is on the performance of the collaboration and therefore on the relation between the two individuals involved."[10] He continues,

> Surprising as it may seem, given the very great intrinsic interest of the story of the other—the informant—in these cases, I argue that the two narratives— Art's and Vladek's—are not offered to us on an equal footing. If my reading is correct, it is the story of the story that has the upper hand. That is to say. . . that *Maus* is in the last analysis Art Spiegelman's autobiography.[11]

I intend to demonstrate that not only is this the case, but also that it is largely through the graphic dimension of the text, as well as through the paratextual apparatus, such as photographs, dedications, chapter headings, and cover "photographs," that issues of family power relations, history, and narrative form are resolved for Artie, if not for Vladek. This is implicit in Rick Iadonisi's comment that "Art Spiegelman's different selves are both within and outside of the printed text, at once influencing the narrative we get and reflecting on the collaboration that results in the narrative."[12] Like the other texts I have mentioned, *Maus* shows the son Artie reconstructing the family both imaginatively and in reality according to his own needs. While some of the ways through which he achieves this are common aspects of family life— such as marriage and parenthood—the text, on both its written and graphic levels, leads us to interpret both Artie's actions and Spiegelman's creative choices in particular ways. However, *Maus* differs from other texts on this theme in that it invites the reader to question its motives, representations, and narrative resolution.

Blurred Generations

Post-war survivor families often reflect a blurring of generational lines from the outset, such as the Jakubowiczs whom Marianne Hirsch remembers from her own childhood, with "their pale and other-worldly daughter Chana, who was only ten, though her parents were in their late fifties."[13] The words "pale and other-worldly" situate Chana as a ghostly echo of her six dead half-brothers and sisters, without whose deaths she would not have been born. In generational terms, this is the position of author Art Spiegelman and the character Artie in *Maus*: Richieu, his older brother, died in the Holocaust. Although both of Artie's parents survived, he was not born until his father was in his forties, at least a decade after his brother's birth. Had Richieu lived, this ten year gap would have seemed substantial, almost a generational difference in itself, to the two children growing up. Because Richieu died when he was "only five or six," however, the matter becomes more complex, with Art rapidly overtaking the age of his "elder" brother. Artie explains to Françoise,

> The photo [of Richieu] never threw tantrums or got in any kind of trouble. . . it was an ideal kid, and *I* was a pain in the ass. I couldn't compete. They didn't *talk* about Richieu, but that photo was a kind of reproach. *He'd* have become a *doctor* and married a wealthy Jewish girl. . . the creep. (*II*, 15)

Artie's virtual or imaginatively constructed relationship with Richieu allows him to feel both child and adult rivalries simultaneously, telescoping his perception of his parents' feelings toward both sons. Artie tells Françoise, "After the war my parents traced down the vaguest rumors, and went to orphanages all over Europe. They couldn't believe he was dead." They had a photo of Richieu in their room but "They didn't need photos of me in their room. . . . I was alive!" (*II*, 15). The depiction of Richieu in the text as a precious object whose safety is his parents' prime concern during the war contrasts sharply with the expectation that Artie will comfort his father after Anja's death and fulfil a role, as we have seen, that is generally secondary to Vladek's.

Bosmajian's comments on the image of "bleeding history," and in particular what she terms "the continuous seepage of repressed and displaced memories that affected Artie every day of his childhood," express the generational confusion that is at once the root and the description of intergenerational trauma. Postmemory, or the continuing impact of parents' experiences, appears to affect many survivors' children dramatically, but its effect can be hard to disentangle from the children's sense that they are not *supposed* to be affected in this way. Artie tells Françoise the following:

> I know this is insane, but I somehow wish I had been in Auschwitz with my parents so I could really know what they lived through! I guess it's some kind of guilt about having had an easier life than they did. (*II*, 16)

This desire to have been in Auschwitz implies a sense of having been born into the wrong generation. If Artie had been his father, for example, his problems would have had an origin that was perfectly comprehensible to both himself and the outside world. Imagining himself back in time supplies a fantasy explanation for his current emotional problems. Yet the extreme *un*imaginability of the older generation's plight, implicit in the young Artie's ability to consider even for a moment that being in Auschwitz would be preferable to his own life, paradoxically renders this imagined situation safe and desirable. What is often referred to as the sanctification of the survivor intensifies Artie's perceptions of his own experience as inauthentic, and any unhappiness as unjustified. His reasoning is still more jumbled generationally, as it is predicated on a sanctified and sympathetic view of survivors that is characteristic of Artie's generation in the present, but would have had little bearing on his father's immediate postwar life.

Artie's empathic link to his parents would seem to imply a premature sense of responsibility, and consequently adulthood, and yet—as we have seen in some of the images from "Prisoner on the Hell Planet"—he is equally an overgrown child. Bosmajian writes:

> During the Holocaust a child had to grow up fast for the sake of survival. The child had to be able to use duplicity consciously or to "pass" as older than he or she was in order to be defined as "workable" in Auschwitz. . . . At age fifteen Elie Wiesel, for example, is able to "pass" as an adult in Auschwitz and develops with his father a relationship that truly has shared adulthood in the nightmare of history (*Night*). Such a relationship is not possible between Artie and Vladek.[14]

By being born "afterwards," Artie is condemned to perpetual childhood in the eyes of his father, who throws out his coat without permission and gives him one of his own old coats by way of replacement. As the quotation above indicates, too, adulthood during the Holocaust became a survival strategy, or performance, in itself. While Richieu never experienced the camps, he was a Holocaust victim. This victimhood accords him a status that, as we have seen, Artie feels he and his problems lack. This sense is caused by Vladek's expectations, as depicted in the opening sequence that shows Artie's friends deserting him. Artie suspects that, for Vladek, Richieu is, and always will be, the "survivor" and therefore the older brother. His attempts at reconstructing this family hierarchy in a manner that acknowledges his own adulthood form a complex struggle that is played out in his and Vladek's relationship in *Maus*.

Vladek and Artie are shown as adopting different positions of maturity as the book progresses. Notably, Artie's crisis following his father's death shows him shrinking in size until he is physically childlike. The child-Artie is shown saying to himself, "sometimes I just don't feel like a functioning adult. I can't believe I'm gonna be a father in a couple of months. My father's ghost still hangs over me" (*II*, 43). The crisis in Artie's own sense of maturity is brought on by his father's death and daughter's imminent birth as definitive markers of his own adulthood. As in other works by children of survivors, an interest in, or need to find out about, his father's Holocaust experiences seems related to a stage in Artie's own development that is, in any case, challenging to his own sense of identity. His father's death has left him parentless, yet, due to his father's refusal to acknowledge his maturity, psychologically unprepared for adulthood, independence, and fatherhood. Chapter 3 of *Maus I* even shows Artie listening childlike at his father's feet, and many of the father/son interview sessions take place in Artie's childhood bedroom, scene of the bedtime story.

Yet Vladek's dominant fatherhood breaks down at certain points. We see the tone of the father/son conversations change, particularly in *Maus II*, when Vladek has heart problems. On one occasion, his talking has tired him out so much that he has to lie down, and Artie, assuming the adult role of the carer, has to talk him out of fixing the roof (*II*, 117). *Maus II* also sees Vladek's capricious behavior worsen, with Artie and Françoise often looking on like embarrassed parents themselves, such as when Vladek returns half-empty boxes of food to the supermarket (*II*, 89). The very end of *Maus II* sees Vladek in bed protesting to Artie that there have been "enough stories," because he wants to go to sleep (*II*, 136). Although it is Vladek who assumes the role of the tired child in bed here, and Artie that of the parent-figure, it is Vladek who has been telling the stories to his son.

Chapter Headings and Auto/biographical Meanings

This generational confusion is one aspect of *Maus* that reduces the temptation to read it as a dual narrative, with alternate sides of the struggle to narrate gaining supremacy at different moments. Dominick LaCapra comments on "the frequent juxtaposition of scenes from the present and scenes from the past, which creates a double or multiple consciousness in the reader and generates both a jarringly ironic discrepancy and an uncanny sense of déjà vu."[15] The frequency and pointedness of these juxtapositions makes it clear that they are present by editorial design rather than mere accident of chronology, and this element of artifice is drawn further to the reader's attention by the punning chapter headings, which often reflect these juxtapositions and serve to muddy the line between the past and the present.

Taking into account the generational fluidity inherent in the story, then, it would appear that something more complex than a relatively straightforward dual narrative is taking place. In LaCapra's opinion,

> the very notion of the present serving as a narrative frame with the Holocaust as an inner or framed story may well be too simple or even misleading, for the past returns to create uneven developments in the present and to pose the problem of the intricate relation between acting-out and working-through for survivors, for children of survivors, and for others born later.[16]

The trauma and dislocation of both generations seem to derive from Spiegelman's apparently conscious resistance to clear divisions between past and present. The chapter titles of both *Maus* books play on this without being consistently explicit. It is on a graphic level, and particularly through the use of chapter headings and their accompanying illustrations, that the cartoonist's sense of historical or generational blurring and problematization is expressed. As Artie and Vladek's relationship is based so heavily around the transmission of Vladek's story, resonances of the past in the present have more to do with "the story of the story" than with Artie's life, at least in the first volume.

The first chapter of *Maus I* is called "The Sheikh," reflecting the young Vladek's supposed resemblance to Rudolph Valentino. It also reflects his success with women at that time, and the potential glamor of his business success, according to Vladek's own interpretation of his life. Despite these apparent concessions to Vladek's vanity, the end of the chapter shows Artie promising his father not to include in his book anything about Lucia, his girlfriend before he met Artie's mother. This very episode has just been represented in the text. This seems to emphasize to the reader that the text is ruthlessly true to Vladek's story, conceding little ground to his vanity. The very dramatization of this dispute in cartoon form works to dispel any questions of veracity that the connotations of the cartoon form might raise. It also introduces the theme of filial disobedience, showing that Artie has moved beyond the circumstances of the preface episode and now has strategies for asserting his own needs over those of his father. Spiegelman thus introduces his agenda clearly and dramatically. He will strive for painstaking accuracy in writing his father's story by representing the dynamics of the story's transmission. What he will not do is sacrifice this accuracy for the sake of his father's feelings.

The subsequent chapter headings continue to reflect the storytelling present, highlighting the dynamics of Vladek and Artie's relationship that facilitated the making of the book. The graphic form, with its use of speech bubbles, is used to demarcate Vladek's narrative clearly within the text as a whole, lending a special clarity to the cartoonist's ongoing assertion of the text's relationship to its primary source. The title of chapter 2, "The Honeymoon," refers to Vladek and Anja's marriage in prewar Poland, and perhaps also to the newly re-established relations between father and son. Yet the picture accompanying the chapter heading is of mice looking up at a swastika flag. Reading the title through the image, the emphasis is on "honeymoon" as a strictly limited period of happiness.[17] Chapter 3, "Prisoner of War," opens with Artie eating dinner with Vladek and Vladek's second wife, Mala. Vladek demands that Artie finish what is on his plate, prompting Artie to tell Mala of his father's rigid implementation of that policy during his childhood. We are then given Vladek's story of how his own father insisted on starving him to ensure that he failed the army medical. Further on, we see Vladek as a prisoner of war being ordered by German soldiers to scrub a stable totally clean in one hour. Immediately afterward, in the following scene, we see him becoming aggressive toward Artie, who has accidentally let cigarette ash fall on the carpet: "You want it should be like a stable in here?" (*I*, 52). These incidents position Artie as a parody of a prisoner of war, especially as the chapter concludes with the comic incident of Vladek throwing away Artie's coat and providing a "new" one, like a prisoner's uniform. Further support for this reading is offered by the fact that this is one of the few occasions in which Artie is depicted as having a tail, a marker that seems to signify vulnerability.[18]

Fittingly, then, chapter 4, "The Noose Tightens," opens with Vladek confronting Artie with the words, "you're late!"(*I*, 73). The honeymoon over, their father-son relationship is beginning to show the strain. In Vladek's story, the Jews of Sosnowiec are gradually disappearing, and some of his friends are hanged on the street. The "mouse holes" of the title of chapter 5 are the Jews' cramped hiding places as the war starts, and also the safe at the bank where the present-day Vladek obsessively hoards anything of value. Equally, "Mouse Trap," the title of the final chapter, shows Anja and Vladek tricked into ending up at Auschwitz, and Vladek's admission—after several attempts at sidestepping the truth—that he burned Anja's diaries. The promise of receiving these diaries has been at least part of what has motivated Artie's regular visits. By now, however, he is too involved in his father's story to abandon it: he is caught in the "trap." As in *The Thousand and One Nights*, maintaining narrative control allows Vladek to keep what he desires, a relationship with his son, which the preservation of his dead wife's diaries would have threatened.

Thus, Artie's discomfort with the existing family relationships is an undercurrent throughout the text. Yet by expressing this so metaphorically, compared to the superficially unproblematic linear narrative of Vladek's story, and by locating his apparently growing unease as an alternative reading in headings and title pages outside the main body of the text, or in the *relationship between* words and pictures, headings and narrative, Vladek's story can easily be read as privileged.[19] The problems Artie experiences as a result of this loyalty to Vladek's reality become increasingly obvious, and are explored in more depth in *Maus II*.

This second volume of *Maus* further develops Artie's role in the text, and the representation of time and parallel events becomes more self-conscious. The dedication to this volume, which frames a picture of Richieu, reads "for Richieu and for Nadja," Spiegelman's own daughter. While Marianne Hirsch has suggested that we cannot be sure who the child in the picture is, she also acknowledges that we are led to assume it is Richieu, and that "in terms of function" it must be.[20] Firstly, Artie discusses the "large blurry photograph"

(15) very early in *Maus II*, while the image is still fresh in the reader's mind. This picture is indeed quite undefined, as if it would be "blurry" when enlarged. The child in the photograph is dressed in similar clothing to that worn by the mouse Richieu in Spiegelman's drawings. Finally, this image completes the "set" of photographs of the Spiegelman family, and it seems notable that this picture, assuming it is Richieu, is placed fully outside the narrative. While he can write about both his parents from personal experience, Spiegelman can only relate his work to his dead brother indirectly, through imagination and commemorative gestures such as dedications. As Hamida Bosmajian has pointed out, the name "Nadja," anagrammatically, can be read as a refiguring of Art/Artie's mother's name, Anja, suggesting that Spiegelman's daughter has been named after her.[21] In addition, the photograph of Richieu, necessarily as a child, situates Spiegelman's brother and Nadja in the same generation. By linking both Richieu and Anja to his daughter in this way, in a dedication placed around an image of a child, Spiegelman could be seen to be situating himself as older than his dead relatives, at last privileging the present and future experience of himself, the living, over the burdensome presence of the dead. It could also be read as an assertion of the importance of childhood experiences throughout any adult's life. In addition, the inclusion of the photograph could be read as a partial capitulation to the view Artie finds implicit in his parents' choice to display a photo of Richieu, that "they didn't need photos of me in their room. . . . I was alive!" (*II*, 15). However, the presence of his daughter's name and the linking of her to both his mother and his brother lay the emphasis on memory through dynamic continuity rather than static memorialization.

Marianne Hirsch has commented on possible reasons for the extensive use of images of children in what she terms "postmemorial work" as follows:

> Culturally, at the end of the twentieth century, the figure of the "child" is an adult construction, the site of adult fantasy, fear, and desire. As recent controversies suggest, our culture has a great deal invested in the children's innocence and vulnerability—and at the same time, in their eroticism and knowledge. Less individualized, less marked by the particularities of identity, moreover, children invite multiple projections and identifications.[22]

While Hirsch suggests that, in keeping with these arguments, the photograph of Richieu at the beginning of *Maus II* "elicits a very specific kind of investment from Spiegelman's readers," Richieu's presence as a photograph in the Spiegelman home is shown to do the same.[23] Richieu is at once a fantasy, to Artie, and a lost object of desire to his parents. If we see Artie as a replacement child then the shape and dynamics of the postwar Spiegelman family are predicated on Richieu's absence. Anja and Vladek are traumatized by their loss, and Artie by his sense of rejection as an inadequate replacement, his fears confirmed in the worst possible way by his mother's suicide. Hirsch argues that "the visual encounter with the child victim is a triangular one, that identification occurs in a triangular field of looking. The adult viewer sees the child victim through the eyes of his or her own child self," thereby producing simultaneous "affiliative and identificatory as well as. . . protective spectatorial looks."[24] In this way, Richieu seems to be at the heart of Artie's traumatic responses as well as those of his parents, and for this reason, too, it is Richieu whose name helps Artie and the narrative toward resolution. In placing the photograph at the front of *Maus II*, the volume in which he poses the most searching questions about his family as well as his chosen mode of representation, Spiegelman invites the reader to consider Richieu's significance. The aligning of Richieu, Nadja, and implicitly Anja in the volume's dedication illustrates this complex process of identification that has children at its heart. Spiegelman's own fatherhood, in this "triangular" system of identification, may be seen as a recovery of his childhood self—an act that has finally enabled him to identify with and mourn for Richieu, as well as help him identify with and recover memories of a mother who has not been present for his adult life. Thus, while Hirsch points out some of the potential misuses of images of children, in this instance the photograph appears to confirm belated family reconciliation: now that the rest of the Spiegelman family is dead, the author/artist can symbolically readmit Richieu into his life.

The narrative in this volume, which is less clearly linear than that of the first volume, reflects the more self-reflexive, meditative approach taken by Spiegelman. Chapter 1 of this second volume is called "Mauschwitz," playfully drawing attention to Vladek's pointless games of cat-and-mouse in which he sneaks past the "guard" into the Pines Hotel to play bingo and use the gym without getting "caught." It also covers the very beginning of Vladek's time in Auschwitz, showing how his strange, miserly habits were skills or tendencies that predated the war, became survival tactics in the camps, and which Vladek has subsequently fetishized. More than in the first volume, in which we saw Artie suffer from his father's tyrannical decisions—such as choosing a new coat for him and burning his mother's diaries—Artie now begins to be gently but decisively critical. The title also hints at the incident at the beginning of the chapter in which Artie discusses with his French wife, Françoise, which animal he should use to represent her in the book. Françoise's indignant assertion that she should be a mouse—"I converted didn't I?"—points to her own reconstruction as Jew in order to become part of the Spiegelman family (*II*, 11). Further, we learn later in the conversation that Artie finds that "middle-class, New York, Jewish women. . . remind [him] too much of [his] relatives to be erotic" (*II*, 12). This emphasizes the artificiality of Françoise's position in the family still more: while her French identity must be overwritten in order for her to become an acceptable equivalent to those "middle-class, New York, Jewish women," her desirability lies in her difference to them. This reinforces the sense of Art/Artie's restructuring of the family according to his own needs, although Françoise's comment that she "only converted to make Vladek happy" attests to his father's pervasive influence (*II*, 12).

Chapter 2, "Auschwitz (Time Flies)," is heavily concerned with Vladek's story of being in Auschwitz, yet the title page shows flies crawling out of the frame of a picture of mice in flames. These flies recur throughout the chapter, appearing first during Artie's depression. He is depicted in despair at his drawing board, on a pile of mouse bodies, with an Auschwitz watchtower visible through the window. The flies rise from the bodies and buzz around him, rising visually as well as metaphorically from the past. Bosmajian comments that the subtitle to *Maus II*—which also serves as title to chapter 3— "And Here My Troubles Began," could refer as much to Artie's troubles beginning at Auschwitz as to Vladek's.[25] The same could be said of the speech bubble that appears to the right of one of the frames showing Artie's depression, which reads "Alright Mr. Spiegelman. We're ready to shoot!" In the double-context, this refers both to the proposals to film *Maus*, which Artie does not favor, and to the shooting in the camp. The chapter ends with Françoise and Artie on the terrace of Vladek's holiday bungalow, flies buzzing around them. Artie zaps them with spray and we see them dead, including one that falls to the ground just outside the frame. This recalls Spiegelman's reasons for choosing to draw cats and mice in his book as follows: "Hitler's rhetoric referred to the Jews as subhuman, as vermin to be exterminated. The gas in Auschwitz, Zyklon B, was actually a pesticide!"[26] The flies buzz outside the frames, like escaping traces of history. Punningly, they also reflect Vladek's statement that "time is flying" while he has been telling the story (*II*, 73), and Artie and Vladek's unsatisfactory attempt to account for how Vladek spent his time in Auschwitz (*II*, 68).

Chapter 3, "And Here My Troubles Began," is illustrated by a picture of walking legs and feet in camp uniform. It deals with the period after Vladek leaves Auschwitz, including a forced march, a journey in cattle trucks, imprisonment in Dachau, and contracting typhus. The implication of the title seems to be that although while in Auschwitz, as we have seen, Vladek found ways of gaining control, or at least the semblance of it, over his own life, the uncertainty that followed was much harder to deal with. Indeed, the strange, obsessive behavior that so exasperates Artie and Françoise in the present seems to stem from survival strategies developed in specific response to his imprisonment in Auschwitz; at least, there is less in the narrative to imply that Vladek has a similarly heroic or self-congratulatory view of his behavior or reasons for survival following this period. In a sense, as his hoarding and miserliness suggest, it is still Auschwitz that he is coping with; as James Young points out, even Vladek's story is carefully bartered in return for Artie's company.[27]

Chapter 4, "Saved" begins with Vladek saying, "Always I saved," referring to his obsessive economizing (*II*, 102). In his story, the difficult times of the war are over. The photographs of Anja's family that he produces have also been saved, yet the fact that they are not Anja's diary, as Artie initially thinks they are, reminds the reader what a deliberate act of destruction Vladek's burning of them was, given his compulsive hoarding of all other things. Vladek's unwillingness to preserve an alternative version of events raises the question of his story's reliability. For instance, Bosmajian points out that Richieu's paternity is called into question "since Vladek at this point has already told the story about Anja's friendship with a young communist"—an issue about which Anja's diaries may have been revealing.[28] The graphic representation of Vladek on page 116, which shows him split by four frames, and partially covered by a family photograph, suggests a link with the photographs scattered at his feet. With the symbolic presence of these other victims and survivors, Vladek is portrayed as fragmented: his story can no longer be framed as a coherent whole in itself.[29] In chapter 5, "The Second Honeymoon," Vladek and Mala are back together after a period of separation, Anja and Vladek are reunited after the war, and Vladek and Anja are finally buried together.

These headings comply with Hirsch's analysis of the photographs in *Maus* in that they "reinforce. . . a past that will neither fade away nor be integrated into the present."[30] Sometimes the parallel incident in the present has more to do with Vladek than with Artie, so that it seems to be concerned with the story of the story rather than with Artie's life. As Terrence des Pres has written of the first volume, "at every moment, finally, the separate stories of Vladek and Artie turn out to be inseparable—a point confirmed by the comic-book format, by the way the two worlds interlock on the page."[31] In a final inadvertent statement on confusion of time and identity, Vladek's closing words to Artie, and to the book are, "I'm tired from talking, Richieu, and it's enough stories for now" (136). Bosmajian is right to say that "it is the lost son Richieu who is present for Vladek, and Artie is blanked out."[32] However, this does not rule out the possibility that, by calling him "Richieu," Vladek is revealing a new view of Artie now that he has shared in his father's experiences through listening, a sense that is emphasized in the childlike image of Vladek in bed, settling down to sleep. The making of the book has been the foundation of their recent relationship, so the dates that Art Spiegelman gives to this process on the last page refer also to a process in family relations; in his own construction, Artie is now the adult son.

Conclusion

Peter Brooks writes that

> the deathbed scene of the nineteenth-century novel eminently represents the moment of summing-up of a life's meaning and a transmission of accumulated wisdom to succeeding generations. Paternal figures within novels write their own obituaries, transmitting to the younger protagonists something of the authority necessary to view the meaning of their own lives retrospectively, in terms of the significance that will be brought by the as yet unwritten end.[33]

This nineteenth-century life narrative and plot is clearly and deliberately deployed as a possibility in *Maus*. Brooks argues that "most viable works of literature tell us something about how they are to be read, guide us toward the conditions of their interpretation."[34] *Maus*, in the interplay between written text and pictures, guides us toward such traditional modes of interpretation, only to confront us with a sense of their inadequacy for dealing with two different and sometimes rival perspectives (those of parent and child) and the manner in which they have influenced one another. The ending of *Maus II*, showing a tired Vladek settling down to sleep, is a symbolic deathbed scene that posits the whole of his just-told story as his death-bed words. This, along with the "happy ending" of the reunion with Anja, points to the possibility of a traditional, linear, monoperspectival narrative interpretation, especially if we choose to see Vladek's testimony as privileged. As LaCapra has suggested, "Artie has an insistent and pervasive preoccupation with recording his father's story, which is dangerously close to becoming the master narrative of his own life," in a version of "transmission of accumulated wisdom."[35] However, Spiegelman's dedication to *Maus II*, with (I have suggested) its indications of a new adult status, suggests a reading of the last page as a coming-of-age for Artie: it is he, after all, who is figured as the "parent" at the "child's" bedside at the end. While Vladek has the last speech bubble of the book, the final picture is of his and Anja's shared gravestone, with their names and dates of birth and death, and beneath is Spiegelman's signature, with the dates 1978–1991 indicating when the books were written (*II*, 136). Thus, echoing the juxtaposition of names of the living and the dead in the dedication, Spiegelman's "living" signature is the final word beneath the memorialized names of his parents.[36] The role of this signature is a complex one. Eakin points out that these [relational autobiographical] texts suggest that the identity of the self who writes and signs as author includes and is included in the identity of the other whose story she presents. The signature on the title page, moreover, reflects the necessarily unequal distribution of power in situations of this kind: once the narrative has been published, whatever the terms of the collaboration may have been, an act of appropriation has occurred, and the self who signs may well be led to reflect on the ethical responsibilities involved.[37]

Once more, it is the *graphic* dimension of the work, in this case Spiegelman's "real" signature at the end of the book, more insistent a marker of identity than a printed name on a title page, that alters the meaning of this ending. After one trying incident with Vladek, Artie tells Françoise, "one reason I became an artist was that he thought it was impractical—just a waste of time" (*I*, 97). In a later conversation that serves to highlight Vladek's lack of knowledge of cartoons, Vladek and Mala discuss the importance of Artie's book in terms of its ability to educate a wider public about the Holocaust, rather than its significance on an artistic level (*I*, 133). These incidents further underscore the importance of reading the graphic dimension to *Maus* as Artie's encoded commentary on his father's story. They suggest that the visual component, used by Spiegelman to problematize representation, is also being used to hide such problematization from a father obsessed with himself and his own story, and who will ignore the graphic dimension as simply "childish." Thus, *Maus* is split into two stories: one that Vladek as "naive reader" can read, and one that he cannot. Young comments that *Maus*

> highlights both the inseparability of his father's story from its effect on Artie and the story's own necessarily contingent coming into being. All this might be lost to either images or narrative alone, or even to a reception that did not remark its own unfolding.[38]

Vladek's burning of Anja's diaries can thus be seen to suggest a personal lack of receptiveness to alternative stories, and not just the desire for an undivided audience. Furthermore, this dual strategy of Spiegelman's also reverses the traditional hierarchy, as it is the graphic novel that requires the more sophisticated readership.

Yet if Vladek's lack of sophistry condemns him to understand only half the semiotic possibilities of the text, Artie himself, or some kind of composite version of Artie and the "real" Spiegelman, becomes part of the paratextual apparatus. Particularly important in the light of what I have said about his signature is *Art* Spiegelman's construction of himself as artist/writer within the *Maus* books. The back flyleaf of the dustjacket in current editions of both volumes shows Spiegelman's color drawing of himself, in a mouse mask, at his drawing board. He looks despondent, his head in his hands, in a manner that recalls the episode of depression in *Maus II* during which he is unable to work: that is the only other time we see the cartoonist with a mouse mask. By choosing to represent himself in this way in his cover "photo," Spiegelman suggests a correspondence between the real cartoonist and the cartoonist figure depicted in the main body of the text. Yet by choosing to draw on the only episode in which he wears a mouse mask for this "photograph," which is also the episode where the cartoonist character is challenged by the ethical problems of representation, Spiegelman aligns himself only with very specific aspects of the cartoonist character. It suggests that he wishes that particular episode to be read as an intrusion by himself—a self characterized by self-doubt and ethical concerns, a "mouse" from outside the text. Yet this proximity works both ways: by placing the mouse figure rather than his own photo on the cover, he is furthering the empowerment of son over father that is played out in the text by bringing their relationship out of the main text and nearer to "reality." This generational battle for genre extends into the materiality of the book, with the character/cartoonist being identified as an author who receives royalties. However, in hiding his physical appearance behind his own devices of artistic style, and within that a mask, Spiegelman is placing physical distance between himself, his books, and their texts. Indeed, it is easiest to read this as Spiegelman's attempt to depict a series of selves, none of which quite corresponds to the person known as Art Spiegelman. The cartoonist in the mask is perhaps most easily understood as his "self" in relation to the text of *Maus*.

There is another issue at work here, however. Where other characters appear in masks, it occurs when they are trying to hide their Jewishness—in Nazi Poland—or are somehow engaged in questioning it—such as in Artie's therapy with Pavel. Amy Hungerford has suggested that

> in *Maus* Spiegelman aims at a literal truth that photographs or realistic drawings would fail to convey: the truth that not only Jewish identity but all identities arise from the Holocaust and, more specifically, from telling Holocaust stories.[39]

If the animal identities in *Maus*, then, "arise from the Holocaust and. . . from telling Holocaust stories," then the cartoonist's identity arises from telling the story of *Maus*. The scene with the therapist serves to address Artie's sense, as someone born after the war, of being inadequately placed to produce his book about the Holocaust. His "Holocaust," and therefore Jewish identity, is what is at stake. Following his visit to Pavel, we see his head become that of a "real" mouse again, and not just a mouse mask. As I discussed at the beginning, the use of animal heads thus raises issues of ethnicity, questioning Nazi ideas about "race" and substituting them with more obviously fluid and constructed concepts of identity and ethnicity. Spiegelman retains Artie's mask for himself on the dustjacket to accord the reader the permanent possibility of not only unmasking him, but determining what lies beneath the mask. This concern with the provisionality of narratives and identities, including those of his father, is Spiegelman's key message, and it is this that means that, in Eakin's formulation, the "story of the story" predominates, rendering the book Spiegelman's autobiography rather than Vladek's. His questioning of ethnicity and identity is also an interrogation of autobiography. I referred earlier to Carolyn Steedman's statement that "children are always episodes in someone else's narrative, not their own people, but rather brought into being for particular purposes."[40] Spiegelman's artful manipulation of the graphic format and its paratextual apparatus, including inserted mini-narratives, chapter headings, dedications, and cover pictures, permits Artie to serve as an "episode in [Vladek's] narrative," and to protect the feelings of the "real" Vladek, but also to redefine, and keep redefining, "his own person," with his own viable sense of family, at the same time. As Tabachnik has written, "out of the Holocaust, Spiegelman has created a modern Jewish epic, whose primary theme is the family and its survival under impossible conditions."[41] The survivor of the title is not Vladek, perhaps, but rather the post-Holocaust family as a whole.

CHAPTER 4

The Fantastic Novel:
Joseph Skibell's *A Blessing on the Moon*

Introduction

Joseph Skibell's powerful novel *A Blessing on the Moon* forms a particularly original addition to the Holocaust "canon." First published in the United States in 1991, the novel has been translated into several languages. The grandchild of a Jew who fled Poland, Skibell has spoken in interviews about the loss of many of his close family members, a topic that was not discussed, as he has described:

> This silence, I think, haunted me as a child and formed my character in a number of ways. . . . So the book is an attempt on my part to recover from the silence a family history that, except for a clutch of photos and whatever is encoded genetically, had all but disappeared.[1]

Consequently, the protagonist of the novel is named for his great-grandfather, Chaim Skibelski, and the author's dedication of the novel to all his great-grandparents attests to the commemorative and recuperative function he claims for it.[2] While the narrators and protagonists discussed in earlier chapters engage with historical details from their families' pasts, Skibell relies to a larger extent on imagination to explore a link that he has said is nonetheless important to him. The nature and scope of this imaginative process is revealed in a brief account of the novel's plot.

It is set in Poland during the war years. Following the massacre of all the Jews in his community, Chaim Skibelski climbs out of a mass grave only to find that he is dead, though still able to suffer from his wounds. His rabbi is also alive, but has been transformed into a crow. Chaim returns to his home, which has been appropriated by a Polish family, only one of whom, the young daughter Ola, shows any pain or guilt over what they refer to as the "disappearance" of the Jews. While Chaim is looking after Ola, who has fallen seriously ill, the moon falls from the sky and disappears. When Ola eventually dies of the illness that apparently stems from her moral unease, Chaim returns to help his dead friends and neighbors out of the grave, and together they wander, under the rabbi's guidance. They are threatened by wolves, and Chaim is threatened by, but then takes pity on, the disembodied head of a German soldier who believes himself to be Chaim's murderer. Eventually, they are welcomed at the mysterious and luxurious Hotel Amfortas. Here, after a reunion with their families, all except Chaim are mysteriously taken away. It is implied that they have been put into the hotel ovens, which are symbolic of the gas chambers. He wanders for a while in despair, his lamentations echoing those of Job, and then comes upon a town that he realizes is his own, though we infer that much time has passed. A trail of strange glowing rocks leads him from his former home to two Hasidic Jews in a hut in the woods who have been waiting for him to help them restore the moon to its rightful place. After they achieve this, with the now elderly Rabbi's help, Chaim is finally released from his sufferings, figured as a kind of "unbirth" in which he diminishes in size in his mother's lap until his awareness of the world around him disappears.

In this chapter, I will argue that such an obviously "literary," fantastic novel supports the claim made by Sue Vice that "Holocaust fiction which is unaccommodating to the reader may be more successful in conveying the disruption and unease that the subject demands than the more seamless, aesthetically pleasing work."[3]

Fairy Tales and Holocaust Memories

Discussions of writing about the Holocaust are underpinned by questions of the nature of memory. And, as Nicola King demonstrates in the opening chapter of *Memory, Narrative, Identity*, "it is impossible to imagine or formulate memory and its operations without the use of metaphor."[4] King explores the problem of formulating memory in relation to the models of archaeological excavation and *Nachträglichkeit* (belatedness) that have informed psychoanalytic theory as accounts of the memory process.[5] The powerful cultural force exerted by the archaeological model has been explored implicitly in the segment of my introduction that deals with images of burial and disinterment, owing to its particular resonances with the second- and third-generation experience. *Nachträglichkeit*, whereby later experiences and impressions effect a reorganization of earlier ones, is a model that, King suggests, "is close to the structure and effect of narrative itself."[6] Consequently, some of the issues it raises reflect certain aspects of the relationship between narrative and memory as follows:

> the concept of *Nachträglichkeit* unsettles the belief that we can recover the past as it was and unproblematically reunite our past and present selves, although the assumption that memory can give us direct access to the preserved or buried past retains a powerful hold on our culture.[7]

This assumption is similar to that which underpins anxiety about representing the Holocaust in any form other than the historical chronicle or eyewitness testimony. The cultural and emotional power of this idea lies in its presupposition of a "pure" form of memory that, if located, removes any problematic obstacle to our relationship with the past. Similarly, James Young writes the following of Holocaust narratives:

> the "docu-novelists" and "docu-dramatists" of the Holocaust work as hard [as the diarists and memoirists] at manufacturing their own testimonial authority as part of their fictional discourse. In many cases, their reasons for reinforcing the factual authority in narrative are similar: all of these writers seem to fear that the rhetoricity of their literary medium inadvertently confers a fictiveness onto events themselves.[8]

However, Young continues, such attempts may be doomed from the outset as,

> if there is a line between fact and fiction, it may by necessity be a winding border that tends to bind these two categories as much as its separates them, allowing each side to dissolve occasionally into the other.[9]

The ideas of "pure" referential narrative and memory nonetheless loom large in discussions of the Holocaust, as if to suggest that their impossibility should not preclude us from striving toward them.

Writers whose families were affected by the Holocaust often start writing about it with (as we have seen) a sense of particular proximity to the event, despite not having been "there." This fact makes particular demands of its own on representation: where "memory" is secondary, does narrative have to be, too? Does Skibell's literary gesture of remembrance (dedicated to his great-grandparents and their children) remember his dead family members' stories, the communication of those stories (directly or indirectly) by his parents, or his own assimilation of those stories as a child? The structure of Skibell's family relationships, and those of others, to the Holocaust dismantles the illusion of "pure" memory right from the beginning, and with it "pure" referential narrative; to whose history does this ostensibly fictional narrative refer?

One of Joseph Skibell's professed starting-points in the writing of this novel is highly pertinent to these questions. The Holocaust, he says,

> seemed foreshadowed in the tales of the Brothers Grimm: the oven in Hansel and Gretel becomes the ovens of Auschwitz; the Pied Piper leading away the rats and then the children of Hamelin is, to me, the story of World War II. Hitler as the mesmerizing entrancer seducing the "rats"—which is how the Nazis characterized European Jewry—to their doom. (272–73)[10]

In this, Skibell may be compared to other writers of the second and third generations. Children and grandchildren of survivors often write from the perspective of having grown up with the more disturbing aspects of their families' history functioning as their childhood stories. Daniel Asa Rose is heavily influenced by Grimm's fairy tales in writing his memoir of himself and his two sons travelling to Europe to find their family's wartime hiding places; he describes the true stories his mother told him as a child as being "like Grimm's fairy tales, updated, with people hiding in laundry hampers and haylofts and wood sheds until the ogres went away."[11] Anne Karpf recalls that

> the Holocaust was our fairy-tale. Other children were presumably told stories about goblins, monsters, and wicked witches; we learned about the Nazis. And while their heroes and heroines (I realise now) must have fled from castles and dungeons, the few I remember had escaped from ghettoes, concentration camps, and forced labour camps.

While, she says, she did read other stories, "no fictional evil could have possibly rivaled the documentary version."[12] Alternatively, in Lisa Appignanesi's family, "no one bothered with Grimm. But at the age when [she] had grown out of fairytales, [her parents' stories] persisted."[13]

The survivor's tale would seem to share certain features with the fairy tale, which is almost by definition a tale of miraculous escape from danger. The woman who survives and saves her family because of the lure of her beauty to a handsome Nazi "prince" is a recurrent theme in memoirs.[14] Others survive due to a special gift, such as Anne Karpf's mother, a concert pianist.[15] The enemy, an unequivocally evil force, is variously misheard and inadvertently fictionalized by children as, for example, "the Not-sees"[16] or "the Nasties."[17] When powerful stories of the Holocaust enter children's frames of reference as they are struggling to differentiate lived and fictional experience, the stories seem to be particularly hard to categorize.

There are particular moments and incidents in *A Blessing on the Moon* in which fairy tales seem especially influential, such as when wolves threaten Chaim by name in the woods (93–95); or when his first wife's face appears to him in the feathers, blood, and snow at his feet (120–21); or again when the dead Jews cross a river that has magical healing powers (134–37). Similarly, when Chaim's search for his family in the Hotel Amfortas leads him to the kitchens, the bakers joke with each other: "Hansel, stick your finger out so I can see if you are fat enough!" (189–90). Such points in which the influence of Grimm is clearly signaled, in this case with reference to the Hansel and Gretel story, are also often entwined with allegory in particularly clear ways. Thus, Chaim wonders about the threatening wolf, "is it possible I know him from somewhere before?" (95), as if he represents a less supernatural threat than it would appear, and the hotel kitchen staff, for all their joking about Hansel being fat enough to eat, tell Chaim as follows that they have "baked" his family: "they have been in our ovens" (191). The head baker is heard singing, "'there will again be sweetness in the world,'. . . rubbing his hands in glee" (190), demonstrating that he is proud of his role in disposing of the Jews.

Skibell exploits his childhood perceptions directly in the instances described above, but also evokes them in the generic uncertainty that characterizes his unusual novel.

Between Genres

Tzvetan Todorov, in his influential book *Introduction à la Littérature Fantastique*, has defined the following three conditions that must be fulfilled for a text to be an example of "fantasy": firstly, a hesitation on the part of the reader as to whether to interpret the events portrayed in natural or supernatural terms; secondly, a replication of this in the experience of a character, so that hesitation is thematized; and thirdly, the reader's refusal to interpret the text in an allegorical or poetic sense. In Todorov's account, the first and third of these conditions *must* be present for a text to fulfil the conditions of the fantastic, while the second usually occurs.[18] If the hesitation in the text is resolved so that a natural explanation is clearly possible, then the story belongs to the category of the *étrange* (strange), while if the events cannot be explained without calling into question our existing knowledge of natural laws, the story belongs to that of the *merveilleux* (marvellous). A text is only *fantastique* (fantastic) for as long as it sustains a hesitation between these two genres that form its borders.[19]

An obvious objection to a reading of *A Blessing on the Moon* in terms of this account of the fantastic is that, as I have already indicated, the novel contains many elements that point to its being an allegory on the theme of the concentration camps. Allegory, or extended metaphor, would certainly seem to account for those unsettling parts of the text that draw uncomfortably and unexpectedly close to historical events. In the first place, Chaim and his neighbors, though dead, appear to be capable of a prolonged, possibly infinite suffering. This fundamental premise of the text makes the reader confront the possibility of physical mutilation in a context that, although apparently belonging to the genre of the *merveilleux*, nonetheless feels uncomfortably real because of the Holocaust theme:

> The soldiers' lime has eaten into their skins. . . .
>   With a dirty hand, Basha Rosenthal wipes a tear from a lost eye. Her child plays at her broken feet, without its jaw.
>   Rivke Siedenberg, my old seductress, bravely holds her disembowelled viscera in with two unsteady arms. (81)

On an obvious level, this is indeed *merveilleux*, for these people have climbed out of their grave, and their injuries are enough, if not to have killed them, then certainly to have prevented their behavior as described above.

Yet, as I have also suggested, this passage may be read as an allegory for the unimaginable prolongation of suffering in the camps, in which the body underwent extreme and grotesque transformations. Primo Levi wrote,

> I turn rotten in the rain, I shiver in the wind; already my own body is no longer mine: my belly is swollen, my limbs emaciated, my face is thick in the morning, hollow in the evening; some of us have yellow skin, others grey. When we do not meet for a few days we hardly recognize each other.[20]

Levi and his fellow deportees are transformed into "a hundred miserable and sordid puppets."[21] While Levi survives, his description of his own body evokes a corpse rather than a living being: it is "rotten" and "grey," and his use of the term "puppet" reflects the Nazi objectification and dehumanization of the living Jewish body. To be alive does not mean that his body is truly his own. Recounting the arrival of his transport, Levi states, "this is hell" and "we are not dead" in close succession, suggesting that the coexistence of these two facts begins to explain his position.[22] In Skibell's novel, when a character, faced with danger, points out that they are already dead, Chaim counters, "you think they can't kill us as often as they wish!" (132).

A second powerful pointer to an allegorical interpretation can be found in Chaim's being criticized for his failure to act ethically. His friend Reb Elimelech berates him for climbing out of the grave (believing himself alive) and leaving the others behind, to which Chaim responds, "You were dead." The conversation continues as follows:

> "But so were you!" he shouts.
> "What did you expect me to do?"...
> "Didn't you even look!."...
> "Yes," I say. "Once. Quickly."
> "But you didn't stop, did you!"...
> "I'd been shot in the head," I scream. "I wasn't thinking clearly!" (92)

In this world without obvious rules, Chaim has not only failed to make the best moral choice, but is unconscious of having made a choice at all. The nature of moral action in extreme circumstances is interrogated here through a fantasy world with rules as incomprehensible to the characters as they are to the reader. The opportunity to save yourself, this passage says, does not absolve you from responsibility toward others. This was, of course, a central dilemma during the Holocaust, for even small gestures of help to those at serious risk could threaten the lives of the helper and his or her family. In such circumstances, the decision *not* to help could be easily rationalized.

An allegorical reading of the novel is further supported by numerous smaller details. For example, Nazi propaganda encouraging elderly Jews to go to Terezin is echoed in the promises of good kosher food and luxurious surroundings offered to the Jews by the German staff of the Hotel Amfortas, who nonetheless coerce the Jews by "block[ing] their path" (129–30). Equally, their instruction to leave clothes behind, as they say, "we have fresh ones for you here" (130), recalls Nazi attempts to create a semblance of normality when directing victims to the gas chambers. Chaim loses all markers of time, just as happened to the prisoners in the camps, as symbolized by both the disappearance of the moon and the fact that he is no longer able to read his watch (15, 18). In the following desecration of kosher law, he finds the shul full of unkosher pigs and (kosher) goats:

> "Can we rely on the villagers for protection?" one of the pigs says, his voice quavering with rage. "Think again, my friends," a goat warns, shaking his grey beard, although none of them seems convinced. (7)

Despite their ambivalence, these animals are clearly being kept for slaughter. Similarly, many Jews debated whether or not to leave, maintaining faith in their non-Jewish friends and neighbors until it was too late. Chaim's failure to understand the rules of the world he has entered—such his inability to recognize immediately that he is dead (3–5) and his sense, when visiting the office of his former business, that his absence is simply unnoticed and unmourned (17)—also permit an allegorical reading.

While the uncanny resemblances between Chaim's afterdeath experiences and the experiences of concentration-camp prisoners are allegorical on a historical and thematic level, the moon is an allegorical emblem that has an important structural function in the novel. According to Jewish tradition, "the moon, on account of its monthly reappearance, is considered as the emblem of Israel; the latter, like the moon, undergoing several phases through persecution without being destroyed."[23] The moon's waning is thus envisaged as persecution. The disappearance and eventual restoration of the moon during the Holocaust, in Skibell's telling, therefore symbolizes an unprecedented threat to the Jews, followed by a resurgence of hope. In addition,

> the reason why the Jews count the days of the year by the moon is that, like the moon, which reigns both in the daytime and at night, the Jews have both this world and the future one. On this account the eclipse of the moon is considered by the Rabbis as a bad sign for the Jews.[24]

Chaim spends much of the novel longing for that future world, the World to Come, and he is only able to leave the world of the living when the moon is restored. There is a further tradition, which gives the novel its title, that the new moon should be blessed on its reappearance each month. One version of this tradition advises the following: "to raise the body on the tips of the toes three times, addressing the moon with the ancient formula: 'As I dance toward thee, but can not touch thee, so shall none of my evil-inclined enemies be able to touch me.'"[25] In the novel, two Hasids land a boat on the moon, the effect of which is to drag it from the sky. The moon is eventually discovered buried in a "hidden grave" (228), "beneath layers and layers of corpses" (240), and soaked with blood and covered with bullet holes (253–54), a description that reflects Chaim's (or Israel's) own state of being "risen" from the grave, albeit permanently scarred.

As I suggested earlier, however, Todorov's definition of allegory as an extended metaphor does not account for the whole of this novel.[26] Although there are a number of incidents that invite allegorical readings, the extent to which they form a coherent extended metaphor is limited. Purely allegorical works like George Orwell's *Animal Farm* present a set of "fictional" circumstances, characters, and events that can be mapped point for point on to real ones. This cannot be done with *A Blessing on the Moon*. For example, while the animals in the shul *do* stand in for the Jews at that moment—the implication being that the animals have taken over the social space that the Jews occupied before their deaths—they do not reappear elsewhere in the text. In fact, the oppressed position they represent will be explored more extensively through the experiences of the dead Jews themselves. Likewise, the Hotel Amfortas, of which the Jews are initially so wary, turns out to be a place where their wounds are healed and they can be reunited with their families in luxurious surroundings. It is true that all the characters except Chaim disappear again, as all but he have appointments "for the steam," but there are no scenes of horror. Ultimately, the episode of comfort in the hotel cannot simply be accounted for as allegory.

At such moments as these, the text exemplifies the *merveilleux*. When Chaim meets the German soldier who shot him, both the man's request for forgiveness and Chaim's refusal to give it recast postwar debates about memory as an allegory or fable. On the other hand, the soldier's headlessness and Chaim's attempt to help the talking head find its body once more are part of a separate network of images. Likewise, the moon's restoration to the heavens may be allegorical and/or symbolic, but the manner in which it happens as follows belongs to the *merveilleux*:

> Poking out from beneath a cluster of bluish elbows is the tip of the crescent's curved horn, about as big and round as a large man's fedora. It shines with a dull yellow light.
> Zalman wraps a tailor's tape around the curving hook and takes its dimensions. (240)

The lengthy account of the attempts of Chaim and the two Hasids to restore the moon to its proper place is superfluous to any allegorical content. These details belong to the *merveilleux* dimension to the text, which is in constant interplay with the allegorical dimension for the full duration of the novel.

In this analysis, *A Blessing on the Moon* is not an example of fantasy, but rather an example of a generic hybrid. Where the *fantastique* is denoted by a hesitation between the *étrange* and the *merveilleux*, and what Todorov calls *allégorie hésitante* by a hesitation between allegory and literality, in Skibell's work the hesitation is between *allégorie* and *merveilleux*. Any attempt to read the novel according to only one of these genres is inadequate. What is important about what would otherwise be a meaningless exercise in generic categorization is that the interplay of the two genres exploits readers' expectations by creating a disorienting space that never resolves itself sufficiently for confident predictions to be made. The resulting confusion (perhaps a better word than "hesitation" in this instance) is shared by Chaim in his bewilderment, mourning, and despair as he tries to understand his position in the shadowy afterlife in which he finds himself.

The key point about allegory and *merveilleux* as the genres that engage in this interplay is that they represent radically different relationships between text and reality. In allegory, the text's bizarreness or distance from everyday life can be a way of encouraging critical contemplation of aspects of reality that might normally be glossed over. In other words, it encourages us to adopt the perspective we might have when looking at more unusual events. The *merveilleux*, on the other hand, understood in its purest form, is not meant to be a representation of reality, but instead a genre in which normal rules are suspended and the impossible or magical can occur.[27] Its only relationship to reality is to reality as other. The genres of allegory and *merveilleux* constantly displace each other in this text so that the reader is shunted between opposing interpretations of the events in the text as "real" or supernatural. This creates precisely the "disruption and unease" that Vice suggests may be the most successful strategy for representing the Holocaust in fiction. As Gila Ramras-Rauch has written, "in Holocaust literature we veer between the believable and unbelievable; the realistic experience touches the dimension of the incredible"; thus the normal "rules" of fantasy do not apply.[28] Skibell lets the child's perspective, in its blurring of real and imaginary, function as a metaphor for that of the adult faced with understanding a history that seems both distant and improbable.

Even those such as Cynthia Ozick, who continues to argue for caution in the exercise of imagination when representing the Holocaust, acknowledges the possibility of overexposure to a few well-worn images. "We must suppose," she writes, "that some of these images, through repetition, have become so recognizable, so clichéd, that the most liberal hearts can be hardened against them."[29] As Gilead Morahg expresses it,

> the psyche recoils reflexively from the pain of such an experience and creates defenses against it. The fantastic has the capacity to breach these defenses without devastating that which they were designed to protect. By defying the codes of reality and reason, the fantastic may provide a protective measure of distance and alternative possibility that makes the horror bearable without diminishing its concreteness. [It] can also serve to recuperate the profound sense of unreality that assailed those who were cast into the concentrationary universe and discovered that all the normative categories that formed the world as they knew it had been horribly reversed.[30]

The Holocaust fantasy story, or "fairy tale," has the potential to make us children again through its function as an instrument of understanding, just as extreme events may be seen to infantilize us in our inability to comprehend them. We move some way toward sharing the horror of the reality, as fantasy disorients us and, by approaching the subject from an unexpected angle, it "breaches the defenses" of cliché that we have unconsciously built up. This provides a rationale for Skibell's decision to use a fantasy-based form for his "imaginative reconstruction" of his family's unspoken, repressed experiences of the Holocaust.

Drawing on Hayden White's suggestion that the "anomalies, enigmas, and dead ends encountered in discussions of the representation of the Holocaust are the result of a conception of discourse that owes too much to realism, which is inadequate in cases such as the Holocaust," Morahg writes that fantastic fiction—at least in the case of Israel—"acknowledges the impossibility of an authentic *representation* of the concentrationary experience," while nonetheless "enabling an authentic *response* to this experience" (emphasis added).[31] The move from "representation" to "response" here is significant. What the writers under discussion in this volume attempt is, after all, not a "realistic" representation of what happened, but a literary response based on their own experience; the issue of representation shifts from the first generation's history to other generations' present and future. It is a means of expressing a theme that on some level we cannot understand in a form that we can comprehend.

The Child's Vision and the Mother's Body

The use of fairy tales is just one way in which the child is a key concept in this novel. Fairy tales are thematized in a network of images that support my reading of Skibell's use of "fantasy." The influence of fairy tales and folktales, both of which are traditionally associated with children, and the manner in which the novel slips between discourses, as if uncertain of what is real and what is imagined, serve to emphasise the link that Skibell makes between his writing and his own childhood perception of his family's history. Specifically, it is the child's *vision* that is constructed as the "other" in opposition to the obtuseness and immorality of the perpetrators (represented by the German soldier) and the bystanders (represented by the Polish family that is only too pleased to take over Chaim's family property as its own). Ola, the young daughter, is able to see the blood that Chaim has smeared on the walls of the house while it remains invisible to the rest of her family, and her grief and distress lead to her fatal illness. This illness is clearly moral. When Chaim starts to help make her comfortable, she protests, "we are intruders here. We have no rights" (34) in contradiction to her father's angry declaration that she is "blubbering over some silly people who'd do the same to us. . . given half the chance" (32). Self-imprisoned in her bedroom, the filthy conditions of her sick room come gradually to resemble those of a concentration camp's barracks, rendering visible through her illness what has been covered over by law, society, and her family: the disappearance and murder of the Jews.[32]

Later, as Chaim and the rabbi are leading the other dead Jews through the town, it is only the children who can see them, and react as follows: "Most ran away in fright, but many threw rocks and jeered" (89). An ability to see the truth does not in itself equip the viewer with morality. However, children in this novel at least have the chance, through their privileged vision, to understand and be appalled. Adults, it would seem, have lost the vision that gives them the capacity for pity and remorse altogether. For Naomi Solokoff, the child in literature, and in Jewish literature in particular, occupies a unique position as follows:

> to the extent that the Jews form a minority culture and so an Other, this figure [of the child] becomes the Other of the Other. In this capacity children serve as a useful instrument for observing, criticizing, or celebrating both their elders and the non-Jewish world in its treatment of the Jews.[33]

The children in *A Blessing on the Moon* occupy a position between the living adults and the dead. They are not so fully caught up in adult ideology as to be unable to see the crime that has been committed, and to recognize its victims as human, even if they then choose to mistreat them. In this they approach the position of the dead Chaim, who notices that, in his former village, "in front of every house were piles of vows and promises, all in broken pieces. How I could see such things, I cannot tell you" (4). Children here stand in for a more usual and desirable state of adult affairs, in which differing opinions are proffered, weighed, and debated. Instead, the adult world portrayed only offers a collective, conspiratorial silence of denial, rooted in endemic anti-Semitism and reinforced by the possibility of personal financial gain. This preoccupation with ideological and economic factors figuratively and literally blinds the novel's non-Jewish, living adults to the moral issues and realities underlying their position of comfort.

Rosemary Jackson, in an argument that may be used to link children in *A Blessing on the Moon* back to matters of fantasy again, has observed that

> the topography of the modern fantastic suggests a preoccupation with problems of vision and visibility, for it is structured around spectral imagery: it is remarkable how many fantasies introduce mirrors, glasses, reflections, portraits, eyes—which see things myopically, or distortedly, or out of focus—to effect a transformation of the unfamiliar into the familiar.[34]

In *A Blessing on the Moon*, the toy telescope belonging to Ola—who, her parents say, "sees things" (24)—produces just such a transformation. Not only is the telescope a child's tool of vision, but the first thing Chaim sees through it is a child as follows:

> The lens has sustained a crack. . . . I scan my town and see it, as it were divided in two, the vein in the lens rendering everything slightly askew. . . .
> The boy is carrying something, food perhaps, and when his hat blows off his head, he does not hesitate or look behind. . . . Instead, he pumps his arms harder, jumps into the air, and disappears through the crack in the lens. (42)

Chaim's speculation that the boy is a Jewish survivor, plus his disappearance "through the crack" is one of the novel's many refusals to clarify its proposed relation between reality and fantasy. His supposed survival, that is, his continued existence in the "real" world, is miraculous, yet his status as survivor is ultimately unclear because he belongs to neither one side of the cracked lens nor the other. Like Ola, who is able to see the dead Jews and grieve for them but who proves too frail for the "real" world of the living, he is part of neither state. Again, it is only *living* adults, and not the dead Jews, who are defined against the children. Despite the telescope lens being fractured in two, it is this that eventually enables Chaim, his rabbi, and the two Hasids to ascertain that the moon has returned to its proper place at the end of the novel.

The girl's telescope is contrasted with another instance of distorted perception: the disembodied head and broken spectacles of a German soldier. The soldier appears while Chaim and his companions are sleeping in a field, and marches the Jews into the woods. Finally, Chaim turns on the soldier in anger and discovers that he is also dead when one of his blows displaces his head. However, when the body runs off confused, Chaim takes pity on the head, despite its persistent arrogance and anti-Semitism as follows:

> "If it weren't for you," he says, "I'd still be at the conservatory, working on my compositions." He stretches his lower lip into a frown.
> "If it weren't for me?"
> "For your people." (102–3)

Chaim's revenge on the head of the soldier, who believes himself to be his murderer, consists in depriving him of an already distorted vision by secretly breaking his damaged glasses. There are now two broken lenses in Chaim's possession, yet it is the child's telescope that he will use again. The head itself discusses childhood and vision:

"I have done things. . . which, as a child or even a young man, I would not have believed myself capable. . . . I've tried to convince myself that it is only a matter of finding my glasses, but I can't lie to myself any longer. My sight is dimming. Is it possible that I am really, finally going to die?" (116)

Contrasting his status as a murderer with memories of his childhood self, the soldier interprets his failing vision as a sign of drawing near to death. This is the inverse of Ola's ability, and that of other children, to "see things" that permit them to have moral choices.[35] Where the child's telescope appears to illuminate the relationship between apparently irreconcilable worlds, metaphorically highlighting the "crack" or disjuncture between them, the German soldier's already imperfect vision—with or without its own cracked lenses—is merely doomed to fade. To the soldier, Chaim is objectified as a Jew within Nazi discourse; the soldier's interest in him is for practical help and forgiveness, the latter of which Chaim refuses to give. In its representation of children, the novel offers a symbol for a freshness of vision that is capable of bypassing adult norms, for better or for worse.

A particularly important component of the novel's understanding of childhood is Chaim, whose fatherhood and the deeply painful experiences he has had in connection with it, do not estrange him from a child's perspective. Instead, Chaim has a special affinity for children that is played out in his relationship with Ola and in the way he allowed his grandchildren to draw in the blank pages of ledger books, to his accountants' consternation (17–18). The fact that his relationship with Ola becomes sexual is something that troubles him, as he reflects, "never while I lived did I place myself in such a compromising circumstance!" (52). This relationship's transgressiveness, however, is a feature that it shares with other aspects of Chaim's afterlife, such as the rabbi's transformation into a distinctly non-kosher crow, which then steals a wedding ring, and pecks out of a man's eyes (9–11).

The child Ola stands in for two other (dead) women in the text: Chaim's first wife, Ida, who "died in childbirth, a girl herself" (121) and is described as "small and frail" and "childlike" (157), and his mother, the other woman he hopes to meet in the afterlife, whose family members were "frail and hopeless. . . such dreamers!" (159). Chaim's love and affection for these women, who are not sufficiently distinguished from each other or from Ola to be truly individual, suggests again that it is the childlike qualities such as Ola's small size and imaginativeness that Chaim values. These qualities merge into one in Chaim's mind as a sensitive, idealized child/woman.

In contrast to this child/woman stands Chaim's second wife, Ester, who is "large, blunt" with a "body as thick as a small tree" (154). Ester is thus described in a similar manner to the Polish peasants at the beginning, and while she is not depicted as an unsympathetic character, Chaim questions the degree of his own affection for her, recalling, "when I married her, also, I was still grieving over Ida, my first wife. She had died some months before, so small and frail and unable to bring a baby into the world" (157). The nature of the discord or discrepancy between himself and Ester is illustrated in part of their conversation at the hotel as follows:

"Are we little children that we should cry?"
[. . .] She is right, of course. . . . But a man can still mourn. Or must he be a child for that? (155)

His relationship with Ester, even though she bears ten children, denies him the proximity to children's sensibility and vision that he desires.

What emerges particularly strongly from Chaim's identification with children and his perception of the women he loves as childlike themselves is a strong contrast between a small, childlike physique and an excessive physicality (which Chaim describes with disgust or disdain). Chaim also develops a correspondingly polarized perception of women as either robust mothers or fragile children. The most important point about the first of these is that Chaim himself is divorced from physicality. The "body" he retains has no physical relationship to much of the world around him, and only serves as a reminder of the human body's potential for injury, illness, suffering, and decay. Ramras-Rauch writes,

in the Holocaust [. . .] : autism, the shattered self-image, minimalized experience, reduced existence, and self-negation—all of these were aspects of survival. The hesitation was directed to oneself, to one's sanity, and to the very possibility of continued consciousness. Many of the characters in Holocaust literature therefore have an amorphous quality to them, a certain weightlessness.[36]

His unburial, from which he emerges surprisingly conscious, if not alive, is an image of rebirth, but rebirth without a body. He is alienated from the physical in "real" terms, reduced to a purely spiritual entity. This goes hand in hand with his revulsion for most things physical. At Ola's funeral, he is revolted by her family's bodies:

How they sigh and heave, these fatuous dreamers, flaunting the very air in their chests. Their exhalations fill my nostrils with a putrid stench. Oh, the living, how they stink! They stink! They do! They rot but do not decompose. (63–64)

At the end of the novel, when the rabbi is transformed into a human being again, Chaim finds himself, to his own dismay, "flooded with revulsion" for the old man (266). His postmortem affection for Ola, Ida, and his own mother is strongly connected to their small, fragile stature, bringing them relatively close to his own bodiless state.

There is another interpretation of this, which relates to the fact that all mothers in the novel (except Chaim's own mother) have excessively oversized bodies. Ola's thinness and illness are accentuated by references to her mother's "thick arms" (22), "enormous breasts" (60), and "fat crab-like hand" (38). Ester is both "tall" and "stout" (13), and an account of the ten children she bore precedes the observation that it was trying to have children that killed Chaim's first wife, the fragile Ida. He remembers Ester's giving birth in terms of her heaviness (47). Even the Virgin Mary, during her brief, comic appearance in a heavenly chariot, is described as a "matronly woman" (60) with "strong arms" (59).

For Chaim, the mother is split into two parts: an excessively physical being whose influence he wishes to escape, and an idealized and forbidden object of desire (this desire was carried to its logical extreme in his sexual relationship with Ola). Marina Warner and Bruno Bettelheim have both written about the process in fairy tales whereby the cruel and undesirable aspects of parents and grandparents are dealt with in the character of a wicked stepmother. In this process, Warner argues, "fairy tales play to the child's hankering after nobler, richer, altogether better origins, the fantasy of being a prince or a princess in disguise, the Freudian 'family romance.'"[37] As I have already explored, this is recurrent in writing by descendants of survivors. Here, it leads my argument back again to the question of Chaim as an adult, but an adult in sympathy with children.

To understand this, it should be noted that the idea of burial alive is felt by many to be "uncanny," a fact attributed by Freud to its being a transformation of the fantasy of being in the womb.[38] In climbing from the mass grave, Chaim is therefore "reborn," but without a mother. His resulting sense of abandonment after this motherless rebirth from the pit gives rise to a resentment that is directed specifically toward mothers' bodies, their nurturing presence. Perhaps in allowing him to be born, his mother was also responsible for all his and his family's sufferings at the hands of the Nazis. This is in turn a displacement of his own self-loathing as a father who has similarly failed in his protective duty, and which an identification with children helps him to deny. Chaim is, of course, a symbolic figure, representing the continued life (*chaim*) of the Jews, the restoration of Israel implicit in the moon's reappearance. David Patterson notes that "if the Holocaust memoir is distinguished by the death of the self, the first signs of that death often come upon the loss of the mother"—the mother also being symbolic of Israel.[39] Chaim's suffering and abandonment symbolize the Jews' abandonment by

God, and the pain of surviving without the comfort of religious ritual and guidance. It is this absence of visible spiritual leadership that leads to his fifty years of wandering.

Chaim's afterlife endures for a lifetime in itself: he undergoes "birth," attempts to make sense of an unfamiliar world, has a sexual relationship, learns moral responsibility, separates from his family, and works. Finally, he returns to (or through) the large maternal body that he has been denying:

> Beneath this large woman's caressing hands, I forget my children's names. . . I no longer recall how I earned my living or why I died. . . . although I find I can still, without difficulty, remember my name.
> Chaim Skibelski.
> "Chaimka, Chaimka," the woman sings, "look at the moon. Can you see the moon?"
> My small body is flooded with well-being. I gurgle in her lap. With her large fingers, she carefully turns my head and the light of the moon fills my eyes, until it is all I see. (267)

As Chaim returns to a state of infancy, his mother's body, previously small, becomes large to him again. Patterson argues that, in Holocaust memoir,

> as the survivor enters into the memory of the mother, this one who had given him life becomes part of his life, in such a way that what survives is not the continuation of one life but a second life, one that now bears the trace of its maternal origin.[40]

Chaim's repression of his mother's body is tied to his own disembodied inability to die: only by bringing her body back into play to enable him to be "unborn" can he rest. The child is thus uncannily present within Chaim, the adult narrator, as that which is both familiar and, on some level, repressed. The child that haunts Chaim, alone and abandoned yet desperately denying this painful state, is like the (literal and figurative) haunting of Poland by the Jews: the former existence of the Jews underlies the wealth and culture that the Polish characters enjoy, yet acknowledging that former existence questions their entitlement to this wealth.

There is another aspect to this ending. Patterson, in his discussion of the loss of the mother in his work on Holocaust memoir, observes the following:

> Initially the man comes into the world as a Jew because his mother is a Jew; then he is reborn as a Jew through the memory of his Jewish origin, a memory manifested through a sense of Jewish responsibility. The process of memory, furthermore, entails a movement towards the womb of origin that arises not

afterward but from the depths of the Horror itself, from the first moment of the origin's obliteration.[41]

Survival is a continuation of the maternal—it is a second birth, the birth of memory. The "unbirth" of the novel's ending represents a return to the very heart of that which was (supposed to have been) annihilated.

This reading shows that Skibell's use of genre calls into question the relationship between real and imaginary in a way that seems suited to representations of the Holocaust, given the reluctance of many people to believe what they heard at the time and afterward. Skibell's comments in an interview, cited earlier in this chapter, on the influence of Grimm's fairy tales on his early understanding of the Holocaust, and also the influence of Jewish traditions of storytelling on his writing, link his use of genre to children. Children's perceptions of the Holocaust are then developed throughout the novel as analogous to the disoriented, abandoned, and marginalized Chaim. Children also represent a distance from the disturbing historical events of the Holocaust; like the dead Jews, children are outside the mainstream social framework that permitted such events to happen, even if in some cases (such as the children who throw stones at the Jews) they choose to participate in that framework's norms. My argument will now move on to illustrate the ways in which Skibell's choice(s) of genre are situated in a broader historical and ethical context.

Fiction and Reality

The foregoing reading lays out the strategies employed by Skibell to re-create his great-grandfather's past from a position of historical and geographical distance. I would also argue that these strategies (specifically the use of generic boundaries and the references to fairy tales) serve a dual purpose, providing a second kind of link to the past. The novel thus serves to critique the enlistment of such literary strategies in the service of anti-Semitic and Nazi ideology.

In an essay entitled "Aliens Among Us," Elana Gomel draws a historical link between fascism and the literary genre of fantasy, arguing that "science fiction and fascism share both a structure and a source. While H. G. Wells was writing his evolutionary fantasies. . . the discourse of evolution was producing its own monsters, eugenics and Social Darwinism."[42] Eugenics, a corruption of Darwin's theory of "natural selection," advocated "selective breeding" to "improve" the human race.[43] Such ideas were adopted by the Nazis in their mass murder of the mentally disabled, as well as Jews. Gomel notes that the rise of Nazism in Germany had been foreshadowed in a number of fantastic works that espoused a radical right-wing ideology and enjoyed unprecedented popularity in the Weimar Republic, outselling almost any other genre.[44]

She suggests that it is precisely in the figure of the "monster" that this link exists, as the "forgotten bestsellers" used a particular symbolism that

> reduced all social, political or even psychological conflicts to corporeal affects. Ideological hatred was translated into the language of nausea caused by the body of the "alien," while revolution became bodily purification.[45]

Such symbolism is, of course, familiar in Nazi depictions of the Jewish body as deformed, intrinsically "inferior," and verminous. Moreover, Gomel points out that "*Mein Kampf* depicts the Jew as a monster, not figuratively but *literally.*"[46] This represents the concept that narrative theorist Peter Brooks has termed a "collapsed metaphor, a metaphor unaware that its tenor and vehicle have become identical."[47] In his representation of the Jewish body as literally monstrous, Hitler completely elided the complex relationships between language, representation, and reality (such as those that Skibell explores) in the service of his political and eugenic objectives. As Daniel Schwarz writes,

> words have instrumentality when the word *Jew* becomes a fact or thing, a star to be worn, a reason to be defiled. Words also have materiality when they fictively render that process into a text that lives its effects on others.[48]

The effect of Hitler's use of language in *Mein Kampf*, with its emphasis on bodily monstrosity, is "that real human bodies are overlaid with literary clichés to the point of becoming invisible. Ironically, the ideology grounded in corporeal discrimination erases the corporeality of its victims."[49]

In writing a "fantasy" novel about the Holocaust, especially from the position of one whose ancestors escaped it, Skibell is reclaiming a genre whose "metaphors of monstrosity," Gomel argues, have "a structural complicity" with "the slogans of racial hatred."[50] This applies not only to fantasy as Todorov defines it in terms of nineteenth-century literature, but also to fairy tales, some of which also exhibit an anti-Semitic conflation of fantasy and reality.

One reason for Skibell's declared wish to write in a Jewish literary tradition rather than in the German tradition that he sees as so pertinent to the perspective of later generations on the Holocaust is the association of Grimm's fairy tales with anti-Semitism. "After 150 years of 'The Jew in the Thornbush' as a bedtime tale," he expresses in an interview, "nothing the Germans did should come as a surprise."[51] In *A Blessing on the Moon*, Skibell is writing specifically *against* this fairy tale and others like it. The Jew of the story's title is the victim of an anti-Semitic stereotype: although there is nothing to indicate that he has an evil or dishonest intention, he is victimized on the assumption that, as a Jew, he will have fleeced people and is therefore a fair target. He is actually "punished" three times, while the man who brings about these punishments escapes unharmed. On the first occasion, a magic violin forces the Jew to dance in a thornbush, he is then forced to hand over his money, and finally he is executed.

However, it seems that the real question here is that of meaning and interpretation. When the Jew goes to the judge, he does not tell him about the magic violin being used to make him a victim of extortion; instead he tells him that he was beaten and robbed. Bruno Bettelheim points out that, unlike myth,

> although the events that occur in fairy tales are often unusual and most improbable, they are always presented as ordinary, something that could happen to you or me or the person next door when out on a walk in the woods. Even the most remarkable encounters are related in casual, everyday ways in fairy tales.[52]

This mostly holds true for "The Jew in the Thornbush," but the Jew calls this generic feature into question by relaying not the *truth* of the supernatural event, but the *meaning* of that event in natural terms. The servant, who is responsible for the Jew's punishment, tells the literal "truth"—that the Jew handed his money over freely—but this truth operates on a level that suppresses the event's moral truth, namely that it is the Jew who has a grievance against the servant, and not vice versa. It is, however, this literal "truth" that effects the performance of anti-Semitism, for the judge deems that a Jew would never hand his money over freely, and as a result of this ruling, the Jew is executed. The servant is described more than once as "compassionate" despite his actions toward the Jew. Likewise, the Jew is groundlessly called a "rogue" by the servant.

The story exposes anti-Semitism's presumption of Jewish guilt as unfounded, even though this presumption is shown to be performative. As Wilhelm Solms writes,

> When the Jew in the thorns acknowledges at the end that the knave had "earned the money honestly," which he had gained from him with the help of the magic fiddle, this is not in fact the truth. Anyone who still feels that his being sentenced to death is his just deserts must be obsessed with the prejudice that a Jew is always in the wrong.[53]

Anti-Semitism is a *fait accompli* in this story to the extent that without it, the story makes no sense. Being incompatible with empirically observable phenomena, the anti-Semitism of the story undermines itself as follows: the Jew in the story shows no evidence of a propensity to dishonesty. Anti-Semitism shows itself clearly as a "belief," just as we are invited to believe in the servant's "honesty" and "compassion." The Jew is the servant's only victim: while the judge and the onlookers at the gallows are also compelled by the violin to dance, they do so only as part of the servant's victimization of the Jew. The "crime" that leads directly to the Jew's execution is his interpretation of the supernatural in natural terms, just as the story unwittingly betrays that there is no "natural" grounds for fear or suspicion of Jews. "The Jew in the Thornbush" exposes anti-Semitism as pure superstition. Herein lies the interest of the story for Skibell's project. After commenting on the resonance of Grimm's fairy tales with the events of the Holocaust, Skibell says, "when I eventually discovered the great wealth of Jewish and Yiddish tales, I knew I had found my form."[54]

The first part of the novel, consisting of nineteen chapters, is entitled "From the Mayseh Book." The Ma'aseh Books, a feature of European Jewish life from the early fifteenth century, were "written in Judaeo-German in Hebrew script, and contained stories, legends, and tales ("ma'asim") on various subjects, most of them relating to Jews and Judaism."[55] Their evolution over the next two centuries, during which time they absorbed many cultural influences, led to the publication in 1602 of "a work known simply as 'Ma'asehbuch,' purporting to be a collection of Jewish legends and historical tales and without any admixture whatever of foreign elements." [56] These collections, therefore, were a mixture of stories from Jewish tradition and the non-Jewish cultures in which the compilers found themselves: *The Jewish Encyclopedia* notes that, "like the name 'ma'asehbuch' itself, this entire literature is a mixture of Jewish and German, both in language and in substance."[57] For Skibell, then, turning to Yiddish folktales does not necessarily represent a turning away from German folktales, for he is drawing on a form that, by its nature, adopted and adapted tales from neighboring, specifically German, cultural traditions.

In the light of centuries of anti-Semitic superstition in Poland, and in keeping with Elana Gomel's argument, the Holocaust was superstition, folk belief, and fairy tale (specifically superstitious anti-Semitism) acted upon and carried to its "logical" conclusion in reality. Jack Zipes' overview of the uses of fairy tale discourse in the Weimar Republic and Nazi Germany includes the following observation:

> Hitler thought of himself as a wise king who wanted to wield power for his
> people and to prevent sinister forces from invading the fatherland. . . .
>
>   Hitler as fairy-tale king. Germany as glorious realm. The aesthetics of poli-
> tics in the service of mystification. This fascist perversion of the bourgeois pub-
> lic sphere and its dire consequences for the German people conditioned the
> literary fairy-tale discourse during the 1930s and 1940s.[58]

As we have seen, Nazi ideology itself can be read as a fairy tale and certainly
as a work of fiction: the "sinister forces" that it sought to conquer came
largely in the form of European Jews.

In *A Blessing on the Moon*, the Jews are not only objects of fear, but provide
grounds for it once they have been killed, for it is implicitly the senseless act
of killing, rather than the Jews themselves, that haunts Poland for fifty years.
In the novel, the nature of superstition and "supernatural" events are repeatedly called into question. For example, Chaim Skibelski returns to his home
and realizes that he cannot be seen or heard by the Poles in his village: "so I
touched them. I grabbed onto their shoulders, [. . .]. At that, they crossed
themselves and shuddered. [. . .] They were peasants. Superstitious." (5) He
derides them for their superstitious belief systems while knowing nevertheless
now that such "superstition" is "real." Such supernatural events become the
topic of rational debate. Chaim's old porter and his niece discuss whether it is
the dead man who has stolen his family photos from the garage, the niece
protesting, "Europe would be crawling with them. Poland. They'd be every-
where"(55–56).

Chaim's perspective is also the inverse of anti-Semitic superstition, as for
example when he remembers seeing priests as follows: "We used to run by, as
children. . . out of fear for these black demons, certain they were neither man
nor woman with their pointy beards and their wide billowing skirts" (44).
This description of these sinister figures forms a counterpart to the figure of
the "evil" Jew. When Ola dies, Chaim's perspective places Christianity on the
plane of superstition as well, despite apparent proof of its truth when Jesus
and Mary descend from the sky to claim her. As they fly up into the sky, Mary
calls out "Shalom aleichem, Reb Chaim!" (60). Not only the reality, but the
Jewishness of Christianity is emphasized, yet Chaim muses on "the misery" of
witnessing this ascent "accompanied by her false gods, those idolatrous
abominations, while our God, the One True God, has left me neglected here
below, answering my pleas with His stony, implacable silence!" (62).

The persistence of Chaim's own beliefs is called into question, as he has
arguably no reason left to believe in God, yet he still does, and considers these
other gods "false" despite having seen them for himself. In his role as Job,
Chaim cannot lack faith, whatever test it is put to. One of his darkest

moments comes when the head of the Polish family who has occupied his house fails to be intimidated by Chaim's poltergeist-like presence at Ola's funeral meal:

> I have jumped to the floor and am about to rip the curtains from their rods, when the drunken old fool leaps upon the table and does a little mazurka of his own, sending forks and knives scattering in all directions. . .
> "Look! Look at me!" he sings out. "I"m a dead yid. I"m the ghost of that Jewish yid!" (66)

In Skibell's post-Holocaust world, superstition is justified: with the Jews dead and still inhabiting Poland, they have acquired the sinister, supernatural dimension that anti-Semites always attributed to them. Yet the power of this ghostly status, such as that which Chaim tries to exercise, is threatened by its very tangibility. The Polish characters, notably pitiable, ignorant bullies like Andrzej and the porter, see such a continued Jewish presence as rationally acceptable as follows: if live bogeymen were plausible, then why not dead ones? Just as Grimm's story inadvertently illustrates the groundlessness of anti-Semitism, the Poles' very willingness to believe in the dead Jews' haunting of their house undermines their assertions that they do not know where the Jews have "disappeared" to.

The story of the two Hasids and the moon is a central structuring motif in the novel, and a brief analysis of its use provides a summary of and conclusion to the current discussion. The story first appears as a bedtime story told by Chaim to Ola, which Chaim believes he has invented. It then appears as an eyewitness account told by the German soldier, in which Chaim, as listener, is markedly deprived of a voice. His response is only implicit in the following "conversation":

> "Can you guess it, Herr Jude?
> "Not a rock, no.
> "Not a cave.
> "Exactly. A boat." (111)

Chaim's (apparent) role as originator of the story is covered over, his role as listener is suppressed, and what the German perceives as the fleeing Hasids' stupidity at debating the morality of taking the boat turns it into an anti-Semitic tale. Finally, the story emerges as the "literal," disastrous truth within the *merveilleux* (and allegorical) context of the novel, as Chaim is called upon to help the two Hasids restore the wounded moon that, as we have seen, represents the persecuted Israel. This three-stage mutation reflects the progress of anti-Semitic discourses from superstition and prejudice to reality, and is a reflection and illustration of the slippage between discourses that the novel exploits.

Alain Finkielkraut wonders whether "anti-Semitism is an outmoded relic, best relegated to the museum of horror and superstitions between the fear of witches, the practice of magic and devil worship?" concluding that "nothing permits such optimism."[59] In support of this conclusion, a 1992 opinion poll showed that twenty-five percent of Poles put the number of Jews then in Poland at between seven hundred and fifty thousand and three and a half million, while another ten percent thought there were between four and seven million. In reality there were around six thousand.[60] The Jews persist as the imaginary "other" even in their absence.

In a particularly striking demonstration of the readiness of history and superstition to merge in surprising ways, Martin Gilbert describes the following incident that occurred in 1961 at the site of the notorious Babi Yar massacre,[61] in which over 30,000 Jews were murdered. The lake that had formed there spilled through its retaining wall:

> Streams of clay and mud, mixed up with the remains of human bones, gushed out into the streets of Kiev below. In the wake of the rushing waters, a garage was completely destroyed, fires broke out, and the stream of liquid clay, reaching the nearby tram depot, overturned tram cars and buried alive in its onward rush both passengers and tramway workers. That night, as soldiers were busy digging out the dead, and searching for survivors in the mud, a second wave of liquid clay burst out from the Yar, wreaking further havoc, and death. In the two disasters, twenty-four citizens of Kiev were killed. A few days later, as a tram passed the site of the disaster, an old woman suddenly began to shout: "It is the Jews who have done this. They are taking vengeance on us. They always will."[62]

The very *destruction* of the Jewish people who, while alive, unwillingly served as a superstitious focus for the Ukrainian population is shown here to preserve and even amplify that population's superstitious unease. Guilt, or at least the consciousness of having inflicted violence, feeds into old superstitions to modify them to the present circumstances.

Alain Finkielkraut considers the effect of the Holocaust on anti-Semitic words. If the Holocaust had not happened, he surmises,

> The insult "dirty kike" would still be part of our daily experience. It is only taboo now because forty years ago it was carried out to the letter by the regime of the Reich. The very goal of Hitlerism was, in effect, destruction of the barrier traditionally raised between hate speech and the murderous act. The classic slogans of anti-Semitism have been so effectively transformed into reality

that they have lost, in a single stroke, all ritualistic or symbolic force. Today one can no longer say "Death to the Jews," because this death has taken place.[63]

That which was figurative and story-like has become real, and in its reality it has effaced the possibility of the figurative discourse that provided its own precondition. The novel's flexible use of genre does not simply have to do with representing events that are hard to comprehend within any single genre. It also reflects, in its slippage between two relationships of words to reality, the shifts that took place, and are still taking place, in history.

Conclusion

Skibell draws on fantasy and its neighboring genres both as a representational strategy for dealing with a history that is hard to comprehend, and as a means of interrogating some of fantasy's less benign generic neighbors: anti-Semitic superstition and eugenic discourse.

Daniel Schwarz suggests that "in truth it is barbaric *not* to write poetry, in part because if we do not write imaginative literature, how can there be a post-Holocaust era"? He consequently proposes that "fifty years later the Holocaust lives because the Nazis' efforts to erase all traces of a people and to deprive the Jews of their private selves have been flouted by word and image."[64] The Holocaust "lives," he implies, in a different form, one that has evolved with and alongside successive generations, through the words and images these generations create.

Naomi Solokoff points out that the word "infant" means "without speech": it is the child's exclusion from discourse altogether that renders it as an "other." As they grow up, children move from their status as "peripheral figures" to become part of the dominant culture themselves. The converse of this fact is that, unlike other oppressed groups, they do not have a literature of their own in which to contest others' portrayals of them.[65] They thus remain a *perpetual* "other," in the service of numerous adult discourses. Specifically in a Jewish literary context,

> the child not yet fully initiated into tradition nor fully understanding of Jewish obligation becomes an indirect spokesman for authors who had themselves moved away from the orthodoxy of their early family life. Secularized adults, the writers sought out characters capable of seeing *other*wise the religious definition of Jewishness.[66]

Thus, implicit in Solokoff's argument is the fact that the child in literature can function as a foil to adults, or as a metaphor for a marginalized (Jewish) adult perspective. In *A Blessing on the Moon*, the child is analogous to the silenced, "infantilized" Jew, abandoned in both religious and social terms.

One thing that Skibell's novel demonstrates is that in the post-Holocaust era, as more descendants of survivors grow up, the silenced voice returns in a new form, even if it is not truly replaced. Shoshana Felman describes the objective of the Nazis as follows:

> To make the Jews invisible not merely by killing them, not merely by confining them to "camouflaged," invisible death camps, but by reducing even the materiality of the dead bodies to smoke and ashes, and by reducing, furthermore, the radical opacity of the *sight* of the dead bodies, as well as the linguistic referentiality and literality of the *word* "corpse," to the transparency of a pure form and to the pure rhetorical metaphoricity of a mere *figure*: a disembodied verbal substitute which signifies abstractly the linguistic law of infinite exchangeability and substitutability. The dead bodies are thus verbally rendered invisible, and voided both of substance and specificity, by being treated, in the Nazi jargon, as *figuren*: that which, all at once, *cannot be seen* and can be *seen through*.[67]

Skibell's novel attempts to resurrect the dead bodies linguistically and historically, reminding us that the choice of whether to see or to see through is a moral decision. In placing his "resurrected" dead bodies on the border of allegory and fantasy, with an uncertain and shifting relationship to reality, he answers the "camouflage" of Nazi rhetoric with a literary strategy that exposes the bodies' existence in, and influence on, the world, and suggests that they are invisible only to those who wish them to be.

CHAPTER 5

The Poetic Novel:
Anne Michaels's *Fugitive Pieces*

Introduction

In the context of the works I have discussed so far, Anne Michaels's novel *Fugitive Pieces* marks a radical departure: it rejects the author's family as a focal point of textual interest.[1] Even Joseph Skibell relies on an imagined figure—based on his real great-grandfather—with whom, he says, he "spent two very intimate years" in the writing of his book.[2] Family as a theme in second-generation texts provides a framework within which to explore questions of selfhood and subjectivity. Furthermore, drawing attention to autobiographical and familial connections to Holocaust-related material provides a kind of ethical and critical safety net for the writer, who can appeal to a contemporary culture that sanctifies both victimhood and the particularity of personal experience, in defence of his or her own responses.

If Michaels's denial of any autobiographical motive is explicit, then so, despite her own reservations, is her sense of a personal link to the Holocaust. Although she has declared in an interview that she is "not the child of survivors," she goes on to say, "it seemed like everyone my family knew, their lives had been completely altered by those years. It was the immediate history that my own life—the life of my generation—rose from."[3] More specifically, Michaels says,

> It's hard to separate what my father and grandfather might say now were the reasons they left, and why they actually did leave [the border of Russia and Poland in 1931]. . . . But I'm sure they were economic; I'm sure there was a question of persecution.[4]

One might conclude from this quotation that Michaels could have written a more autobiographical work, or a family- or community-based book on the subject, but Michaels's ambitions are for a further-reaching literary project that moves beyond the personal. In the same interview, she states that "[she] took a lot of pains to write the book in a certain way; and [she doesn't] want that to be side-tracked by anyone saying, 'Oh well, it's her story, and nobody else's.'"[5]

Instead of an autobiographical structure, Michaels relies on language, specifically poetic language, to forge her links with the past, to the extent that one reviewer described *Fugitive Pieces* as "less a novel than a 300-page prose-poem."[6] The text is also structured as an imperfect or distorted family history: the narrators of its two parts represent two generations without being biologically related, and it is precisely silence and the breakdown of intergenerational family narrative that the novel thematizes.

The novel begins as the fictional Polish poet Jakob Beer, then seven years old, escapes the Nazis who have just murdered his parents. He is found by archaeologist Athos Roussos who takes him to his native Greece for safety. They spend the war hiding on the island of Zakynthos and subsequently move to Toronto for Athos to take up an academic post. After Athos's death and a failed marriage, the still-traumatized Jakob leaves Canada for the Greek island of Idhra in order to write. Revisiting Toronto, he falls in love with Michaela, who helps him work through his childhood trauma, focusing on his failure to notice that, at the time of his parents' murder, his older sister Bella had simply disappeared. The couple move to Idhra, but die shortly afterward in a car accident in Athens.

Here, the novel turns to Ben, a young academic who has inherited his survivor-parents' trauma and is drawn to Jakob's writings as an alternative to the silence surrounding his own father's Holocaust experience. Partly as a break from his faltering marriage, Ben visits the poet's house on Idhra in search of his diaries. While there, he has an affair with Petra, an American, who eventually ransacks the house, thereby uncovering Jakob's elusive note-books. At this point—which also represents his break up with Petra—Ben realizes the value of his now-dead parents' relationship, and consequently of his marriage to Naomi. As the novel ends, he heads back to Toronto to make a fresh start: his time on the island has brought about a significant change in him, but we do not know what the outcome of this change will be.

The novel thus works its way back to the very familial territory that Michaels tries, on one level, to leave behind. Her denial of the autobiographical, adoption of a highly aestheticized style, and declared and implied strong personal commitment to a responsible representation of the past make *Fugitive Pieces* a near-ideal case study for a discussion of the "ethics" of representation. These elements additionally make the novel a focus of particular kinds of critical attention from within the field of Holocaust studies.

Despite the climate of critical anxiety surrounding representations of the Holocaust, most critics have adopted a largely positive stance toward Michaels's novel, possibly because it refrains from direct representation of the camps. Both Ann Parry and Annick Hillger have approached this topic from a philosophical perspective that gives little space to concerns of the "appropriateness" of the novel's form and language to its content.[7] Norma Rosen doubts that poetry can heal such trauma, but concludes that "this small, brilliant book is intent on healing. And so—would that it were so—let it be."[8] From a perspective firmly grounded in the study of "Holocaust literature," Nicola King calls *Fugitive Pieces* "a moving, poetic meditation upon love, loss, memory and time" that is "clearly based on extensive research in Holocaust history and survivor testimony." She also recognizes that the text carefully "acknowledges silence" in its reference to lost and buried stories.[9] However, she indicates a degree of unease with Michaels's heavily poeticized style by qualifying her positive assessment with concerns about it's the book's "mystification of human and political agency" in some of Jakob's "poetic meditations" on the past and his grief.[10]

King's response is echoed in those of Méira Cook and Adrienne Kertzer who similarly contend that *Fugitive Pieces* tends to "distract and console" by dwelling on those who survived.[11] "Of what benefit," Kertzer asks, "is our willingness to listen now to the few Holocaust survivors who still live? The appeal of trauma narrative is that it avoids such political questions. It makes the Holocaust accessible and reparable."[12] Finally, a more extreme position on this novel is adopted by Sue Vice who effectively dismisses it in a short paragraph in the introduction to her book *Holocaust Fiction*. Raising similar issues to those highlighted by King, Cook, and Kertzer concerning the consolatory and redemptive potential of the text, Vice concludes a forceful argument with the view that such poetization of the Holocaust is deeply suspect.[13]

Underlying the concerns of all these critics, and much criticism of other literary texts written about the Holocaust, is an anxiety generated by Holocaust deniers who have used lies and distortion to deny that the Holocaust ever occurred. Such worthy concerns also entail the danger that in our desire to take account of such dishonest "scholarship" we allow it to dictate the boundaries of our discussions, thereby capitulating to it indirectly.

Finding the Space for Fiction

Every Holocaust survival narrative is a story of the triumph of improbability, and Michaels takes many opportunities to point out the historical unlikelihood of survival in this fictional work. Firstly, Jakob, the child survivor who narrates the first and larger part of the novel, survives only by virtue of his size, as he squeezes into a hiding place behind the wallpaper in his parents' house when the Nazis arrive. Later, the text refers to those who were squeezing themselves into "strange graves" all over Europe, trying to make themselves invisible to history. Jakob's size is also vital in facilitating his flight from Poland, hidden under the coat that Athos is wearing; and later, in enabling him to be concealed in a sea chest whenever anyone approaches the house. The adult Jakob, who narrates the story of his life, is aware of his good fortune as follows:

> while I had the luxury of a room, thousands were stuffed into baking stoves, sewers, garbage bins. In the crawlspaces of double ceilings, in stables, in pigsties, chicken coops. A boy my age hid in a crate; after ten months he was blind and mute, his limbs atrophied. (45)[14]

Jakob correctly narrates his own experience of the war, which he spent "living with Athos. . . learning Greek and English, learning geology, geography, and poetry" (45) as exceptional. Given that a fictional survivor is essential to the nature of her project, Michaels consistently contrasts Jakob's life with more likely outcomes through his own first person narrative and through two of his short stories that are included in italics in the body of the text.[15] However, the text is marked by an awareness of the potential ethical difficulty of writing about survivorhood at all.

Owing to remarkable acts of resistance by the mayor and the archbishop of Zakynthos, who refused to hand over the names of the Jews residing on the island, and by the rest of the islanders, who worked together to conceal the Jewish population in the mountains, most of the Jews of Zakynthos survived the Nazi occupation and the war. The fact of their survival is implied, rather than stated explicitly, by Michaels, who is nonetheless ready to recount how elderly Jews who were unable to flee disappeared in an SS truck. She is careful not to take the unusual circumstances of the Zakynthos Jews' survival out of historical context and thereby provide a happy ending, telling us instead of the disturbing events that occurred on the neighboring islands Crete and Corfu. These are told with great difficulty to Jakob and Athos by Ioannis, an islander who is married to a Jewish woman from Corfu. Firstly, he tells of the Corfu Jews' deportation by boat, and secondly, with increasingly visible distress, of the deliberate sinking of the boat carrying the Jews of Crete's ancient ghetto (42–43). These images of drowning become part of the landscape of Jakob's nightmares for many years to come (44). The reader is encouraged to understand the fate of the Jews of the Greek islands as a whole, particularly when we see the elderly Jews of Zakynthos escape deportation (but not death) only because the boat that comes for them is already full of Jews from Corfu.

The use and integration of historical data within the text makes it impossible to dwell for too long on the happy anomalies that enable the fictional Jakob's survival.[16]

Yet too much preoccupation with the use of history in fiction about the Holocaust may simply result in a circular argument that tells us little about the workings of the text and much about the preferences of the critic. As the preceding discussion has indicated, for Anne Michaels, the rejection of the autobiographical goes alongside a deep commitment to historical truth, raising the following question that Berel Lang has asked: "What space is left for authors who commit themselves to images of a composite event so dense morally and historically as to leave the imagination little room in which to move or act?"[17] Lang refers to the example of Aharon Appelfeld's parable *Badenheim 1939*, in which Jewish vacationers at a spa resort find their lives gradually curtailed, until, in its closing pages, they board a train for the east. The resort has gradually taken on the character of a concentration camp, yet the Jews fail to comprehend what is going on around them. While the vacationers are strangely reassured by the poor condition of the train carriages, inferring from this that "the journey. . . could not be a long one under those circumstances," the reader is left to fill in the blanks rather differently with historical knowledge.[18]

The book creates a parable of Jews' disbelief in 1930s Europe without trying to represent it directly. Similarly, Lang argues, ending the novel at the moment of deportation allows room for the complex historical events to unfold according to the reader's knowledge (or indeed lack of it). In keeping with this, Anne Michaels's careful research and embedding of historical information within her narrative show that she is at pains to provide an accurate historical context for the representation of purely fictional events. By attempting to imagine the feelings and lives of imagined characters who "escaped" the Holocaust, or were born afterward, her writing largely steers clear of rewriting the past, focusing instead on a fictional particular in the context of the historical generality. This strategy is one answer to the question of critical unease with novels that lack historical awareness.

Historical realities haunt the novel's poetic texture in another way, despite the text's apparent commitment to the power of language to heal the wounds of history. As we shall see, history constantly threatens to undermine the apparently obvious messages of the text that emerge as Jakob finds a means to escape his traumatic past through language. The text exposes the limitations of history in a novel that is less a prose poem than a meditation on the availability, or unavailability, of the past to those who exist in the present. Not only does it open up the question of whether or by what means the past is available at all, but it also suggests that memory and poetry share a capacity to transform and contain a past that threatens to take overwhelming possession of the future.

Poetic Language and Language as Metaphor

Anne Michaels has explained her use of poetic language to describe disturbing and traumatic events in the following way:

> The book could have been written in very brutal language. It could have been ugly to read. But I realised in a way that that would be less true. It would separate one from the horror even more in a way by pretending to be closer. Rather than do that, I wanted to make the images work in a certain way so that the brutality or potency of an image would hit the reader before one had a chance to defend oneself against them, in such a way that you respond to them emotionally and then very quickly start to think about what the image means.[19]

This strategy is an extension of her rejection of the autobiographical: language for Michaels is a link to the past through imagination, not direct or obvious reference. As Jakob says in the novel, "Never trust biographies. Too many events in a man's life are invisible" (141). His role as a translator of posthumous war writing confirms his position as analogous to that of Michaels: in identifying the invisible, he creates, in a new language, a story that might not otherwise be told. Such posthumous tales are already belated, and the shift between languages adds cultural and linguistic difference to the existing discrepancy between the occurrence of an event and its telling.

Fugitive Pieces is primarily concerned not with the historical events of the Holocaust, but with the invisible processes of witnessing that unfold when the events are over. Its meditations on the ability and inability of experience to be passed on without being radically transformed also operate as a forum in which to discuss the role of writing after the event.

Witnessing the Human Body: Athos as Witness to Jakob

It is fitting that a novel so preoccupied with the capacity of language to unearth the past should begin with an exhumation. The seven year old Jakob Beer emerges from the ground to find himself before a witness at the ancient and newly excavated city of Biskupin. Since the murder of his family by the Nazis, he has been fleeing at night and burying himself to hide during the day. Writing from the perspective of adulthood, the character portrays his seven-year-old self as a body preserved in peat:

> I squirmed from the marshy ground. . . like the boy they unearthed in the
> middle of Franz Josef Street. . . six hundred cockleshell beads around his
> neck, a helmet of mud. Dripping with the prune-coloured juices of the peat-
> sweating bog. (5)

This image represents his body as preserved rather than living, as if his
exhumation is a return from the dead.

Even in the eyes of his witness, Athos the archaeologist, the newly emerged
Jakob only attains full, living humanity by passing through other states:

> I limped towards him, stiff as a golem, clay tight behind my knees. I stopped a
> few yards from where he was digging—later he told me it was as if I'd hit a glass
> door, an inarguable surface of pure air—"and your mud mask cracked with
> tears and I knew you were human, just a child. Crying with the abandonment
> of your age". . .
>
>   I screamed into the silence the only phrase I knew in more than one lan-
> guage, I screamed it in Polish and German and Yiddish, thumping my fists on
> my own chest: dirty Jew, dirty Jew, dirty Jew. (13)

The archaeological artifact of the peat-preserved body becomes a legendary
man-made golem in this passage before it becomes human, a transformation
that is shown through his tears. A journey through a discourse of archaeology
(dead human), and then of golem legend (supernatural or inhuman), is
finally completed in the Nazi discourse of dehumanization, signaled in the
child's choice of the words, "dirty Jew." As the text reminds us, Jews were, to
the Nazis,

> not considered human. . . . Non-Aryans were never to be referred to as human,
> but as "figuren," "stücke,"—"dolls," "wood," "merchandise," "rags." Humans
> were not being gassed, only "figuren," so ethics weren't being violated. (165)

Jakob's witness sees beyond the literal and figurative "dirtiness" of Jakob's
condition to the humanity of the body beneath.

Athos's excavation of the preserved city of Biskupin is itself at a crossroads
of meaning. Apart from its importance as an archaeological find, a recent
chapter in its archaeological history lends it specific resonance. The SS-
Ahnenerbe (Ancestral Inheritance), founded by Himmler in 1935, set out to
show by willful misinterpretation of archaeological data "that Germans or
Germanic tribes were the first settlers bringing civilisation to areas previously
inhabited only by a few nomadic Slavonic savages, or that previous settlement
had been that of Untermenschen inferior to the incoming Germanics."[20] The
"magnificent timber city" of Biskupin, with its "ingenious nail-less wooden

houses" (6) was inconvenient counter-evidence to their false claims, and as such would eventually be destroyed. Athos' act of interpretation on first seeing Jakob is therefore one for which he is uniquely qualified. As an archaeologist, he is equipped to save relics of lost cultures—such as Jakob—and bring them back into reference. Athos' resistance of Nazi "interpretation" is apparent in his witnessing of Jakob as human, but also in his exposure of Nazi archaeology after the war. Later he recounts despairingly the career of one of his student contemporaries as follows: "He falsified digs to prove that Greek civilization started in. . . Neolithic Germany! Just so the Reich could feel justified in copying our temples for their glorious capital" (104). Greek himself, Athos is part of the culture that Himmler attempted to appropriate and will thus reclaim his own national history as well as Jakob's humanity at this site of contested meanings.

Athos's full recognition of Jakob's humanity, which permitted the boy's translation into a new history, quickly moves beyond the status of archaeological relic to become suggestive of a shared subjectivity. He smuggles the boy to Greece in the back seat of a car as follows:

> the man I came to know as Athos, wore me under his clothes. My limbs bone-shadows on his strong legs and arms, my head buried in his neck, both of us beneath a heavy coat. . . .
>
> Another man drove and when we were signalled to stop, Athos pulled a blanket over us. In Greek-stained but competent German, Athos complained he was ill. He didn't just complain. He whimpered, he moaned. He insisted on describing his symptoms and treatments in detail. Until, disgusted and annoyed, they waved us on. (13)

Jakob survives by disappearing into Athos's body as an illness or abnormality, and by thus sheltering Jakob, Athos in turn survives, for soon after they leave, all of Athos's colleagues at the excavation are either shot or deported (51). The maternalization of Athos is completed in his temporary abandonment of his professional activity to serve the interests of the child protectively in a domestic setting. The fact that the women in the novel function collectively as a powerful image of domesticized femininity only serves to enhance this reading.[21] Jakob's emergence from the earth is depicted as a rebirth, as he calls the dampness of the peat "afterbirth of earth" and observes that "no one is born just once" (5). The form of Athos's rescue seemingly re-enacts this birth that is already a re-enactment. Athos's first act, that of interpretation, is clearly not enough: the interpretation must be played out in the realm of physical action in order to bring Jakob to real safety. It also requires the reburying of Jakob—this time under Athos's clothes—to allow a full and satisfactory emergence. The act of witnessing here is thus a double one.

The shared subjectivity implied in the maternalized process of sheltering another within one's own body—particularly in the context of a shared replaying of an earlier event—is a figure for the role of the witness, whose link through listening is more important than a historical understanding. According to Dori Laub, the witness does not listen passively to the narrative of trauma. As the trauma victim has been unable to experience the event fully, the witnessing process marks the "creation of knowledge" rather than the passing on of a narrative.[22] Laub contends that

> by extension, the listener to trauma comes to be a participant and a co-owner of the traumatic event: through his very listening, he comes to partially experience trauma in himself. . . . The listener has to feel the victim's victories, defeats and silences, know them from within, so that they can assume the form of testimony.[23]

Michaels's project, too, is essentially empathic, and Athos's witnessing and re-enacting (or even re-experiencing) of Jakob's "rebirth" at Biskupin introduces and frames this concern.

Jakob's position as a child survivor, however, gives him a highly particularized role as a witness. Firstly, he "witnesses" his parents' fate from a hiding place behind the wallpaper, "a blind man, a prisoner of sound" (17). This "witnessing" occurs completely aurally; only later through the images Jakob draws from the landscape around him, and from his education with Athos, does he fill in the darkness from which he heard his parents' deaths. For Adrienne Kertzer, Jakob Beer, in his failure to "witness" his family's catastrophe visually, may be read as representing the child of survivors who learns about trauma only through listening. This is in direct contrast to the visual, physical nature of Athos's witnessing of Jakob. Indeed, for Kertzer, this novel pays "obsessive attention to listening."[24] She finds this particularly marked in relation to the characteristically visual terminology of trauma and witnessing. Consequently, when Michaels deliberately positions Jakob in the cupboard so that he will not see what happens, she creates a protagonist who on a literal level is a Holocaust survivor, yet repeatedly emphasizes his belatedness, the inadequacy of the visual, and the necessity of the aural.[25]

In this sense Jakob is caught between the status of eyewitness to trauma and the status of the "witness who listens" who, in Laub's formulation, assists the eyewitness in the construction of memory. As such, Jakob bridges the gaps between the first and second generations, a position that his age confirms.[26] He stands in the middle of the generation gap between Ben and his parents—a position that is key to an understanding of his role in Ben's life later in the novel.

Jakob's relationship to sound and to silence—his witnessing by sound, but his failure to hear his sister's fate, which is the very thing he needs to hear— also has the function of suspending him between generations and between the positions of primary and secondary witness. Do Jakob's lack of visual witnessing and his inability to account for Bella's disappearance in the sounds that he hears stand for the missed or, in Caruth's term, the "unclaimed" experience of first-hand trauma? Or is the failure of his senses meant to represent a protective barrier that separates him experientially from the rest of his family and, as Kertzer suggests, inserts him into the "second generation," akin to the position of children of survivors? A silence that simultaneously excludes and communicates is at the center of Nadine Fresco's view of second-generation experience as "litanies of silence, which outline an invisible object enclosed in an impossible evocation."[27] Yet according to Laub, the process of witnessing begins with the first-generation survivor, or eyewitness, "breaking the internal silence."[28] Jakob's silence in the earlier part of his narrative is both internal *and* external: his failure to hear Bella's fate is external—unless it represents the "traumatic deafness" suggested by Kertzer[29]—yet the traumatic silence of his story, a story that is only fully heard with the arrival of Michaela, his second wife, is internal. This duality also replays Athos's "double witnessing" of Jakob's trauma.

A similar dual process is at work in Jakob's dreams, where the dead have a deeply physical presence, "their hair in tufts, open sores where ears used to be, grubs twisting from their chests. . . heaving into humanness; until they grew more human than phantom and through their effort began to sweat" (24). Jakob characterizes these presences as "the embodied complexity of desires eternally denied," and he embodies them in turn: "Their strain poured from my skin, until I woke dripping with their deaths." In his torment at "the possibility that it was as painful for them to be remembered as it was for me to remember them" (25), the traditional relationship of haunting is twisted to become reciprocal, and the line between living and dead is one that Jakob cannot demarcate. As Cathy Caruth suggests, "it is the inextricability of the story of one's life from the story of a death, an impossible and necessary double telling, that constitutes. . . historical witness."[30] Jakob as witness is both imperfect and ideal: he is imperfect in his failure to conform to primary- or secondary-witness status, and ideal in the way in which this status seems to reflect the very paradoxes and complexities that trauma theory brings to his interpretation.

Finally, the character of Jakob is pivotal to the novel's thematization of language: his story concerns a process of negotiation with language and languages in an attempt to regulate the processes of memory and forgetting. Language functions paradoxically in Jakob's life, as both a route to his unknown past and a way of living in the present, as, for example, when Athos makes sure the boy studies Hebrew and Greek (21–22). While these ancient languages carry memory themselves, for Jakob, Greek is a language of the future, as opposed to Yiddish, which is "a melody gradually eaten away by silence" (28). This correlation between language and the processes of memory and forgetting is mentioned throughout the novel. Jakob compares the individual who has lost loved ones to one of the migrating birds that were experimentally kept in darkened rooms, revealing that their migration instincts required no sight of the sky. Similarly, Jakob writes,

> [the loved ones'] limbs will follow when you lie down, a shadow against your own, curving to every curve like the Hebrew alphabet and the Greek, which cross the page to greet each other in the middle of historia. (169)

Once again, the dual subjectivity of witnessing trauma is reflected within the text, with the vision of "limbs" as "shadows" echoing Jakob's journey under Athos's clothes, representing the culmination of the man's witnessing of the boy. Just as the witness arguably helps to create knowledge, so does language and, as Jakob's previously cited comments on language imply, one language replacing another has the power to create new knowledge. Consequently, when Jakob came to write about the events of his childhood "in a language foreign to their happening, it was a revelation. English could protect [him]; an alphabet without memory" (101). Language appears to Jakob to be an easy way to leave behind him the traumatic parts of his past.

Yet this feat of linguistic forgetting never quite equates to the desired memory loss that obliterates experience. Much as Jakob "tried to bury images, to cover them over with Greek and English words, with Athos's stories," and later with "a different avalanche of facts: train schedules, camp records, statistics, methods of execution"(93), images of his dead family and best friend return to him at night: forgetting words does not mean forgetting experience. For Jakob, trauma cannot be held in language, but rather, as it was experienced through sound, in silence:

> I felt that this was my truth. That my life could not be stored in any language but only in silence. . . . But I did not know how to seek by way of silence. So I lived a breath apart, a touch-typist who holds his hands above the keys slightly in the wrong place, the words coming out meaningless, garbled. . . . I thought of writing poems this way, in code, every letter askew, so that loss would wreck the language, become the language. (111)

Given the failure of language to adequately represent, and the failure of Jakob as a poet to work with silence, the only alternative is to disrupt language in order to represent its failure to correspond to his experiences. The resonance with critical debates surrounding the fictional representation of Holocaust experiences is clear.

Yet eventually, Jakob "feel[s] his English strong enough to carry experience" (162), marking a linguistic mastery of his life through a new language. This occurs on the island of Idhra, immediately before he meets Michaela, whose love seems to effect the full witnessing Jakob has been waiting for. This development in his relationship to language thus seems to prepare him for this final step toward "cure." It also contradicts most of what has come before about language and, as we shall see, what comes after, when Ben finally orients himself toward a productive future through the very "gap between the words and the man" in whose existence he had come to disbelieve. These contradictions open the question of whether, like the Nazi soldiers who accepted the lie of Jewish dehumanization, Jakob has found his own "lie." As he writes shortly after describing the "surrender" of English on Idhra, "there's a precise moment when we reject contradiction. This moment of choice is the lie we will live by. What is dearest to us is often dearer to us than truth" (166). This section of the book, entitled "Terra Nullius," ends with the following passage:

> To remain with the dead is to abandon them.
>   All the years I felt Bella entreating me, filled with her loneliness, I was mistaken. . . . Like other ghosts, she whispers; not for me to join her, but so that, when I'm close enough, she can push me back into the world. (170)

Rather than developing a special relationship to language, whereby it is "strong enough to carry experience," the relationship that Ben will be drawn to explore and interrogate may be read as Jakob's own lie—a necessary one by which he leaves his traumatic nightmares behind.

Puns, Euphemism, and the Illusion of Mastering Language

In trauma theory, the state of traumatization is itself understood to prevent or preclude certain linguistic functions, namely narrative and metaphor, for the victim is only able to relive the traumatic event in full, and not narrate it as a story. When this becomes possible, the narrator is by definition no longer traumatized.[31] Language, and specifically poetry, in its sophisticated manipulation of language, functions as therapy for Jakob against the traumatic loss of metaphor and the Nazi corruption of metaphor in euphemism. Questioning dishonest uses of language such as propaganda is, for Jakob and Athos, an essential means of resistance, and this questioning, as we have seen, enables Athos to recognize Jakob as human in order to rescue him. Such dishonest use of language undermines even itself, as Jakob writes,

> If the Nazis required that humiliation precede extermination, then they admitted exactly what they worked so hard to avoid admitting: the humanity of the victim. To humiliate is to accept that your victim feels and thinks, that he not only feels pain, but knows that he's being degraded. And because the torturer knew in an instant of recognition that his victim was not a "figuren" but a man, he suddenly understood the Nazi mechanism. . . . When the soldier realized that only death has the power to turn "man" into "figuren," his difficulty was solved. And so the rage and sadism increased: his fury at the victim for suddenly turning human; his desire to destroy that humanness so intense his brutality had no limit. (166)

The alternative to this path is represented by Athos who "never confused objects and humans, who knew the difference between the naming and the named" (167).

The issue of the recognition of victims' humanity also surfaces in the descriptions of bog bodies that recur throughout the novel. We have already seen Jakob's passage from bog body to boy in the opening pages. Athos is interested in such bodies, too, and the horrific story of their fate is misleadingly recast as one of comfort:

> They had steeped for centuries, their skin tanning to dark leather, umber juices deep in the lines of palms and soles. In autumn. . . men had been led out into the moor as sacrificial offerings. There, they were anchored with birch and stones to drown in the acidic ground. Time stopped. And that is why, Athos explained, the bog men are so serene. Asleep for centuries, they are uncovered perfectly intact; thus they outlast their killers—whose bodies have long dissolved to dust. (49)

These bodies are accorded dignity due to their remaining intact. Their human form, recognizable after so many centuries, paradoxically removes the true human horror of their deaths, recalling Jakob's feeling when in hiding on Zakynthos that "to go back a year or two was impossible, absurd. To go back millennia—Ah! that was. . . nothing" (30).

Similarly, Ben, whose parents have confronted him all his life with images and stories of the concentration camps, is soothed by the vision of death that these preserved corpses afford:

> These were not like the bodies in the photos my father showed me. I drew the aromatic earth over my shoulders, the peaceful spongy blanket of peat. I see now that my fascination wasn't archaeology or even forensics: it was biography. The faces that stared at me across the centuries, with creases in their cheeks like my mother's when she fell asleep on the couch. (221)

These bodies are so easily recognizable as human, despite the years that have passed, that Ben even conceives of their comforting effect in terms of metaphors of sleep.

The camps, in contrast, distorted and disfigured human bodies before killing them, or even without killing them at all. They questioned what it meant to be human not only with respect to the brutal, "inhuman" actions of the perpetrators, but in the way these actions were played out in a physically and psychologically dehumanizing fashion on the bodies of the victims. Thus, Ben and Jakob try to resist identifying with Holocaust victims, and the text shares their aversion to images of such deaths, hinting instead through imagery at the Holocaust's uncomfortable disruptions of the dying process. The living Jews of Zakynthos must find "strange graves" (45) in which to hide, and Jakob's experience that "at night, my mother, my father, Bella, Mones, simply rose, shook the earth from their clothes, and waited" (93) evokes tales of ghosts, hauntings, and unquiet graves.

In these attempts by Jakob and Ben to come to terms with recent, disturbing deaths by containing them in a far-off past and images of sleep, a similar process to that of Nazi euphemism is at work. In being seen as "serene" and "intact," "comfort" can only be found in the bog bodies if they are reduced to the purely bodily, for the intactness of their bodies overwrites the mental torment of their executions. In Jean Améry's words, "torture is ineradicably burned into [the victim], even when no clinically objective traces can be detected."[32] This reduction to the bodily that Jakob and Ben unconsciously perform on the bog men, thereby neutralizing their power to disturb, is complicit with the violence of their deaths, as Laura Tanner has theorized as follows:

> The dynamics of violence often involve a violator who appropriates the victim's subjectivity as an extension of his own power, turning the force of consciousness against a victim for whom sentience becomes pain, consciousness no more than an agonizing awareness of the inability to escape embodiment.[33]

Where textual representation is concerned, Tanner argues, a text that refuses to represent the act of violence may "jolt the reader into becoming the author of the crime."[34] In a text that does not directly describe, just as in the way an event, which has not been witnessed, may nonetheless have overpowering effects on one's life, the issue of what or how much to "author" is left open, theoretically in the reader's control. This "freedom," which may lead to inaccurate or dishonest constructions as readily as to honest or revealing constructions, is inherent in the different manifestations of the lack of witnessing that impact both Ben's and Jakob's lives.

The description of the bog bodies offers a contrast with another descriptive passage that represents Jakob's attempts to visualize what he failed to witness. This passage, which I quote in full as follows, has provoked critical unease, leading critics to either pass over *Fugitive Pieces* or qualify their otherwise positive responses to it:

> Some gave birth while dying in the chamber. Mothers were dragged from the chamber with new life half-emerged from their bodies. Forgive me, you who were born and died without being given names. Forgive this blasphemy, of choosing philosophy over the brutalism of fact.
>
> We know they cried out. . . . It is impossible to imagine those sounds.
>
> At that moment of utmost degradation, in that twisted reef, is the most obscene testament of grace. For can anyone tell with absolute certainty the difference between the sounds of those who are in despair and the sounds of those who want desperately to believe? The moment when our faith in man is forced to change, anatomically—mercilessly—into faith.
>
> In the still house, the visitation of moonlight. . . . It has taken me years to reach this fabrication. Even as I fall apart I know I will never again feel this pure belief. (168–69)

For Sue Vice, this scene is

> a way of trying to wring aesthetic and meaningful comfort from an event which offers no redemption of any kind. By contrast to the poetic option, I argue that crude narration, irony, black humour, appropriation, sensationalism, even characters who mouth antisemitic slogans, do not seem as suspect.[35]

For Jakob, this is a "fabrication," a moment of "pure belief" that he will never again attain, but which, like his vision of the bog bodies, is a therapeutic necessity. Only when he has entertained this vision, felt his "English strong enough to carry experience" (162), and began to envision the memories that torment him as also tormenting for those he remembers, is he ready to meet Michaela and move with her into a future of his own, away and apart from the dead. In his "fabrication," he exploits what Tanner calls the "freedom" to "author the crime" by constructing it in a way he can cope with, which "[extricates] the story of his life from the story of a death, [in] an impossible and necessary double telling."[36] At this point, his status begins to shift from that of a primary witness with his own traumatic history to that of a secondary witness with a clear distance between his present and the past of his family.

Van der Kolk and van der Hart write that

> many traumatized persons. . . experience long periods of time in which they live, as it were, in two different worlds: the realm of the trauma and the realm of their current ordinary worlds. . . . This simultaneity is related to the fact that the traumatic experience / memory is, in a sense, timeless.[37]

Throughout the novel, Jakob repeatedly senses that "every moment is two moments," an apparent reflection of this aspect of his traumatic memories. The climactic resolution of this, after he meets Michaela, comes with his detaching his trauma from nature. The birch forest in *Fugitive Pieces* recurs as an emblem of persecution right from the beginning of the novel, where such a forest is the site of the immediate aftermath of his trauma. Dori Laub has argued that an "internal witness," especially when no other kind is available, can be important to the victim of trauma. Laub cites the case of a young boy for whom, while he was forced to fend for himself when his parents were imprisoned by the Nazis, a photograph of his mother held such a witnessing function.[38]

A similar process seems to be at work in Jakob's projections on to the landscape. This process is internal both in Laub's sense, and in the sense that the boundary between the body and the landscape is all but breached:

> The river was the same blackness that was inside me; only the thin membrane of my skin kept me floating.
>
> From the other bank, I watched darkness turn to purple-orange light above the town; the colour of flesh transforming to spirit. They flew up. The dead passed above me, weird haloes and arcs smothering the stars. The trees bent under their weight. (8)

At this point he begins to work through the losses of his parents, first sensing his mother's presence in the following excerpt:

> I knew suddenly my mother was inside me. Moving along sinews, under my skin. . . . She was stopping to say goodbye and was caught, in such pain, wanting to rise, wanting to stay. It was my responsibility to release her, a sin to keep her from ascending. I tore at my clothes, my hair. She was gone. (8)

The proximity of the traumatic event overwhelms Jakob's happy memories and images of the river and forest where he grew up, turning this landscape into a screen for the projection of his recent calamity.

Van der Kolk and Van der Hart describe the following therapeutic process by which traumatic images are gradually modified by positive images in the patient's mind:

> One contemporary therapist of a Holocaust survivor had the patient imagine a flower growing in the assignment place in Auschwitz—an image that gave him tremendous comfort. . . . Once flexibility is introduced, the traumatic memory starts losing its power over current experience. By imagining these alternative scenarios, many patients are able to soften the intrusive power of the original, unmitigated horror.[39]

A fiction, or an image much like a poetic fiction, is deliberately introduced with the aim of altering the memory of the event. This is what happens for Jakob, as it is in "a birch forest growing out of white sand" that he leaves traumatic simultaneity behind him. He writes, "This is where I become irrevocably unmoored. The river floods. I slip free the knot and float, suspended in the present" (188). The sight of Jakob's parents, the novel leads us to believe, is not the source of his trauma. It is the silence and absence of Bella, the unknown trauma, that becomes projected on to the landscape of Jakob's hiding. When the simple, clean vision of white sand frees this landscape of birch trees from the horrific images with which he overlaid it, it no longer troubles him. Metaphor is thus the key to Jakob's trauma as well as to its cure. Jakob's vocation as poet and translator is tied to his traumatized state. It is as if, through writing, he can finally bear witness to himself.

The freedom to "author" or to not "author" the act of violence is one that, by implication, most people should be able to exercise without much thought. For Jakob, mastering his trauma means mastering his ability to control his internal representations of something he never experienced directly. The double indirectness of his trauma—his failure to "see" events as well as his failure to "witness" them in the primary traumatic sense—emphasizes the view that our relationship to the past involves a working-through of imagined connections. The reason readers are not as traumatized as Jakob simply by reading about the Holocaust, however distressing that reading process might be, is that their experience does not inevitably force them to confront what they would rather not; by putting down the book, for example, they can go some way to mastering these images themselves. The passage that Sue Vice objects to is, then, a reflection of what happens within many of us reading "after": it is too difficult to stay too close to the horror of the truth. Language, this novel seems to be saying, may be destructive or therapeutic, but representing experience as it occurred is simply beyond its—and our—capacity. Indeed as we have seen, for the trauma victim, what is represented in narrative can never, by definition, be truly representative of the traumatic experience itself.

The Child of Survivors

In its change of focus in the latter part of the novel to a narrator who is a child of survivors, *Fugitive Pieces* stages language's illusion of total authorial presence. In doing so, it goes further in exploring the limits of witnessing. This second section of *Fugitive Pieces* is narrated by Ben, a member of the "second generation" who goes to Idhra with the purposes of finding Jakob's diaries, separating himself from his wife, Naomi, and finding out what enabled Jakob to work through his trauma successfully in the latter part of his life. While it appears to be written in the first person, much of this section is presented in the second person, for despite containing long first-person passages, it is addressed to Jakob Beer, such as in the following example: "I finally understood the meaning of that winter night and that moment with my mother in the garden, Jakob Beer, when I read your poems" (206). While the reader's only access to Jakob's past in this novel is through his own narrative, Ben draws heavily on Jakob's life story in his own attempt to evaluate his experiences and those of his family. The reader thus has a critical perspective to bring to Ben's interpretation of events as he tells them in the novel's second part. Because Jakob is already dead (255), Ben's narrative is a direct address in the knowledge of an absent interlocutor. The narrative is thus an apparently futile gesture, motioning to a listener and a past that it cannot hope to reach or understand. Ben's relationship with Jakob exists purely through language, but Ben has yet to discover this absence for himself, as noted in the following excerpt: "in your case," says Ben to the dead Jakob, "there seemed to be no gap between the poems and the man" (107).

Nonetheless, Ben attempts to reach Jakob directly, as he leaves his own life behind to step into Jakob's life by searching his house on Idhra for his diaries. Moving through the house, which has been left as it was when Jakob died, he is patrolling the dead man's memory and he recognizes, "A house, more than a diary, is the intimate glimpse" (265). It is moreover a "glimpse" that must be physically entered into. This "embodiment" of Ben in the house, which Ben hopes will bring him closer to Jakob, is illusory and always leads him back to himself and his relationship to his own parents. A truer embodiment is in Ben's head, where Jakob has been "incorporated" as a (dead) father figure or imago, indistinct from the role of Ben's own father. Addressing Jakob, Ben says, "you died not long after my father and I can't say which death made me reach again for your words" (255). This confusion is precisely what Ben's time in Jakob's house allows him to clarify: the importance of his father in his life over the imagined importance of Jakob. As Ben writes, "the memories we elude catch up to us, overtake us like a shadow. A truth appears suddenly in the middle of a thought, a hair on a lens" (213). Having been "born into absence" (233) or postmemory as a child of survivors, and lacking a full context and presence of his own, Ben seeks his own frame of reference in the life of Jakob Beer, a man whose communication with him is all language. His parents, who lacked "the energy of a narrative" (204), could not provide this. Like the bog bodies, which provide such comfort for both Jakob and Ben by providing a site on which to work through their traumas, Jakob is for Ben a transferential figure.[40]

Ben thus attempts to replace something that should exist within the family with an act of interpretation: "I would spend weeks inside your house, an archaeologist examining one square inch at a time" (261). He assumes Athos's role of archaeologist and interpreter, with a link to his material based neither on history nor on personal relationships, but on poetry. As he wanders around the house, he notices a number of curious items for which the reader, but not Ben himself, can provide an explanation. The "pocketwatch with a sea monster engraved on the case" belonged to Athos, a present from his father, and the dish of buttons is apparently Jakob's memorial to the last sound of his mother that he heard, as the dish of buttons she had been using for sewing hit the floor (264). What Ben sees as "an obviously mislaid copy of Pliny's *Natural History*" (265) in the kitchen was in fact used by Athos as a cookbook when wartime desperation led him to hunt out unaccustomed edible plants and roots (38). Ben's inability to understand these objects signals him as a failed interpreter, an over-interpreter, who eventually comes to acknowledge that his "mistake would be to look for something hidden" (263).

Jakob's house is not the first that Ben has excavated; the careful sifting of his parents' belongings after their deaths turned up a picture of the secret dead children of whose existence his mother had told Naomi while concealing it from Ben. Ben is left feeling doubly inadequate, for he was unable to properly replace the dead children, who were by their nature irreplaceable, and because Naomi superseded him as the object of his mother's confidences and, in Ben's mind, affection. Indeed, Naomi fits effortlessly and sensitively into the family, as demonstrated by the following quotation: "Right from the start," Ben says, "Naomi seemed to know us" (233). His mother's reluctance to confide in him consequently manifested itself "more frequently once Naomi entered our lives" (231). According to Abraham and Torok's model of the "transgenerational phantom," a child may unconsciously inherit the traumas and buried secrets of previous generations, and manifests this knowledge in apparently unrelated behaviors.[41] Ben's choosing to marry Naomi may be read as an instance of this, in which he attempts to replace the daughter that he unconsciously knows his parents lost. Even Naomi's name recalls the biblical tale of Naomi and Ruth, which centers on a daughter-in-law's loyalty to her mother-in-law. Yet Ben's success in fulfilling this unconscious goal dismays him; the revelation of the secret children and the fact that Naomi knew this secret consequently marks the deterioration of Ben's relationship with his wife. This also precipitates his trip to Greece, making his excavation of Jakob's house a response to that of his parents' house. Working in his parents' flat also inspires Ben to go to the banks of the Humber, near his Toronto home, where

> objects [from the great flood of 1954] had been eroded from the early-spring banks—a souvenir spoon, a doorknob, a rusted mechanical toy. I rinsed them in the river and kept them in a box in the trunk of the car. I didn't find anything I recognised. (253)

Ben's relationship with his parents and both his personal and professional interest in Jakob are unsuccessful means for finding and understanding a hidden past as a way of understanding himself.

Jakob's notebooks provide the key to the secret meanings of all the other books and objects in his house, including the sea monster watch, dish of buttons, and Pliny's *Natural History*. Yet all Ben will come to understand in the course of the novel is himself. Shortly after the unearthing of the notebooks that, rather than through Ben's methodical searching, are uncovered by the random rampaging of Petra, a scarf identical to one owned by his wife is also revealed. Its appearance shocks Ben, who writes, "I know it isn't hers; I know she has one just like it. The scarf is a tiny square of silence" (285). In recognizing the scarf's silence, Ben tacitly acknowledges that its significance depends on his own interpretation. It calls him back into his own life, including his relationship with Naomi. This marks a rejection of his earlier methods, which were based on an exaggerated reverence for the lives of others, including both his parents' and Jakob's survivor experiences. Like Jakob, Ben is reborn.

Ben also finds a note left by Michaela for Jakob, announcing her pregnancy. His decision to leave this behind, rather than take it back to Maurice Salman with, and as an appendix to, the diaries, is made in the immediate aftermath of the uncovering of both the notebooks and the scarf. Instead of the artificially constructed relationship he has struggled to have with Jakob, the finding of "Naomi's" scarf, coupled with the discovery of the notebooks (his objective in being on Idhra), leads him back to his own family relationships and to a recognition of his parents' love for one another (294). The second generation that Ben represents cannot be the same second generation that Michaela and Jakob's unborn child would have represented, for this child would have been Jakob's true biological heir. Jakob's relatively advanced age on becoming a father, with Michaela's considerably younger age on reaching motherhood, places his unborn child where Jakob himself seems to be: between generations. Ben turns back to the memory of his biological father, who was much older than Jakob. As a *child* survivor, as we have seen, Jakob belongs neither to the first generation nor to the second. In this part of the book, he clearly mediates between the two.

"Child I long for. . . if you are born": Michaela and the Breakdown of Witnessing

Ben's discovery of Michaela's note belatedly recasts her role as witness. Like Athos's earlier witnessing of Jakob, her witnessing also now centers on images of rebirth, which Jakob refers to on the very first page of the novel: "No one is born just once. If you're lucky, you'll emerge again in someone's arms; or unlucky, wake when the long tail of terror brushes the inside of your skull" (5).

The first image of pregnancy centered on Michaela arises with Jakob's belief in her ability to take into herself the other body that he has been carrying with him: that of Bella, whom Jakob has, in psychoanalytic terms, incorporated. After seeing Michaela "crying for Bella," Jakob dreams that "Bella sits on the edge of the bed and asks Michaela to describe the feel of the bedcover under her bare legs, 'because you see, just now I am without my body'" (182). Through his proximity to Michaela, Jakob is able to share his burden of grief as follows: "Each night heals gaps between us until we are joined by the scar of dreams. My desolation exhales in the breathing dark" (183). It is not simply that Michaela carries part of the grief within her, but also that by witnessing it, she enables it to leave Jakob and herself—she expels the body that is within and part of both of them.

Jakob is finally able to let go of his memories on seeing Michaela's birch forest growing out of white sand culminates in the following scene in which they spend the night together among the trees:

> We sleep among the wet birches, nothing between us and the storm except the fragile nylon skin of the tent, a glowing dome in the blackness. . . . What does the body make us believe? That we're never ourselves until we contain two souls. For years corporeality made me believe in death. Now, inside Michaela yet watching her, death for the first time makes me believe in the body. (189)

Finally "suspended in the present" (188), Jakob's being "inside Michaela yet watching her" is both a physical, sexual presence within her, which replaces Bella's phantasmic presence, and a recognition of the life within himself.

If Michaela's early incorporation of Bella is symbolic and interpretive—like Athos's witnessing of Jakob's "rebirth" from the ground—her pregnancy with a child that is to be called Bela or Bella mirrors Athos's act of physical witnessing. Her giving birth would represent the final step in Jakob's freeing himself from Bella in a symbolic end to his incorporation of her, and the child's name would memorialize Bella. Crucially, however, Michaela and Jakob are killed early in Michaela's pregnancy, and Jakob dies without knowing that Michaela has conceived. That Michaela's note was left for Ben to find is a breakdown of witnessing, for Jakob's reading of the note would have been the end of the witnessing process, the birth of the child a movement into the future. Ben's discovery of the note is both undesired and unexpected. He is looking to Jakob, the older man, for clues as to how to lead his own life, and this note only serves to remind him that he is not Jakob's son.

Conclusion: Between Language and History

Like Michaels's own references to actual historical events within the text, Ben's failed attempt to find healing through Jakob, whom he knows only through language, operates figuratively as a giant question mark over Michaels's literary project. Put differently, why should a novel that foregrounds the therapeutic potential of language and witnessing throughout its first two-thirds portray the breakdown of these processes as it draws to a close? In an essay about writing published during the time that she was working on *Fugitive Pieces*, Michaels insists on the necessary failure of language to convey experience: "Language abandons experience every time. We hammer and measure, build our lines to the right length; but by the time the fence is up, the field seems empty."[42] As Michaels says in the following excerpt, poems do not succeed because of what they represent, but because of the gaps in representation poetry can acknowledge:

> Great poems are steeped in failure. Their measure is the depth of ignorance they reach in us. The mystery contained in the best poems is bottomless. We read them again and again. We remember certain lines or images; we repeat them, over the years, to ourselves. The depth changes go on and on.[43]

The poem's "mystery" alone can never represent physical experience, though it can lead us back to it. In Michaels's words, "the senses bypass language: the ambush of a scent or weather, but language also jump starts the senses."[44]

Fugitive Pieces testifies to this failure and to this achievement in its concern with language and the Holocaust. Like the reader's imagined relationship to the poet, our perceived relationship with distant historic events is often linguistic, and to recognize this is not to deny the reality of the historic event, nor that the present day individual has some link to a particular event or to a phenomenon that springs from it.

A tension between history and language is manifested in this novel: language can help us move away from history as well as bring us closer to it and, in cases of trauma, moving away may be precisely what is desirable. History and language bound together in this tension produce the memories that first keep Jakob traumatized and subsequently allow him to leave the traumatic past behind him. Witnessing—whether primary or secondary—is a transformative process that uses language to turn history into memory and, eventually, poetry.

This status of witnessing as neither fully historic nor fully linguistic is representative of the particular historical phase in which we find ourselves with regard to the Holocaust and the dilemmas we are currently having to address regarding its representation. As Sue Vice has pointed out, the fact that anxiety about the representation of earlier massive traumas, such as the First World War, does not approach that surrounding literature of and about the Holocaust suggests that many of these questions of representation are a result of our proximity to the event.[45] Given that many critics are linked by specific family history, or Jewishness, to the traumatic events in question—quite apart from the sense of proximity that in-depth reading and scholarship may bring—a sense of personal involvement with the Holocaust is only normal.

While Vice is wary of the "literary" evaluations of works about the Holocaust that slip over into ethical judgements, it is worth considering to what extent such evaluations might not be both inevitable and desirable aspects of critical discourse around the Holocaust for the time being. The passing of time will undoubtedly reduce the personal and collective sensitivity that makes itself so firmly felt in the field in the present. This sensitivity is manifested in a tendency to frame critical works with personal experiences and a self-censoring of any comment on fiction about the Holocaust—a tendency to qualify often with Adorno's infamous statement about the barbarity of poetry after Auschwitz.

Rather than language serving as or attempting to construct a representation of history, it interacts with history to carve out the terrain of both memory and poetry. Memory and poetry function indistinctly from one another in this novel to serve a therapeutic function. In using poetic language that is also aesthetically pleasing, Michaels elicits an empathy from her readers that using historical fact alone cannot achieve. In this novel in which names and naming are so relevant, Michaels's inclusion of a character called Michaela is significant.[46] Michaels draws a comparison between the lover and the poem, and consequently between reading and seduction, in the following quotation:

The sensual mirage is the heart of the poem. It's the moment, however brief, we take the poet's experience as our own. This connection can be so buried as to be completely mysterious. . . or overt as an image overwhelming in its familiarity. And if the poem is able to forge an intellectual bond in the guise of the sensual illusion, the seduction is complete.[47]

In Michael's apparent identification of herself with Michaela, this analogy has been modified to align the fictional lover with the real poet. The fictionality of the lover (Michaela) renders her part of the poem or text, while the poet (Michaels) exists in reality, engaged in processes of love and memory. This intertwining of lover and poet is also reflected in Jakob Beer himself, who occupies both roles, and whose poetry is wound into the story of his life as it appears in his notebooks, which make up most of the novel. The "sensual mirage" of "taking [another's] experience as our own" is precisely what the images of witnessing as shared subjectivity that occur throughout the novel refer to. Recalling Laub's words from earlier in my argument, "the listener to trauma comes to be a participant and a co-owner of the traumatic event: through his very listening, he comes to partially experience trauma in himself."[48] Even more suggestively, Laub writes that "the listener has to feel the victim's victories, defeats, silences, know them *from within*, so that they can assume the form of testimony."[49] In the light of Michaels's lover-poem analogy and her consistent positioning of the trauma victim and listener within a single subject position, it is possible to read the text as an assertion of the relevance and value of writing for memory and testimony. The proximity of the lover, particularly as we have seen in the case of Michaela and Jakob, implies a shared subjectivity. Meanwhile, the reader of this poetic work, given access to the traumatized characters' thoughts and feelings rather than their actions, is encouraged to identify with the victims of violence and trauma rather than with the perpetrators. As Laura Tanner writes, "the disparity between the disembodied reader and the embodied victim may lead to a sense of detachment that is perpetuated by the distanced dynamics of the reading process." There is, therefore, a danger that "the reader's freedom parallels the autonomy of the violator."[50] Michaels, with her use of an interiorized style and staging of a process of witnessing much akin to that described by Laub, attempts to position the reader in the same place as the victim, restricting the reader's freedom while also showing how attaining that freedom can be a therapeutic necessity. In the post-Holocaust world presented by Michaels, the traumas of the past are fully available neither to history nor to memory. Although poetry cannot represent this world, it may begin to approach it.

Literature of the Second Generation: Who Owns the Story?

The texts discussed in this book address not the past in itself, but its intersection with the present at a particular time and place. Many texts explore the nuances of this intersection in imaginative or ostensibly documentary retellings of real or imagined family pasts but, in the texts I have considered, those who experienced the Holocaust first-hand do not constitute the true subject. These texts are, whether fictional or autobiographical, stories of the Holocaust's afterlife, or family romances that both formulate and attempt to answer questions that are pertinent to a postwar present. In this they show that while the historical events of the Holocaust are in the past, "the Holocaust" as a subject of literature is still far from being truly behind us. Instead, the nature and extent of its significance is constantly evolving. While processes of working-through and memorialization may be at work in literature and in cultural and social life more generally, they are, these texts suggest, not nearing an end.

As an encapsulation of the struggles for ownership of narrative that I have explored in the preceding chapters, I will turn briefly to Cheryl Pearl Sucher's novel *The Rescue of Memory*. Rachel, the novel's protagonist, is a daughter of survivors who is working on her first feature film. Her film-making career began in school, where her first subject was an interview with her survivor father about his wartime experiences. Ostensibly science fiction, her current film is in fact a version of her father's war stories in which he and his friends seem to Rachel like "the Lodz ghetto's caped crusaders. . . ordinary men forced to commit extraordinary acts of unwelcome greatness" (24).[1] In her film, her father and his fellow immigrants are "Drummond's band of archangels. . . in search of a fertile constellation, leaving behind an earth ravaged by nuclear holocaust" (25). Meanwhile, in her personal life, Rachel is planning her wedding. This is to be an elaborate affair in line with the wishes of her domineering father, so that "after a while [she] stopped thinking that [she] was getting married and started to pretend that [she] was producing [her] first live-action feature film" (19). It is Rachel's own life (her wedding) that seems inauthentic to her, while her father's life is so real to her that it gives her nightmares and needs to be contained as a "mnemonic futuristic fantasy" (24).

Like Artie's use of the comic strip in *Maus*, Rachel's use of the feature film puts her in command of media technology with which her father—whose closet is full of old photographs and Super-8 film—is not conversant. It thus not only enables her to tell her father's story from her own perspective, but also allows her to do so without his overt interference. For Artie and Rachel, their chosen media and idioms also serve to situate them as members of the postwar generation, laying claim to their own identities while simultaneously acknowledging how they have been shaped by their parents' pasts. In common with Skibell's imagining of his great-grandparents, and Spiegelman's *Maus* books, it is through a genre more commonly associated with fantasy and superheroes that Rachel represents her father's experiences. Such genres offer a strategy for representing how far removed survivors' experiences seem from these writers' lives. They also express how mundane the writers' own postwar lives can seem by comparison.

The retelling of survivors' and victims' stories is central to all of the texts in my corpus. Helen Epstein's conscious search for a second-generation iden-tity hinges on her role as transmitter of her parents' histories. For Louise Kehoe, culture and identity emerge belatedly after she uncovers the story her father would not tell. In common with *Maus*, the struggle for discovery and ownership of narrative in Kehoe's memoir is troubled—even traumatic—in itself, and this is explicitly thematized. Skibell and Michaels, too, are con-cerned with the transmission and ownership of stories. Both *A Blessing on the Moon* and *Fugitive Pieces* use fictional family narratives—albeit in very differ-ent ways—to dwell on language's role in representing past events. In second-generation texts, a tension between the spoken and the unspoken, the known and the unknown, is always not merely present, but is also the motor of fam-ily dynamics and the narrative itself.

The stories that any family tells about itself are motivated by concerns that, as Marianne Hirsch argues in relation to family photographs, "perpetu-ate family myths while seeming merely to record actual moments in family history."[2] The autobiographers I have considered depict themselves and/or their narrators variously exploring and dismantling these myths in the con-text of family lives in the present. It is because such myths have real power over lives currently being lived that this process is important.

Postmemorial Positions: Beyond the Second Generation

That Hirsch developed the concept of postmemory with reference to the medium of photography is particularly interesting. Indeed photography has often been discussed in relation to the representation of trauma. In the context of children of survivors—or what we might more broadly term the second generation—who are subjects or agents of postmemory, the points of analogy between the photograph and the individual are numerous. The child of survivors, like the photograph, transmits memory beyond the death of those who experienced the remembered events. Children of survivors' experience of postmemory is by its nature belated—like the emergence of the captured image in the developing tray—for they obtain their historical connection to the events of the Holocaust in spite of generational and chronological distance. They are mediators of memory, transforming a memory that is itself the transformation of lived experience. They rely on interpretation to wrest meaning from an original referent whose exact status can only be guessed. The suspicions of "inauthenticity" that cling to photographic art forms are reflected in children of survivors' sense of their own histories' secondary or mediated natures. Their lives, they often feel, refer to a history that they have never experienced, and that they can verify only through recourse to the experiences of others.

The existing structure of academic discussion of the topic, with its tendency to use terms like "transgenerational transmission" and "postmemory" in ways that avoid discussion of questions of volition and familial or other personal relationships, makes it hard to keep any discussion of "second-generation" texts too restricted. My readings show that, rather than fixedly defining identity positions, it is more productive for distinctions to be made between "transmission" in terms of the domestic family or milieu and the more general identity-based "transmission" of Ruth Leys's and Walter Benn Michaels's arguments, which I discussed in my introduction. Members of the second, third, or fourth generations are part of their own generations more generally, and also have a particular relationship to survivors or refugees. Their experience as part of those generations, and as part of a distinct group or groups within these generations, is in constant evolution—as is the experience of the "sub-group" of second/third/fourth generation *writers*. Merely to draw lines between voluntary and involuntary transmission, pathological and non-pathological, Jewish and non-Jewish communities, would be an unjustifiable simplification.

The range of the family relationships to the Holocaust in the texts I discuss alone is extensive: Skibell's is imagined, based both on a real family figure and an awareness of how the past has affected his own life; Michaels, in rejecting an autobiographical approach to or interpretation of her work, creates fictional families in order to explore the nature of imagined connections to the past; Epstein grows up with a particular "world-view" and sense of responsibility that comes from her parents' experiences; and Kehoe and Spiegelman have difficulties in defining their own identities as distinct from those of their parents', the result being that their difficulties lead implicitly to anorexia and other psychological issues. Within Jewish families (however they might be defined) there appears to be a continuum of relationships to the Holocaust rather than a question of whether such relationships exist or not. At the end of the spectrum occupied by Kehoe and Spiegelman, aspects of the narrators' lives have been so difficult that they might be said to be traumatized by experiences of their own that are a direct result of their parents' experiences. On the other hand, toward the end of Epstein's book, it becomes increasingly hard to separate the chosen identity position from the imposed one.

Does a child of survivors have to be classified as "traumatized" for her relationship to the Holocaust to be distinct from the "weak" model of cultural transmission described by Leys and Benn Michaels? The primary difference between this and a family-based formulation of postmemory is that a traumatic transmission depends on the *individual's* relationship to history, as opposed to the collective relationship that Benn Michaels presupposes. It could therefore be argued that many texts would fit both models at once. The "second generation" is not a small, discrete entity but a contested area, and in exploring the problems surrounding it, the value of such narrow definitions in a literary context is called into question. In order to look productively at Holocaust literature written by later generations, we need a more differentiated approach to terms like "second generation" and "postmemory" that can account for a range of sub-positions that recognize the diversity of literature and experience, and also the complex dynamics of possible relationships between the two.

Notes

Introduction

1. Efraim Sicher, Introduction to *Breaking Crystal: History and Memory after Auschwitz*, ed. Sicher, 1–16 (Urbana: University of Illinois Press, 1998), 7.

2. I am thinking, among other works, of Peter Novick, *The Holocaust in American Life* (New York: Mariner, 2000); James E. Young, *The Texture of Memory: Holocaust Memorials and Meaning* (New Haven, CT: Yale University Press, 1993); Tim Cole, *Selling the Holocaust: From Auschwitz to Schindler: How History Is Bought, Packaged, and Sold* (New York: Routledge, 2000); and Alan Mintz, *Popular Culture and the Shaping of Holocaust Memory in America* (Seattle: University of Washington Press, 2001).

3. It should be noted that the vast majority of second-generation texts, especially autobiographies, are written by women.

4. Anne Karpf, *The War After* (Portsmouth, NH: Heinemann, 1996; London: Minerva, 1997), 239. Citations are from the Minerva edition.

5. Ibid.

6. Ibid.

7. Ibid.

8. Ibid., 240.

9. Binjamin Wilkomirski, *Fragments: Memories of a Childhood 1939–1948*, trans. Carol Brown Janeway (London: Picador, 1996). Wilkomirski's "memoir," in which he gives an account of "his" experiences in Nazi concentration camps, is now discredited. In fact, he grew up in Switzerland in orphanages and with foster parents, his "Holocaust identity" apparently constructed as a validation of less "impressive" kinds of suffering. Elena Lappin concludes her investigative study of the Wilkomirski case with the observation that "to Bruno Dössekker [Wilkomirski], being a Jew was synonymous with the Holocaust. Swiss history has nothing remotely similar to offer, nothing so dramatic to survive, or to explain to a man where he came from, or how he is." "The Man with Two Heads," *Granta* 66 (1999): 65.

10. A recent example of this was the panel and discussion on "Conceptual Definitions of Survival" at the "Beyond Camps and Forced Labour" conference at the Imperial War Museum, January 2003.

11. Lawrence L Langer, *Versions of Survival: The Holocaust and the Human Spirit* (Albany: State University of New York Press, 1982), 12.

12. Joseph Skibell, *A Blessing on the Moon* (New York: Berkley, 1999), 273. This is the term Skibell uses in interviews. Whether he means that his grandfather "escaped" by the good fortune of having emigrated already, or was a refugee from persecution, is not clear.

13. Mick Brown, "A Labour of Love," *Telegraph Magazine* (January 31, 1998): 55. Despite an implied family connection, Michaels has refused to make any capital out of her family circumstances, and asserts in the same interview that she is not the child of survivors. My decision to write on her powerful fictional account of intergenerational transmission of trauma is a key instance of literary criteria taking precedence.

14. Melvin Jules Bukiet, "A Note on Method and Category," in *Nothing Makes You Free: Writings by Descendants of Jewish Holocaust Survivors*, ed. Bukiet, 25–29 (New York: W. W. Norton, 2002), 28.

15. Bukiet's novel *After* is dedicated to the survivors in his family, and in the introduction to *Nothing Makes You Free*, he sets forth a polemical position framed primarily by his own experiences as a child of survivors rather than as a writer. *After* (New York: Picador, 1997); *Nothing Makes You Free* (New York: W. W. Norton, 2002).

16. Cathy Caruth, Introduction to *Part I: Trauma and Experience*, in *Trauma: Explorations in Memory*, ed. Caruth, 3–12 (Baltimore: Johns Hopkins University Press, 1995), 4.

17. Ibid., 3. In an essay entitled "Not Outside the Range: One Feminist Perspective on Psychic Trauma" in the same volume, Laura S. Brown argues that many of the traumas experienced by women result from situations of poverty and abuse that occur too commonly to be described as "outside the range of human experience." Laura S. Brown, "Not Outside the Range: One Feminist Perspective on Psychic Trauma," in *Trauma: Explorations in Memory*, ed. Cathy Caruth (Baltimore: Johns Hopkins University Press, 1995), 100–103.

18. Caruth, Introduction to *Part II: Recapturing the Past*, in Caruth, ed., *Trauma: Explorations in Memory*, 153.

19. Walter Benn Michaels, "'You Who Never Was There': Slavery and the New Historicism—Deconstruction and the Holocaust," in *The Americanization of the Holocaust*, ed. Hilene Flanzbaum, 181–97 (Baltimore: Johns Hopkins University Press, 1999), 195; Ruth Leys, chapter 8: "The Pathos of the Literal: Trauma and the Crisis of Representation," in *Trauma: A Genealogy* (London: University of Chicago Press, 2000), 284–85.

20. Michaels, "You Who Never Was There," 187.

21. Alan L Berger, *Children of Job: American Second-Generation Witnesses to the Holocaust* (Albany: State University of New York Press, 1997), 1.

22. Carolyn Steedman, *Landscape for a Good Woman: A Story of Two Lives* (London: Virago, 1986), 122.

23. Berger, *Children of Job*, 71.

24. Ibid., 5. See also Karpf, *The War After*, 233.

25. Dina Wardi, *Memorial Candles* (London: Routledge, 1992), 27. Wardi's ideas have been fairly influential, and for that reason I present them here in reasonable

detail. However, she freely uses literary examples as evidence alongside clinical case studies without any explanation or justification. It is unclear from reading the book what implications this has for her methodology.

26. Ibid., 31–32.

27. Ibid., 39. See also Dani Rowland-Klein and Rosemary Dunlop, "The Transmission of Trauma across Generations: Identification with Parental Trauma in Children of Holocaust Survivors," *Australian and New Zealand Journal of Psychiatry* 31 (1997): 358–69.

28. Wardi, *Memorial Candles*, 144.

29. Cathy Caruth, "Parting Words: Trauma, Silence and Survival," *Cultural Values* 5, no. 1 (2001): 10.

30. Cathy Caruth, *Unclaimed Experience: Trauma, Narrative, and History* (Baltimore: Johns Hopkins University Press, 1996), 136.

31. James Herzog, "World Beyond Metaphor: Thoughts on the Transmission of Trauma," in *Generations of the Holocaust*, ed. M. S. Bergmann and M. E. Jucovy (New York: Basic Books, 1982), 103–20.

32. Rowland-Klein and Dunlop, "The Transmission of Trauma across Generations," 359.

33. Ibid., 367.

34. Ibid., 366.

35. See Paul John Eakin, *How Our Lives Become Stories: Making Selves* (Ithaca, NY: Cornell University Press, 1999); and Nancy K. Miller, "Representing Others: Gender and the Subjects of Autobiography," *differences* 6 (1994): 1–27.

36. Esther Faye, "Missing the 'Real' Trace of Trauma: How the Second Generation Remember the Holocaust," *American Imago: Studies in Psychoanalysis and Culture* 58, no. 2 (2001): 526.

37. Ibid., 525–26.

38. Nicolas Abraham, "Notes on the Phantom: A Complement to Freud's Metapsychology," in *The Shell and the Kernel Volume I*, ed. Nicolas Abraham and Maria Torok, trans. Nicholas T. Rand, 171–76 (Chicago: University of Chicago Press, 1994), 173. This process may, of course, equally relate to the mother.

39. Ibid., 174–75.

40. Ibid., 174.

41. Joy Schaverien, "Inheritance: Jewish Identity and the Legacy of the Holocaust Mediated Through Art Psychotherapy Groups," *British Journal of Psychotherapy* 15 (1998): 73.

42. Barbara Kessel, *Suddenly Jewish: Jews Raised as Gentiles Discover their Jewish Roots* (Hanover, NH: Brandeis University Press, 2000), 15.

43. Helen Epstein, *Children of the Holocaust: Conversations with Sons and Daughters of Survivors* (New York: Penguin, 1988), chapter 12.

44. Schaverien, "Inheritance: Jewish Identity and the Legacy of the Holocaust Mediated Through Art Psychotherapy Groups," 67.

45. Lisa Appignanesi, *Losing the Dead: A Family Memoir* (London: Vintage, 2000), 8. I am grateful to Dr. Anne Whitehead for drawing this aspect of Appignanesi's writing to my attention.

46. To give just a few very different examples, Marianne Hirsch introduces some of the chapters in *Family Frames: Photography, Narrative and Postmemory* (Cambridge, MA: Harvard University Press, 1997) with stories about her own family and experiences; the preface to Martin Gilbert's historical work *The Holocaust: The Jewish Tragedy* (London: Fontana, 1997) recounts his first two visits to Treblinka and mentions in passing that he is Jewish; and Alan and Naomi Berger, in their edited collection *Second Generation Voices: Reflections by Children of Holocaust Survivors and Perpetrators* (Syracuse, NY: Syracuse University Press, 2001), include a photograph of and dedication to Naomi's half brothers and half sisters who were murdered at Auschwitz.

47. Sigmund Freud, "Family Romances," in *The Penguin Freud Library* vol. 7, *On Sexuality: Three Essays on the Theory of Sexuality and Other Works*, trans. and ed. James Strachey (London: Penguin, 1977), 221–22.

48. Ibid., 224–25.

49. Examples of the former are Art Spiegelman's mother's suicide and his own mental illness in *Maus: A Survivor's Tale: My Father Bleeds History* (New York: Pantheon, 1986; London: Penguin, 1987), citations are from the Penguin edition; the anorexia of Louise Kehoe in *In This Dark House: A Memoir* (London: Penguin, 1997) and of Lara in Helen Fremont's *After Long Silence: A Memoir* (New York: Delta, 1999); and Helen Epstein's mother's despairing crying fits in *Children of the Holocaust*. Anne Karpf, after years of self-mutilation by scratching, realized that a place on her inner arm that she scratched repeatedly was exactly the place of her mother's concentration camp tattoo (*The War After*, 106).

50. Nadine Fresco, "Remembering the Unknown," *International Review of Psychoanalysis* 11 (1984): 424–25.

51. The "mythical" qualities of young, pre-traumatized parents in narratives by children of survivors take many forms. Anne Karpf's mother was a concert pianist, her talent ensuring her survival. Julie Salamon talks about the good looks and talent of her father, who was a doctor, and the beauty of his first wife, as well as the confidence and self-assurance of her mother, with her precocious talent for arithmetic. Helen Epstein's mother, she informs us, ran her own business at fifteen and her father was well-known at Terezin for being incorruptible.

52. Gary Weissman, *Fantasies of Witnessing: Postwar Efforts to Experience the Holocaust* (Ithaca, NY: Cornell University Press, 2004), 19.

53. Fresco, "Remembering the Unknown," 421.

54. Ibid., 418.

55. Descendants of survivors who offer differing perspectives on this topic are Helen Fremont, Louise Kehoe, and several interviewees in Barbara Kessel's *Suddenly Jewish*. Jewish writers who are not children of survivors who deal with this issue include Susan Jacoby and Mary Gordon.

56. Fresco, "Remembering the Unknown," 418.

57. Art Spiegelman, *Maus: A Survivor's Tale II: And Here My Troubles Began* (London: Penguin, 1992), 15.

58. Fresco, "Remembering the Unknown," 424.

59. Freud, "Family Romances," 224.

60. Hamida Bosmajian, "The Orphaned Voice in Art Spiegelman's *Maus I & II*," *Literature and Psychology* 44 (1998): 9; Spiegelman, *Maus I*, 30. I discuss this subject in a different context in my chapter on *Maus*.

61. Henri Raczymow, "Memory Shot through with Holes," *Yale French Studies* 85, *Discourses of Jewish Identity in Twentieth-Century France*, ed. Alan Astro (1994): 99.

62. Ibid., 102–3.

63. Sigmund Freud, "Moses and Monotheism," in *The Penguin Freud Library*, vol. 13, *The Origins of Religion*, ed. Albert Dickson, trans. and ed. James Strachey, 237–386 (London: Penguin, 1990), 309.

64. Raczymow, "Memory Shot through with Holes," 105.

65. Caruth, *Unclaimed Experience*, 17.

66. Raczymow, "Memory Shot through with Holes," 102.

67. George Steiner, "A Kind of Survivor," in *Language and Silence* (London: Faber and Faber, 1985), 164.

68. Ibid.

69. Kessel, *Suddenly Jewish*, 14.

70. Alain Finkielkraut, *The Imaginary Jew*, trans. Kevin O'Neill and David Suchoff (Lincoln: University of Nebraska Press, 1994), 7.

71. Shoshana Felman and Dori Laub, *Testimony: Crises of Witnessing in Literature, Psychoanalysis, and History* (New York: Routledge, 1992), 225.

72. Hanna Yablonka, "The Formation of Holocaust Consciousness in the State of Israel: The Early Days," in *Breaking Crystal: History and Memory after Auschwitz*, ed. Efraim Sicher (Urbana: University of Illinois Press, 1998), 120.

73. Gilead Morahg, "Breaking Silence: Israel's Fantastic Fiction of the Holocaust," in *The Boom in Contemporary Israeli Fiction*, ed. Alan Mintz, 143–83 (Hanover, NH: University Press of New England, 1997), 149–50.

74. Yablonka, "The Formation of Holocaust Consciousness," 121.

75. Shoshana Felman, "The Return of the Voice: Claude Lanzmann's *Shoah*," in *Testimony: Crises of Witnessing in Literature, Psychoanalysis, and History*, by Shoshana Felman and Dori Laub (New York: Routledge, 1992), 240.

76. Peter Brooks, *Reading for the Plot: Design and Intention in Narrative* (Cambridge, MA: Harvard University Press, 1984), 221. An interesting example of this concept is the character Grandfather Anshel in David Grossman's *See Under: Love*, trans. Betsy Rosenberg (London: Picador, 1991). His great-nephew is desperate to learn about what happened to him "Over There," but the old man is too senile to be able to tell him.

77. George Steiner, "A Season in Hell," in *In Bluebeard's Castle: Some Notes Towards the Re-definition of Culture*, by Steiner, *31–48* (London: Faber and Faber, 1974), 47.

78. See Jan Bondeson, *Buried Alive: The Terrifying History of Our Most Primal Fear* (New York: Norton, 2001), for a detailed history of this fear.

79. Brooks, *Reading for the Plot*, 223.

80. Dan Bar-On, "Transgenerational Aftereffects of the Holocaust in Israel: Three Generations," in *Breaking Crystal: History and Memory after Auschwitz*, ed. Efraim Sicher, 91–118 (Urbana: University of Illinois Press, 1998), 94.

81. Although not a child of surviors, Mary Gordon's account of researching her Jewish father's past makes a fascinating point of reference here. It differs crucially from many other family memoirs in that Gordon fully enacts her father's disinterment, exhuming his body and reburying it at a site of her own choosing. *The Shadow Man* (New York: Vintage, 1997).

82. Cathy Caruth, "The Claims of the Dead: History, Haunted Property, and the Law," *Critical Inquiry* 28 (2002): 423.

83. Ibid., 427.

84. Victoria Aarons, *A Measure of Memory: Storytelling and Identity in American Jewish Fiction* (Athens: The University of Georgia Press, 1996), 73.

85. Epstein, *Children of the Holocaust*, 345.

86. Louise Kehoe and Helen Fremont both write the stories of the Holocaust that their families wished had remained hidden. For Mary Gordon and Susan Jacoby, the Holocaust is not an obvious presence in their family histories, but was perhaps a contributing factor to their fathers' desires to conceal their Jewishness.

87. Caruth, "Parting Words," 21.

88. Helen Fremont, Louise Kehoe, and Art Spiegelman are all writers who make their battle for ownership of history and identity the major theme of their books.

89. Hirsch, *Family Frames*, 22.

90. Ibid.

91. I take the term "relational autobiography" from Paul John Eakin's book *How Our Lives Become Stories: Making Selves*, and deal with these ideas more fully in Chapter 1.

92. Marianne Hirsch, "Projected Memory: Holocaust Photographs in Personal and Public Fantasy," in *Acts of Memory: Cultural Recall in the Present*, ed. Mieke Bal, Jonathan Crewe, and Leo Spitzer (Hanover, NH: University Press of New England, 1999), 8–9.

93. See also Gary Weissman's critique of Hirsch's "blurred distinctions," in *Fantasies of Witnessing*, 16–18.

94. See Mick Brown, "A Labour of Love," 55, for Anne Michaels's comments on this; and see Pierre Nora "Between Memory and History: Les Lieux de Mémoire," *Representations* 26 (1989): 7–25. Artist Lynn Rotin, speaking at the 2003 Association of Jewish Canadian Studies / Association des études juives conference in Halifax, expressed her own experience of growing up in Toronto—and consequent interest in the Holocaust—in strikingly similar terms to Michaels.

95. Dominick LaCapra, *Representing the Holocaust: History, Theory, Trauma* (Ithaca, NY: Cornell University Press, 1994), 210.

96. Her interview with Yehudah Cohen in chapter 14 is a case in point. Likewise, Gabriela Korda's experiences, described in chapter 8, raise questions about identification with the perpetrator that Epstein finds disconcerting.

97. Gary Weissman makes a similar point about Rosenbaum's story "Cattle Car Complex," which he sees as "a romantic fantasy staging the second-generation American Jew's transformation into full-fledged Holocaust victim" (*Fantasies of Witnessing*, 15).

98. Thane Rosenbaum, *Second Hand Smoke: A Novel* (New York: St. Martin's, 1999), 2.

99. Michelle A. Friedman, "The Labor of Remembrance," in *Mapping Jewish Identities*, ed. Laurence J. Silberstein (New York: New York University Press, 2000), 98.

100. Ibid., 108.

101. Aharon Appelfeld, "After the Holocaust," in *Writing and the Holocaust*, ed. Berel Lang (New York: Holmes and Meier, 1988), 84.

102. Cindy McCormick Martinusen, *Winter Passing* (Wheaton, IL: Tyndale, 2000) is a particularly striking example of this, following every convention of a Hollywood-style plot.

103. Dominick LaCapra, *History and Memory after Auschwitz* (Ithaca, NY: Cornell University Press, 1998), 8. James E. Young makes the following similar point in his analysis of *Maus*: "Born after Holocaust history into the time of its memory only, this media-conscious generation rarely presumes to represent events outside of the ways they have vicariously known and experienced them." "The Holocaust as Vicarious Past: Art Spiegelman's *Maus* and the Afterimages of History," *Critical Inquiry* 24 (1998): 670.

104. Sara R. Horowitz, *Voicing the Void: Muteness and Memory in Holocaust Fiction* (Albany: State University of New York, 1997), 1.

105. David Brauner, *Post-War Jewish Fiction: Ambivalence, Self-Explanation and Transatlantic Connections* (Basingstoke, England: Palgrave, 2001), 186.

106. Cole, *Selling the Holocaust*, 6.

107. Ellen S. Fine, "Transmission of Memory: The Post-Holocaust Generation in the Diaspora," in *Breaking Crystal: History and Memory after Auschwitz*, ed. Efraim Sicher, 186–200 (Urbana: University of Illinois Press, 1998), 197.

Chapter 1

1. Journalist-memoirists include Fern Schumer Chapman, Anne Karpf, Daniel Asa Rose, and the authors under discussion in Chapters 1 and 2 of this text.

2. Nancy K. Miller "Representing Others: Gender and the Subjects of Autobiography," *differences* 6 (1994): 1–27 gives a helpful summary of the development of the concept within this field.

3. Laura Marcus, *Auto/biographical Discourses: Theory, Criticism, Practice* (Manchester: Manchester University Press, 1994), 273–74.

4. Paul John Eakin, *How Our Lives Become Stories: Making Selves* (Ithaca, NY: Cornell University Press, 1999), 85.

5. Marcus, *Auto/biographical Discourses*, 3.

6. Ibid., 21.

7. Ibid., 151.

8. Alan L. Berger, *Children of Job: American Second-Generation Witnesses to the Holocaust* (Albany: State University of New York Press, 1997), 16. The first book to which Berger refers is *Living after the Holocaust: Reflections by Children of Survivors in America*, ed. Lucy Y. Steinitz and David M. Szony (New York: Bloch, 1979).

9. Daniel Asa Rose, discussed later, is one writer who refers to Epstein, but to no other similar writers, in his own second-generation autobiography *Hiding Places: A Father and His Sons Retrace Their Family's Escape from the Holocaust* (New York: Simon and Schuster, 2000), 43. Epstein also features in Helen Fremont's acknowledgments to *After Long Silence: A Memoir* (New York: Delta, 1999) for her personal help and support. Fremont's book appeared twenty years after Epstein's book was published.

10. While this is certainly true, it is nonetheless worth noting that many historians and interviewers—including Dan Bar-On—who deal with Holocaust-related topics contextualize their research with a foreword or introduction outlining an aspect of their *personal* relationship to the topic. There are good scholarly reasons for a critical openness about one's own motivations, provided it is not done to replace scholarship with assertions of a moral authority over the subject matter. See the introduction to Gary Weissman, *Fantasies of Witnessing: Postwar Efforts to Experience the Holocaust* (Ithaca, NY: Cornell University Press, 2004) for a discussion of this tendency in Holocaust scholarship.

11. Eakin, *How Our Lives Become Stories*, 58.

12. Ibid.

13. Ibid., 55–56.

14. Ibid., 181. See also Carolyn Steedman, *Landscape for a Good Woman: A Story of Two Lives* (London: Virago, 1986), 122.

15. Helen Epstein, *Children of the Holocaust: Conversations with Sons and Daughters of Survivors* (New York: Penguin, 1988), 9–14. Page references in parentheses within the text refer to this edition.

16. Eakin, *How Our Lives Become Stories*, 176.

17. Dani Rowland-Klein and Rosemary Dunlop, "The Transmission of Trauma Across Generations: Identification with Parental Trauma in Children of Holocaust Survivors," *Australian and New Zealand Journal of Psychiatry* 31 (1997): 360.

18. Aaron Hass, *In the Shadow of the Holocaust: The Second Generation* (Cambridge: Cambridge University Press, 1996), 27.

19. Nanette C. Auerhahn and Dori Laub, "Intergenerational Memory of the Holocaust," in *International Handbook of Multigenerational Legacies of Trauma*, ed. Yael Danieli, 21–41 (New York: Plenum, 1998), 22.

20. Ibid., 38.

21. Epstein indicates that the name "Deborah Schwartz" is a pseudonym.

22. Eakin, *How Our Lives Become Stories*, 61.

23. Laura Browder, *Slippery Characters: Ethnic Impersonators and American Identities* (Chapel Hill: University of North Carolina Press, 2000), 5.

24. Ibid.

25. See also chapter 6 of *Children of the Holocaust*, in which Epstein discusses the limitations of clinical writings, especially their tendency toward over-generalization, in attempting to describe the psychological condition of survivors once their problems were finally recognized.

26. See Peter Novick, *The Holocaust in American Life* (New York: Mariner, 2000), 188–91 for an account of the growth in Jewish self-perception as "honorary

survivors" in the context of American identity politics. One of Epstein's interviewees in *Children of the Holocaust*, Ruth Alexander, states, "I felt the strongest
Jewish experience I had was the Holocaust. *That's* where I identified being Jewish,
and not with anything else" (195).

27. Susan Jacoby is the only one of the writers I refer to who resists and interrogates
this tendency explicitly. *Half-Jew: A Daughter's Search for Her Family's Buried Past*
(New York: Scribner, 2000), 236–41. Amy Hungerford's essay on Spiegelman's
Maus, "Surviving Rego Park: Holocaust Theory from Art Spiegelman to Berel
Lang," in *The Americanization of the Holocaust*, ed. Hilene Flanzbaum, 102–24
(Baltimore: Johns Hopkins University Press, 1999) offers some interesting reflec-
tions on this issue.

28. This is further suggested by the preoccupation with parental deaths, particularly
those of fathers, that is apparent in many memoirs by American, Canadian, and
British Jews of the postwar generation, including those by Julie Salamon, Susan
Jacoby, Lisa Appignanesi, Anne Karpf, Art Spiegelman, Louise Kehoe, Mary
Gordon, and Helen Epstein. All of these texts have endings or narrative climaxes
that involve a representation of the death of the author's father, often presented
regardless of chronology and whether the mother or father died first.

29. Nancy Chodorow explores the relational model in psychoanalysis as an attempt
to reconstruct a "whole" self from the fragmented self that psychoanalysis itself
portrays. See chapter 7: "Toward a Relational Individualism: The Mediation of
the Self Through Psychoanalysis," in *Feminism and Psychoanalytic Theory* (New
Haven, CT: Yale University Press, 1989).

30. It is true that, in the latter part of her book, Epstein makes tentative connections
with her own childhood and that of other *firstborn* children of survivors (253).
As I shall discuss later, such distinctions are foregrounded by Natan P. F.
Kellerman's synthesis of clinical studies of survivors' children. However, Epstein
does not attempt to draw out any implications from this, or to acknowledge that
her brothers' childhood experiences, and those of other children of survivors,
may have been qualitatively different from her own. To do so would require
modifications to the particular autobiographical structure she has chosen. To
return to the context of other memoirs, Eva Hoffman's *Lost in Translation*
(London: Vintage, 1998) is one autobiographical text in which the author refuses
to be dominated by her parents' experiences hiding out in the woods for the
duration of the war. Instead, this work presents her biggest trauma as her postwar
emigration from Poland to Canada.

31. Gary Weissman makes this point about the distorting effect of the dominant second-generation discourse in *Fantasies of Witnessing*, 19 and n. 42.

32. These criteria have been synthesized by Kellerman as follows: "1. [He or she was]
born early after the parents' trauma; 2. [He or she was] the only, or the first-born
child; 3. Both parents were survivors; 4. [He or she was a] replacement [child] to
children who had perished; 5. Parents had endured extraordinary mental suffering and significant loss and were highly disturbed as a result; 6. Symbiotic relations were dominant between parents and children and family relations were
characterised by enmeshment; 7. The trauma was talked about too little or too

much." "Psychopathology in Children of Holocaust Survivors: A Review of the Research Literature," *Israeli Journal of Psychiatry and Related Sciences* 38, no. 1 (2001): 43.

33. It is worth noting that the circumstances of Artie in Art Spiegelman's *Maus: A Survivor's Tale: My Father Bleeds History* (New York: Pantheon, 1986; London: Penguin, 1987), can be seen to coincide with at least six of the seven criteria listed above. Citations are from the Penguin edition.

34. Miller, "Representing Others: Gender and the Subjects of Autobiography," 19.

35. Eakin, *How Our Lives Become Stories*, 93.

Chapter 2

1. This is not to say that the matter might not be more complex than Albright claims. Susan Jacoby, whose own father's Jewish origins were a shameful secret to him at a time of increasing anti-Semitism, writes, "While it is not surprising that Madeleine the girl believed what her parents told her, it is difficult to credit her assertion that as an adult—and a diplomat with wide-ranging international contacts—she never suspected what was well known to many of her contemporaries, including surviving Czech Jewish relatives of whose existence she was fully aware (and whom she stonewalled. . .). Even in this day and age, there are still Jews—some with positions in society that would seem to render them impregnable—who fear that a clear-eyed glance backward can only consign them to the fate of Lot's wife." *Half-Jew: A Daughter's Search for Her Family's Buried Past* (New York: Scribner, 2000), 23–24.

2. Joy Schaverien, "Inheritance: Jewish Identity and the Legacy of the Holocaust Mediated Through Art Psychotherapy Groups," *British Journal of Psychotherapy* 15 (1998): 73.

3. Barbara Kessel, *Suddenly Jewish: Jews Raised as Gentiles Discover Their Jewish Roots* (Hanover, NH: Brandeis University Press, 2000), 7.

4. Ibid., 15.

5. Gabriele Rosenthal gave striking examples of such ambivalence in second- and third-generation memory in a paper entitled, "Three Generation Families of Holocaust Survivors: The Intergenerational Impact of the Concrete Past on the Children and Grandchildren," presented at the "Beyond Camps and Forced Labour" conference at the Imperial War Museum, London, January 2003.

6. Jacoby, *Half-Jew*, 24–25.

7. See for example, Martin S. Bergman and Milton E. Jucovy's compendious edited volume, *Generations of the Holocaust* (New York: Basic Books, 1982).

8. David Brauner, *Post-War Jewish Fiction: Ambivalence, Self-Explanation and Transatlantic Connections* (Basingstoke: Palgrave, 2001), 138.

9. Most second-generation memoirists include a prefatory note detailing where they stand on this question. For example, in *After Long Silence*, Helen Fremont declares in an "Author's Note" that she has "imagined details" in order to present "emotional truths," and she even draws the reader's attention to such details with

phrases like, "I don't know if he said this. . . . I wasn't there." *After Long Silence: A Memoir* (New York: Delta, 1999), 233.

10. Brauner, *Post-War Jewish Fiction*, 138.

11. Louise Kehoe, *In This Dark House: A Memoir* (New York: Penguin, 1997), 3. Page references in parentheses within the text refer to this edition.

12. Brauner, *Post-War Jewish Fiction*, 139.

13. Nicolas Abraham, "Notes on the Phantom: A Complement to Freud's Metapsychology," in *The Shell and the Kernel Volume I*, ed. Nicolas Abraham and Maria Torok, ed. and trans. Nicholas T. Rand, 171–76 (Chicago: University of Chicago Press, 1994), 171.

14. This play with his name can be read as representative of other strategies he uses to deflect his children's interest in their past. Kehoe suggests, "that Dad's disdain for facts was not the product of some lofty philosophical purism, nor even of simple sophistry, but came instead from the desperate desire he felt to escape from the awful realities of his own sad past" (34). The concealment of his past seems to rely on the relationship between naming and paternal authority.

15. This also suggests, in the context of later information about Lubetkin's Jewish origins, an identification with the Nazi perpetrator. Kehoe writes that he "was a rationalist through and through" and that "to him [religion] was not only the opium of the people, it was hemlock, cyanide from the intellect" (38); and in the modernist zoo buildings which were "his personal favourites," "animals became living monuments to rationalism, imprisoned not so much by bars or cages, but by their intellectual inferiority to humankind" (39).

16. The question of Jewishness seems to be strictly limited in this text to where it intersects with family identity and power relations. While the performative dimension to Vicky's identity crisis is drawn out by her assertion that "if I had been able to verify [my Jewishness] while I was still in Paris, I think we would have eloped" (185), it is unlikely that the truth would have made any difference to her "very traditional" boyfriend, for whom the Jewishness of the maternal line would probably have been the significant factor.

17. Haim Bresheeth, Stuart Hood, and Litza Jansz, *Introducing the Holocaust* (Cambridge: Icon Books, 2000), 93. Examples of such letters can be seen at the Museum of the Dutch Resistance in Amsterdam.

18. Anne Whitehead, "A Still, Small Voice: Letter-writing, Testimony and the Project of Address in Etty Hillesum's *Letters from Westerbork*," *Cultural Values* 5 (2001): 93.

19. Abraham, "Notes on the Phantom," 173.

20. Anne Karpf, *The War After* (Portsmouth, NH: Heinemann, 1996; London: Minerva, 1997). Citations are to the Minerva edition.

Chapter 3

1. Hugh Frey and Benjamin Noys, "History in the Graphic Novel," *Rethinking History* 6, no. 3 (2002): 255.

2. James E. Young, "The Holocaust as Vicarious Past: Art Spiegelman's *Maus* and the Afterimages of History," *Critical Inquiry* 24 (1998): 669.

3. Spiegelman highlights this point elsewhere, when Vladek tells him of an anti-Semite who considered himself German but was imprisoned alongside him in Auschwitz as a Jew. During his protest he is drawn as a mouse and as a cat, but when he is being beaten by a guard he becomes a mouse again. Art Spiegelman, *Maus: A Survivor's Tale II: And Here My Troubles Began* (London: Penguin, 1992), 50.

4. Hamida Bosmajian, "The Orphaned Voice in Art Spiegelman's *Maus I & II*," *Literature and Psychology* 44 (1998): 7–8. I am adopting what has already become widespread convention in writing about this text by referring to the protagonist as Artie to distinguish him from the author.

5. Page references in parentheses refer to Art Spiegelman, *Maus: A Survivor's Tale: My Father Bleeds History* (New York: Pantheon, 1986; London: Penguin, 1987), citations are to the Penguin edition; and Art Spiegelman, *Maus: A Survivor's Tale II: And Here My Troubles Began* (London: Penguin, 1992) unless otherwise indicated. The figure in brackets before the page number denotes volume *I* or *II*.

6. Bosmajian also makes this point in "The Orphaned Voice," 11.

7. The angry accusations hurled at the mother by the son, and the corresponding silence in the other direction, serve to emphasize what James E. Young has seen as "a void at the heart of *Maus*": Anja's story. *At Memory's Edge: After-Images of the Holocaust in Contemporary Art and Architecture* (New York: Yale University Press, 2000), 31. This in turn symbolizes the absence at the heart of all Holocaust narration, as "for every survivor story that is spoken and heard, another remains unvoiced, forever lost." Sara Horowitz, "Auto/biography and Fiction after Auschwitz: Probing the Boundaries of Second-Generation Aesthetics," in *Breaking Crystal: History and Memory after Auschwitz*, ed. Efraim Sicher, 276–94 (Urbana: University of Illinois Press, 1998), 280. Marianne Hirsch reads the diaries' destruction as part of a pattern of silenced female voices in and around *Maus. Family Frames: Photography, Narrative and Postmemory* (Cambridge, MA: Harvard University Press, 1997), 35. However, it is notable that Vladek could not be totally silent on the topic of the diaries, despite having been their destroyer. Either a sense of guilt, or the need for truth, prevents him from covering over Anja's story entirely. Yet this in turn feeds into a sense of guilt in the next generation, represented by his son, who is aware "that his entire project may itself be premised on the destruction of his mother's memoirs, their displacement and violation." Young, "The Holocaust as Vicarious Past," 686.

8. Paul John Eakin, *How Our Lives Become Stories: Making Selves* (Ithaca, NY: Cornell University Press, 1999), 92.

9. Michael Rothberg draws attention to this aspect of the date's significance, and also notes that "the late sixties inaugurated a new era for Jews in North America, one which would provide the sociological setting in which and against which Spiegelman would create *Maus*." "'We Were Talking Jewish,': Art Spiegelman's *Maus* as Holocaust Production," *Contemporary Literature* 35 (1994): 679–80.

10. Eakin, *How Our Lives Become Stories*, 59.

11. *Ibid.*, 60.

12. Rick Iadonisi, "Bleeding History and Owning His [Father's] Story: *Maus* and Collborative Autobiography," *CEA Critic* 57, no. 1 (1994): 50.

13. Hirsch, *Family Frames*, 17.

14. Bosmajian, "The Orphaned Voice," 3–4. S. E. Tabachnik makes a similar point about Artie's permanent infantilized state in "Of *Maus* and Memory: The Structure of Art Spiegelman's Graphic Novel of the Holocaust," *Word and Image* 9 (1993): 156.

15. Dominick LaCapra, *History and Memory after Auschwitz* (Ithaca, NY: Cornell University Press, 1998), 175.

16. Ibid., 154.

17. Gillian Banner suggests that "perhaps the 'honeymoon' refers ironically to the period between Hitler's takeover of power in Germany and the effects upon the population in Poland of German policies towards the Jews." *Holocaust Literature: Schulz, Levi, Spiegelman and the Memory of the Offence* (London: Vallentine Mitchell, 2000), 137.

18. For example, Artie and Vladek both have tails in the "mini-narrative" that opens *Maus I* in which Artie is deserted by his friends. Richieu has a tail in chapter 3, before his death in chapter 4. Anja has a tail for part of chapter 6, when her visible Jewishness makes her vulnerable to exposure. Jeanne C. Ewert offers a reading of the use of tails in *Maus* that is consistent with this interpretation. She also points out that, by volume *II*, Spiegelman has stopped drawing tails on mice at all: "Did Spiegelman simply forget that he had been drawing mice with tails? Given his attention to detail, that explanation doesn't seem plausible. It seems more likely the telltale marking of the Jews is knowingly abandoned in Volume II, that in the depiction of the concentration camps there is a deliberate refusal of racial, cultural difference." She goes on to propose that this is part of Spiegelman's "move towards the universal and away from the particular" that is detectable throughout the *Maus* books. "Reading Visual Narrative: Art Spiegelman's *Maus*," *Narrative* 8, no. 1 (2000): 99–101.

19. Jeanne C. Ewert's remarks on this strategy suggest Spiegelman's sensitivity to his material in making a clear division: "he restricts this kind of punning to the chapter titles and accompanying illustrations; the metaphor is never insisted on in the level of Vladek's own story" ("Reading Visual Narrative," 93).

20. Hirsch, *Family Frames*, 36–37.

21. Bosmajian, "The Orphaned Voice," 21.

22. Marianne Hirsch, "Projected Memory: Holocaust Photographs in Personal and Public Fantasy," in *Acts of Memory: Cultural Recall in the Present*, ed. Mieke Bal, Jonathan Crewe, and Leo Spitzer, 3–23 (Hanover, NH: University Press of New England, 1999), 13.

23. Ibid., 12.

24. Ibid., 15.

25. Bosmajian, "The Orphaned Voice," 7.

26. Art Spiegelman, "Looney Tunes, Zionism and the Jewish Question," in *Comix, Essays, Graphics and Scraps: From Maus to Now to Maus to Now*, by Spiegelman, *14–16* (Rome: Sellerio Editore—La Centrale dell'Arte, 1999), 14.

27. Young, *At Memory's Edge*, 35.
28. "When Vladek says that Richieu was a big baby weighing three kilos at birth, Artie questions 'If you were married in February, and Richieu was born in October, was he premature?' Vladek, hesitatingly answers 'Yes, a little' and immediately swerves to the matter of Artie's premature birth. . . . Since Vladek at this point has already told the story about Anja's friendship with a young communist, the question of paternity insinuates itself and could be supported by the events of Vladek's courtship of Anja" (Bosmajian, "The Orphaned Voice," 9). However, as we are told that Anja's original diaries from the camps were lost, and that she rewrote them specifically for the sake of her son, a question mark is placed over their reliability.
29. Marianne Hirsch has read this another way as follows: "Vladek, deploring the absent photos of his own side of the family, sadly stands in for them, filling up an entire page with his own body" (*Family Frames*, 29).
30. Hirsch, *Family Frames*, 40.
31. Terrence Des Pres, "Holocaust *Laughter*?" in *Writing and the Holocaust*, ed. Berel Lang, 215–33 (New York: Holmes and Meier, 1988), 231.
32. Bosmajian, "The Orphaned Voice," 21. S. E. Tabachnik also takes a negative view of this, saying that it merely, "reduces Art to the status of child again" ("Of *Maus* and Memory," 156). However, such a reading seems to ignore the visual dimension of the text that, as I argue, works against the written dimension here.
33. Peter Brooks, *Reading for the Plot: Design and Intention in Narrative* (Cambridge, MA: Harvard University Press, 1984), 246.
34. Ibid., xii.
35. LaCapra, *History and Memory after Auschwitz*, 177.
36. As Bosmajian writes, "the signature is handwritten—the artist and his orphaned voice are alive" ("The Orphaned Voice," 21).
37. Eakin, *How Our Lives Become Stories*, 176.
38. Young, "The Holocaust as Vicarious Past," 676.
39. Amy Hungerford, "Surviving Rego Park: Holocaust Theory from Art Spiegelman to Berel Lang," in *The Americanization of the Holocaust*, ed. Hilene Flanzbaum (Baltimore: Johns Hopkins University Press, 1999), 124. Hungerford's insightful analysis of the use of "masks" throughout the *Maus* books in this article informs much of my thinking on this aspect of the text.
40. Carolyn Steedman, *Landscape for a Good Woman: A Story of Two Lives* (London: Virago, 1986), 122.
41. Tabachnik, "Of *Maus* and Memory," 156.

Chapter 4

1. Interview printed in Joseph Skibell, *A Blessing on the Moon* (New York: Berkley, 1999), 273.
2. "Chaim" is the Hebrew word meaning "life."
3. Sue Vice, *Holocaust Fiction* (London: Routledge, 2000), 161.

4. Nicola King, *Memory, Narrative, Identity: Remembering the Self* (Edinburgh: Edinburgh University Press, 2000), 25.

5. King, *Memory, Narrative, Identity*, 11.

6. Ibid., 17.

7. Ibid., 12.

8. James E. Young, *Writing and Rewriting the Holocaust: Narrative and the Consequences of Interpretation* (Bloomington: Indiana University Press, 1990), 51.

9. Ibid., 52.

10. Parenthetical citations in this chapter refer to Skibell, *A Blessing on the Moon*.

11. Daniel Asa Rose, *Hiding Places: A Father and His Sons Retrace Their Family's Escape from the Holocaust* (New York: Simon and Schuster, 2000), 21.

12. Anne Karpf, *The War After* (Portsmouth, NH: Heinemann, 1996; London: Minerva, 1997), 94. Citations are to the Minerva edition.

13. Lisa Appignanesi, *Losing the Dead: A Family Memoir* (London: Vintage, 2000), 22. Victoria Stewart presents a useful discussion of the function of fairy tales in second-generation writing, specifically in works by Karpf, Appignanesi, and Eva Hoffman. *Women's Autobiography: War and Trauma* (Basingstoke, England: Palgrave Macmillan, 2003), 144–48.

14. Examples are Helen Fremont's aunt Zosia in *After Long Silence: A Memoir* (New York: Delta, 1999); and Lisa Appignanesi's mother in *Losing the Dead: A Family Memoir* (London: Vintage, 2000).

15. Karpf, *The War After*. The film adaptation of Wladyslaw Szpilman's memoir *The Pianist* is a more famous example of this.

16. Rose, *Hiding Places*, 21.

17. Daniel Weissbort, "Memories of War," in *Passionate Renewal: Jewish Poetry in Britain Since 1945: An Anthology*, ed. Peter Lawson (Nottingham: Five Leaves, 2001), 337.

18. Tzvetan Todorov, *Introduction à la littérature fantastique* (Paris: Seuil, 1970), 37–38.

19. Ibid., 46.

20. Primo Levi, *If This Is a Man*, trans. Stuart Woolf (London: Abacus, 1987), 43.

21. Ibid., 32.

22. Ibid., 28.

23. *The Jewish Encyclopedia*, vol. 9, 679.

24. Ibid.

25. Ibid., 244.

26. Todorov, *Introduction à la littérature fantastique*, 68.

27. Todorov points out that fairy tales, an example of the *merveilleux*, can themselves be allegorical or symbolic. However, for a text to be allegorical, there must be clear indications within the text that it is to be read as such (Ibid., 68–69).

28. Gila Ramras-Rauch, "The Holocaust and the Fantastic: A Negative Revelation?" in *The Scope of the Fantastic—Culture, Biography, Themes, Children's Literature*, ed. Robert A. Collins and Howard D. Pearce, 33–42 (Westport, CT: Greenwood, 1985), 41.

29. Cynthia Ozick, "The Rights of History and the Rights of Imagination," *Commentary* 107 (1999): 22.

30. Gilead Morahg, "Breaking Silence: Israel's Fantastic Fiction of the Holocaust," in *The Boom in Contemporary Israeli Fiction*, ed. Alan Mintz, 143–83 (Hanover, NH: University Press of New England, 1997) 163–64.

31. Ibid., 162–63.

32. The fact that Ola's illness fulfills the function of rendering visible the invisible supports Susan Sontag's observation about tuberculosis (the disease that Ola's coughing up blood and wasting body suggest) as an illness that is metaphorized in terms of its visibility on the body. It is characterized as being "rich in visible symptoms," and having aphrodisiac and spiritualizing qualities—all of which apply to the course of Ola's disease. In the Holocaust context, it is relevant, too, that it "is often imagined as a disease of poverty and deprivation—of thin garments, thin bodies, unheated rooms, poor hygiene, inadequate food"—of everything, in other words, that also symbolizes the lingering deaths of those in concentration camps. However, crossing over with this imagery, Ola's death also partakes of the characteristics of a literary heroine's ideal death. *Illness as Metaphor and AIDS and Its Metaphors* (London: Penguin, 1991), 13–14. Despite her sympathy with Chaim and the other Jews, Ola is not subjected to a brutal death such as theirs. Thus, while her illness renders visible the hidden suffering of the concentration camps, it also serves to highlight the gulf between her experiences and those of the Jews.

33. Naomi B. Solokoff, *Imagining the Child in Modern Jewish Fiction* (Baltimore: Johns Hopkins University Press, 1992), 8.

34. Rosemary Jackson, *Fantasy: The Literature of Subversion* (London: Routledge, 1991), 43.

35. It should be noted that, as the soldier is dead, his being able to see Chaim is not a special privilege as it is for Ola.

36. Ramras-Rauch, "The Holocaust and the Fantastic," 41.

37. Marina Warner, *From the Beast to the Blonde: On Fairytales and Their Tellers* (London: Chatto and Windus, 1994), 210. Warner also notes that this was a mechanism that the Grimm Brothers used consciously as a means to "soften the harshness" of stories. In the "Hansel and Gretel" story that they initially collected, for example, both parents wished to abandon their children. In their final version, however, the father is reluctant and the mother is a wicked stepmother (211). Bettelheim sees a separation of good and bad mother figures in Red Riding Hood's grandmother's temporarily being "consumed" by the wolf. Bruno Bettelheim, *The Uses of Enchantment: The Meaning and Importance of Fairy Tales* (Harmondsworth, England: Penguin, 1978), 66–67.

38. Sigmund Freud, "The Uncanny," in *The Standard Edition of the Complete Psychological Works of Sigmund Freud*, vol. 17, *An Infantile Neurosis and Other Works*, ed. and trans. James Strachey, 219–52 (London: Hogarth, 1955), 244.

39. David Patterson, *Sun Turned to Darkness: Memory and Recovery in the Holocaust Memoir* (Syracuse, NY: Syracuse University Press, 1998), 39–41.

40. Ibid., 43.

41. Ibid.
42. Elana Gomel, "Aliens among Us: Fascism and Narrativity," *Journal of Narrative Theory* 30, no. 1 (2000): 138.
43. *The New Fontana Dictionary of Modern Thought*, ed. Alan Bullock and Stephen Trombley (London: HarperCollins, 1999), 288.
44. Gomel, "Aliens among Us," 131.
45. Ibid., 132.
46. Ibid., 134.
47. Peter Brooks, *Reading for the Plot: Design and Intention in Narrative* (Cambridge, MA: Harvard University Press, 1984), 223.
48. Daniel Schwarz, *Imagining the Holocaust* (New York: St. Martin's, 1999), 22.
49. Gomel, "Aliens among Us," 137.
50. Ibid., 133.
51. Skibell, *A Blessing on the Moon*, 273. This quotation is from an interview printed in the Berkeley edition of the novel.
52. Bettelheim, *The Uses of Enchantment: The Meaning and Importance of Fairy Tales*, 37.
53. Wilhelm Solms, "On the Demonising of Jews and Gypsies in Fairy Tales," in *Sinti and Roma: Gypsies in German-Speaking Society and Literature*, ed. Susan Tebbut, 91–106 (New York: Berghahn, 1998), 94.
54. Skibell, *A Blessing on the Moon*, 273. This quotation is from an interview printed in the Berkley edition of the novel.
55. *The Jewish Encyclopedia*, vol. 8, ed. Isidore Singer (New York: Funk and Wagnalls, 1904), 236.
56. Ibid., 237.
57. Ibid., 236–37. The encyclopedia entry also notes as a matter of curiosity that non-Jewish material tended to be preferred by its Jewish readers.
58. Jack Zipes, *Fairy Tales and the Art of Subversion: The Classical Genre for Children and the Process of Civilization* (New York: Routledge, 1991), 166.
59. Alain Finkielkraut, *The Imaginary Jew*, trans. Kevin O'Neill and David Suchoff (Lincoln: University of Nebraska Press, 1994), 12–13.
60. Bernard Wasserstein, *Vanishing Diaspora: The Jews in Europe Since 1945* (London: Penguin, 1997), 262.
61. The records of the Einsatzkommando unit that carried out the massacre record the exact number of deaths as 33,771. See Martin Gilbert, *The Holocaust: The Jewish Tragedy* (London: Fontana, 1997), 206.
62. Martin Gilbert, *The Holocaust: The Jewish Tragedy* (London: Fontana, 1997), 821.
63. Finkielkraut, *The Imaginary Jew*, 13.
64. Schwarz, *Imagining the Holocaust*, 22–23.
65. Solokoff, *Imagining the Child*, 3.
66. Ibid., 9.
67. Shoshana Felman, "The Return of the Voice: Claude Lanzmann's *Shoah*," in *Testimony: Crises of Witnessing in Literature, Psychoanalysis and History*, by Shoshana Felman and Dori Laub, 204–83 (New York: Routledge, 1992), 209–10.

Chapter 5

1. An earlier version of some of the material in this chapter appeared as Marita Grimwood, "Postmemorial Positions: Reading and Writing after the Holocaust in Anne Michaels's *Fugitive Pieces*," in *Canadian Jewish Studies /Études juives canadiennes* 11 (2003): 111–30.

2. Joseph Skibell, *A Blessing on the Moon* (New York: Berkley, 1999), 273. This quotation is taken from an interview printed in the book.

3. Mick Brown, "A Labour of Love," *Telegraph Magazine* (January 31, 1998): 55.

4. Ibid.

5. Ibid.

6. Caroline Gascoigne, "The human race," *The Sunday Times*, February 7, 1997.

7. See Ann Parry, "'. . . to give. . . death a place': Rejecting the 'ineffability' of the Holocaust: The Work of Gillian Rose and Anne Michaels," *Canadian Literature* 160 (1999): 28–45; and Annick Hillger, "'Afterbirth of Earth': Messianic Materialism in Anne Michaels' *Fugitive Pieces*," *Canadian Literature* 60 (1999): 28–45.

8. Norma Rosen, "Poetry after Auschwitz," *Partisan Review* 65 (1998): 317.

9. Nicola King, "'We Come After': Remembering the Holocaust," in *Literature and the Contemporary: Fictions and Theories of the Present*, ed. Roger Luckhurst and Peter Marks (Harlow: Longman, 1999), 102.

10. Ibid., 105–6.

11. See Méira Cook, "At the Membrane of Language and Silence: Metaphor and Memory in *Fugitive Pieces*," *Canadian Literature* 164 (2000): 12–33; and Adrienne Kertzer, "*Fugitive Pieces*: Listening as a Holocaust Survivor's Child," *English Studies in Canada* 26, no. 2 (2000): 203–4.

12. Kertzer, "*Fugitive Pieces*," 206.

13. Sue Vice, *Holocaust Fiction* (London: Routledge, 2000), 9.

14. Parenthetical citations in this chapter refer to Anne Michaels, *Fugitive Pieces* (London: Bloomsbury, 1998).

15. These appear on pages 149 and 157–59.

16. Many of the well-known English-language histories of the Holocaust give little space to the experience of Greek Jews.

17. Berel Lang, *Holocaust Representation: Art within the Limits of History and Ethics* (Baltimore: Johns Hopkins University Press, 2000), 37.

18. Ibid., 38–39.

19. Mick Brown, "A Labour of Love," *Telegraph Magazine* (January 31, 1998): 55.

20. W. J. McCann, "'Volk and Germanentum': The Presentation of the Past in Nazi Germany," in *The Politics of the Past*, ed. Peter Gathercole and David Lowenthal, 74–88 (London: Routledge, 1994), 84. Anne Michaels cites this book as a source in her acknowledgments in *Fugitive Pieces*, 295.

21. Norma Rosen remarks in her review of the book that "each woman, including Ben's wife, Naomi, is abstract enough to resemble the others." "Poetry after Auschwitz," *Partisan Review* 65 (1998): 316.

22. Dori Laub, "Bearing Witness or the Vicissitudes of Listening," in *Testimony: Crises of Witnessing in Literature, Psychoanalysis, and History*, by Shoshana Felman and Dori Laub, 75–92 (New York: Routledge, 1992), 57.

23. Ibid., 57–58.

24. Kertzer, "*Fugitive Pieces*," 196.

25. Ibid., 204–5.

26. Jakob Beer is born in 1933, just as Nazism is taking hold of Germany, and dies in 1993, nearly fifty years after the end of the Second World War. After his parents' murders he is concealed by Athos for the remainder of the war's duration, and the greater part of his life is lived out after the war.

27. Nadine Fresco, "Remembering the Unknown," *International Review of Psychoanalysis* 11 (1984): 420.

28. Laub, "Bearing Witness," 67.

29. Kertzer, "*Fugitive Pieces*," 208.

30. Cathy Caruth, *Unclaimed Experience: Trauma, Narrative, and History*. (Baltimore: Johns Hopkins University Press, 1996), 8.

31. For a discussion of Pierre Janet's concepts of "traumatic memory" and "narrative memory," see Bessel A. Van der Kolk and Onno Van der Hart, "The Intrusive Past: The Inflexibility of Memory and the Engraving of Trauma," in *Trauma: Explorations in Memory*, ed. Cathy Caruth, 158–82 (Baltimore: Johns Hopkins University Press, 1995), 163.

32. Jean Améry, *At the Mind's Limits: Contemplations by a Survivor on Auschwitz and Its Realities*, trans. Sidney Rosenfeld and Stella P. Rosenfeld (Bloomington: Indiana University Press, 1980), 34.

33. Laura Tanner, *Intimate Violence: Reading Rape and Torture in Twentieth Century Fiction* (Bloomington: Indiana University Press, 1994), 3.

34. Ibid., 19.

35. Vice, *Holocaust Fiction*, 9.

36. Tanner, *Intimate Violence*, 3

37. Van der Kolk and Van der Hart, "The Intrusive Past," 176–77.

38. See Dori Laub, "An Event without a Witness: Truth, Testimony and Survival," in *Testimony: Crises of Witnessing in Literature, Psychoanalysis, and History*, by Shoshana Felman and Dori Laub (New York: Routledge, 1992), 86–87.

39. Van der Kolk and Van der Hart, "The Intrusive Past," 178.

40. J. Laplanche and J.-B. Pontalis, *The Language of Psycho-Analysis*, trans. Donald Nicholson-Smith (London: Hogarth, 1973), 211, 455–56.

41. See Abraham, "Notes on the Phantom."

42. Anne Michaels, "Cleopatra's Love," *Poetry Canada Review* 14, no. 2 (1994): 14.

43. Ibid., 15.

44. Ibid., 14.

45. Vice, *Holocaust Fiction*, 8.

46. Jakob Beer was born in 1933, and Michaela is twenty-five years his junior, meaning that she shares with Michaels the birth year of 1958 (Michaels's age and year of birth are mentioned in many reviews and interviews, including Mick Brown's "A Labour of Love" and Lisa Jardine's "Pieces of Mind," *Times* metro section,

week from December 2–January 2, 1998). The twenty-five year age gap—a full generation—gives Michaela and Michaels a firm "second-generation" identity in relation to the Holocaust. This character and the author also share European parentage.

47. Michaels, "Cleopatra's Love," 14.
48. Laub, "Bearing Witness," 57.
49. Ibid., 58, emphasis added.
50. Tanner, *Intimate Violence*, 9–10.

Conclusion

1. Parenthetical citations in this chapter refer to Cheryl Pearl Sucher, *The Rescue of Memory* (New York: Berkley, 1998).
2. Marianne Hirsch, *Family Frames: Photography, Narrative and Postmemory* (Cambridge, MA: Harvard University Press, 1997), 7.

Bibliography

Primary Works

Aleichem, Sholem. *Tevye the Dairyman and the Railroad Stories*. Translated by Hillel Halkin. New York: Schocken, 1987.

Améry, Jean. *At the Mind's Limits: Contemplations by a Survivor on Auschwitz and its Realities*. Translated by Sidney Rosenfeld and Stella P. Rosenfeld. Bloomington: Indiana University Press, 1980.

Amis, Martin. *Time's Arrow*. London: Quality Paperbacks Direct, 1992.

Antin, Mary. *The Promised Land*. New York: Penguin, 1997.

Appelfeld, Aharon. *The Iron Tracks*. Translated by Jeffrey M. Green. New York: Random House, 1998.

Appignanesi, Lisa. *Losing the Dead: A Family Memoir*. London: Vintage, 2000.

Ascher, Carol. *The Flood*. Willimantic, CT: Curbstone, 1996.

Balzac, Honoré de. *Le Colonel Chabert*. Paris: Livre de Poche, 1984.

Bellow, Saul, *Mr. Sammler's Planet*. New York: Penguin, 1996.

Berger, Alan L., and Naomi Berger, eds. *Second Generation Voices: Reflections by Children of Holocaust Survivors and Perpetrators*. Syracuse, NY: Syracuse University Press, 2001.

Bukiet, Melvin Jules, *After*. New York: Picador, 1997.

———. Introduction to *Nothing Makes You Free: Writing by Descendants of Jewish Holocaust Survivors*, edited by Melvin Jules Bukiet, 11–23. New York: W. W. Norton, 2003.

———. "A Note on Method and Category." In *Nothing Makes You Free: Writing by Descendants of Jewish Holocaust Survivors*, edited by Melvin Jules Bukiet, 25–29. New York: W. W. Norton, 2003.

———, ed. *Nothing Makes You Free: Writings by Descendants of Jewish Holocaust Survivors*. New York: W. W. Norton, 2002.

———. *Signs and Wonders: A Novel*. New York: Picador, 1999.

Chametzky, Jules, John Felstiner, Hilene Flanzbaum, and Kathryn Hellerstein, eds. *Jewish American Literature: A Norton Anthology*. New York: Norton, 2001.

Chapman, Fern Schumer. *Motherland: Beyond the Holocaust: A Mother-Daughter Journey to Reclaim the Past*. New York: Penguin, 2001.

Ciresi, Rita. *Pink Slip*. New York: Delta, 1999.

Cohen, Matt. *Emotional Arithmetic*. New York: St. Martin's, 1990.

Delbanco, Nicholas. *What Remains: A Novel*. New York: Warner, 2000.

Eisenberg, Robert. *Boychiks in the Hood: Travels in the Hasidic Underground.* San Francisco: HarperCollins, 1996.

Eliach, Yaffa. *Hasidic Tales of the Holocaust.* New York: Vintage, 1988.

Englander, Nathan. *For the Relief of Unbearable Urges.* New York: Vintage International, 2000.

Epstein, Helen. *Children of the Holocaust: Conversations with Sons and Daughters of Survivors.* New York: Penguin, 1988.

———. *Where She Came From: A Daughter's Search for her Mother's History.* New York: Plume, 1998.

Finkelstein, Barbara. *Summer Long-a-coming.* Sarasota, FL: Disc-Us, 1987.

Florsheim, Stewart J., ed. *Ghosts of the Holocaust: An Anthology of Poetry by the Second Generation.* Detroit: Wayne State University Press, 1989.

Fremont, Helen. *After Long Silence: A Memoir.* New York: Delta, 1999.

Friedman, Carl. Excerpts from *Nightfather.* Translated by Arnold and Erica Pomerans. In *Nothing Makes You Free: Writings by the Descendants of Jewish Holocaust Survivors*, edited by Melvin Jules Bukiet, 33–47. New York: W. W. Norton, 2002.

Friedmann, Thomas. *Damaged Goods.* Sag Harbor, NY: Permanent Press, 1984.

Goldstein, Rebecca. *Strange Attractors.* New York: Penguin, 1994.

Gordon, Mary. *The Shadow Man.* New York: Vintage, 1997.

Grant, Linda. *Remind Me Who I Am, Again.* London: Granta, 1999.

Grimm, Jakob, and Wilhelm Grimm, eds. *Household Stories.* London: Routledge, Warne, and Routledge, 1864.

———. "The Jew Among Thorns." In *Household Stories*, edited by Jakob Grimm and Wilhelm Grimm, 349–52. London: Routledge, Warne, and Routledge, 1864.

Grossman, David. *See Under: Love.* Translated by Betsy Rosenberg. London: Picador, 1991.

Harris, Mark Jonathan, and Deborah Oppenheimer. *Into the Arms of Strangers: Stories of the Kindertransport.* London: Bloomsbury, 2001.

Heaney, Seamus. *New Selected Poems 1966–1987.* London: Faber and Faber, 1990.

Hershman, Marcie. *Tales of the Master Race.* New York: Harper Perennial, 1992.

Hoffman, Eva. *Lost in Translation.* London: Vintage, 1998.

Jacoby, Susan. *Half-Jew: A Daughter's Search for Her Family's Buried Past.* New York: Scribner, 2000.

Kalman, Judith. *The County of Birches: Stories.* New York: St. Martin's, 1998.

Karpf, Anne. *The War After.* London: Minerva, 1997. First published 1996 by Heinemann.

Katchor, Ben. *The Jew of New York.* New York: Pantheon, 1998.

Kaufman, Alan. *Jew Boy.* London: Robinson, 2001.

Kehoe, Louise. *In This Dark House: A Memoir.* New York: Penguin, 1997.

Keneally, Thomas. *Schindler's Ark.* London: Sceptre, 1996.

Kertesz, Imré. *Kaddish for a Child Not Yet Born.* Translated by Christopher C. Wilson and Katharina M. Wilson. Evanston, IL: Northwestern University Press, 1997.

Lawson, Peter, ed. *Passionate Renewal: Jewish Poetry in Britain Since 1945: An Anthology.* Nottingham: Five Leaves, 2001.

Levi, Primo. *If This Is a Man.* Translated by Stuart Woolf. London: Abacus, 1987.

Martinusen, Cindy McCormick. *Winter Passing.* Wheaton, IL: Tyndale, 2000.

Matza, Diane, ed. *Sephardic-American Voices: Two Hundred Years of a Literary Legacy.* Hanover, NH: Brandeis University Press, 1997.

Michaels, Anne. "Cleopatra's Love." *Poetry Canada Review* 14, no. 2 (1994): 14–15.

———. *Fugitive Pieces.* London: Bloomsbury, 1998.

———. *The Weight of Oranges/Miner's Pond.* Toronto: McClelland and Stewart, 1997.

Miller, Nancy K. *Bequest and Betrayal: Memoirs of a Parent's Death.* New York: Oxford University Press, 1996.

Morrison, Toni. *Beloved.* London: Picador, 1988.

Moses, Miriam Israel. "From 'Survivors and Pieces of Glass.'" In *Jewish American Literature: A Norton Anthology*, edited by Jules Chametzky and others, 1111–20. New York: Norton, 2001.

Newman, Louis I., ed. *The Hasidic Anthology: Tales and Teachings of the Hasidim.* New York: Schocken, 1975.

Ozick, Cynthia. *The Shawl.* New York: Vintage, 1990.

Perec, Georges. *W ou le Souvenir d'Enfance.* Paris: Gallimard, 1993.

Perera, Victor. *The Cross and the Pear Tree: A Sephardic Journey.* London: Flamingo, 1997.

Raphael, Lev. *Winter Eyes.* London: Gay Men's Press, 1992.

———. "Writing a Jewish Life." *Tikkun* 17, no. 6 (2002): 49–56.

Rose, Daniel Asa. *Hiding Places: A Father and His Sons Retrace Their Family's Escape from the Holocaust.* New York: Simon and Schuster, 2000.

Rosen, Jonathan. *The Talmud and the Internet: A Journey Between Worlds.* London: Continuum, 2000.

Rosenbaum, Thane. *Elijah Visible: Stories.* New York: St. Martin's, 1996.

———. *Second Hand Smoke: A Novel.* New York: St. Martin's, 1999.

Rosenthal, Gabriele. "Three Generation Families of Holocaust Survivors: The Intergenerational Impact of the Concrete Past on the Children and Grandchildren." Paper presented at the "Beyond Camps and Forced Labour" conference at the Imperial War Museum. London: January 2003.

Roth, Philip. *The Ghost Writer.* Harmondsworth, England: Penguin, 1980.

———. *The Human Stain.* London: Vintage, 2001.

———. *Operation Shylock: A Confession.* London: Vintage, 1994.

———. *Patrimony: A True Story.* London: Vintage, 1991.

Sacco, Joe. *Palestine.* London: Jonathan Cape, 2003.

Salamon, Julie. *The Net of Dreams: A Family's Search for a Rightful Place.* New York: Random House, 1996.

Schiff, Hilda, ed. *Holocaust Poetry.* New York: St. Martin's Griffin, 1995.

Schlink, Bernhard. *The Reader.* Translated by Carol Brown Janeway. London: Phoenix, 1997.

Sebald, W. G. *Austerlitz.* Translated by Anthea Bell. London: Hamish Hamilton, 2001.

———. *The Emigrants.* Translated by Michael Hulse. London: Harvill, 1997.

Segal, Lore. *Other People's Houses*. New York: New Press, 1994.

Singer, Isaac Bashevis. *Enemies: A Love Story*. Harmondsworth, England: Penguin, 1977.

Skibell, Joseph. *A Blessing on the Moon*. New York: Berkley, 1999.

Spiegelman, Art. *Maus: A Survivor's Tale: My Father Bleeds History*. London: Penguin, 1987. First published 1986 by Pantheon Books.

———. *Maus: A Survivor's Tale II: And Here My Troubles Began*. London: Penguin, 1992.

———. *The Complete Maus* CD-ROM. New York: Voyager, 1994.

———. "Mein Kampf. My Struggle." In *The Familial Gaze*, edited by Marianne Hirsch, 99–100. Hanover, NH: University Press of New England, 1999.

Steinfeld, J. J. "The Apostate's Tattoo." In *Dancing at the Club Holocaust: Stories New and Selected*, by J. J. Steinfeld, 12–19. Charlottetown, PE: Ragweed, 1993.

———. *Dancing at the Club Holocaust: Stories New and Selected*. Charlottetown, PA: Ragweed, 1993.

Steinitz, Lucy Y., and David M. Szony, ed. *Living after the Holocaust: Reflections by Children of Survivors in America*. New York: Bloch, 1979.

Stern, Steve. *Lazar Malkin Enters Heaven*. London: Abacus, 1998.

———. *The Wedding Jester*. St. Paul, MN: Graywolf, 1999.

Stollman, Aryeh Lev. *The Far Euphrates*. New York: Riverhead, 1997.

Sucher, Cheryl Pearl. *The Rescue of Memory*. New York: Berkley, 1998.

Thomas, D. M. *The White Hotel*. London: Penguin, 1981.

Velmans, Edith. *Edith's Book*. London: Penguin, 1999.

Weissbort, Daniel. "Memories of War." In *Passionate Renewal: Jewish Poetry in Britain Since 1945: An Anthology*, edited by Peter Lawson, 337. Nottingham: Five Leaves, 2001.

Wilkomirski, Benjamin. *Fragments: Memories of a Childhood 1939–1948*. Translated by Carol Brown Janeway. London: Picador, 1996.

Yolen, Jane. *Briar Rose*. New York: Starscape, 2002.

The Holocaust in Greece: Zakynthos. http://www.ushmm.org/greece/eng/zakyntho.htm. Accessed October 7, 2002.

Secondary Works

Aarons, Victoria. *A Measure of Memory: Storytelling and Identity in American Jewish Fiction*. Athens: University of Georgia Press, 1996.

Abraham, Nicolas. "Notes on the Phantom: A Complement to Freud's Metapsychology." In *The Shell and the Kernel Volume I*, by Nicolas Abraham and Maria Torok. Edited and translated by Nicholas T. Rand, 171–76. Chicago: University of Chicago Press, 1994.

Abraham, Nicolas, and Maria Torok. *The Shell and the Kernel Volume I*. Edited and translated by Nicholas T. Rand. Chicago: University of Chicago Press, 1994.

Allison, James, Chris Jenks, and Alan Prout. *Theorizing Childhood*. Cambridge: Polity, 1998.

Anderson, John C., and Bradley Katz. "Read Only Memory: *Maus* and Its Marginalia" on CD-ROM. In *Considering* Maus*: Approaches to Art Spiegelman's "Survivor's Tale" of the Holocaust*, by Deborah R. Geis, 159–74. Tuscaloosa: University of Alabama Press, 2003.

Anderson, Linda. *Autobiography*. London: Routledge, 2001.

Appelfeld, Aharon. "After the Holocaust." In *Writing and the Holocaust*, edited by Berel Lang, 83–92. New York: Holmes and Meier, 1988.

———. *Badenheim 1939*. Translated by Dalya Bilu. Boston : D. R. Godine, 1980. Originally published as *Badenheim Ir Nofesh* (Tel Aviv: Hakibbutz Hameuchad, 1979).

Ariès, Philippe. *Centuries of Childhood*. Translated by Robert Baldick. London: Jonathan Cape, 1962.

Auerhahn, Nanette C., and Dori Laub. "Intergenerational Memory of the Holocaust." In *International Handbook of Multigenerational Legacies of Trauma*, edited by Yael Danieli, 21–41. New York: Plenum, 1998.

Bach, Gerhard. "Memory and Collective Identity: Narrative Strategies against Forgetting in Contemporary Literary Responses to the Holocaust." In *Jewish American and Holocaust Literature: Representation in the Postmodern World, edited by Alan L. Berger and Gloria L. Cronin*, 77–91. Albany: New York State University Press, 2004.

Bal, Mieke, Jonathan Crewe, and Leo Spitzer, eds. *Acts of Memory: Cultural Recall in the Present*. Hanover, NH: University Press of New England, 1999.

Banner, Gillian. *Holocaust Literature: Schulz, Levi, Spiegelman and the Memory of the Offence*. London: Vallentine Mitchell, 2000.

Bar-On, Dan. "Transgenerational Aftereffects of the Holocaust in Israel: Three Generations." In *Breaking Crystal: History and Memory after Auschwitz*, edited by Efraim Sicher, 91–118. Urbana: University of Illinois Press, 1998.

———. *Legacy of Silence: Encounters with Children of the Third Reich*. Cambridge, MA: Harvard University Press, 1991.

Barrington, Judith. *Writing the Memoir: From Truth to Art*. Portland, OR: Eighth Mountain Press, 1997.

Baumgarten, Murray. *Expectations and Endings: Observations on Holocaust Literature*. New York: Yeshiva University Holocaust Studies Program, 1989.

Berger, Alan L. *Children of Job: American Second-Generation Witnesses to the Holocaust*. Albany: State University of New York Press, 1997. First published by Heinemann, 1996.

Bergmann, Martin S., and Jucovy, Milton E., eds. *Generations of the Holocaust*. New York: Basic Books, 1982.

Bettelheim, Bruno. *The Uses of Enchantment: The Meaning and Importance of Fairy Tales*. Harmondsworth, England: Penguin, 1978.

Bloom, Lynn Z. "Auto/bio/history: Modern Midwifery." In *Autobiography and Questions of Gender*, edited by Shirley Neuman, 12–24. London: Frank Cass, 1991.

Bohm-Duchen, Monica, ed. *After Auschwitz: Responses to the Holocaust in Contemporary Art*. Sunderland, England: Northern Centre for Contemporary Art and Lund Humphries, 1995.

Bondeson, Jan. *Buried Alive: The Terrifying History of Our Most Primal Fear*. New York: Norton, 2001.

Bosmajian, Hamida. "The Orphaned Voice in Art Spiegelman's *Maus I & II.*" *Literature and Psychology* 44 (1998): 1–22.

Brauner, David. *Post-War Jewish Fiction: Ambivalence, Self-Explanation and Transatlantic Connections*. Basingstoke, England: Palgrave, 2001.

Bresheeth, Haim, Stuart Hood, and Litza Jansz. *Introducing the Holocaust*. Cambridge: Icon Books, 2000.

Brooks, Peter. *Reading for the Plot: Design and Intention in Narrative*. Cambridge, MA: Harvard University Press, 1984.

Broughton, T. L. "Women's Autobiography: The Self at Stake?" In *Autobiography and Questions of Gender*, edited by Shirley Neuman, 76–94. London: Frank Cass, 1991.

Browder, Laura. *Slippery Characters: Ethnic Impersonators and American Identities*. Chapel Hill: University of North Carolina Press, 2000.

Brown, Laura S. "Not Outside the Range: One Feminist Perspective on Psychic Trauma." In *Trauma: Explorations in Memory*, edited by Cathy Caruth, 100–12. Baltimore: Johns Hopkins University Press, 1995.

Brown, Michael. "Of *Maus* and Men: Problems of Asserting Identity in a Post-Holocaust Age." *Studies in American Jewish Literature* 12 (1993): 134–40.

Brown, Mick. "A Labour of Love." *Telegraph Magazine* (January 31, 1998): 52–57.

Budick, Emily Miller. "Acknowledging the Holocaust in Contemporary American Fiction and Criticism." In *Breaking Crystal: History and Memory after Auschwitz*, edited by Efraim Sicher, 329–43. Urbana: University of Illinois Press, 1998.

Caruth, Cathy. "The Claims of the Dead: History, Haunted Property, and the Law." *Critical Inquiry* 28 (2002): 419–41.

———. Introduction to *Part I: Trauma and Experience*. In *Trauma: Explorations in Memory*, edited by Cathy Caruth, 3–12. Baltimore: Johns Hopkins University Press, 1995.

———. Introduction to *Part II: Recapturing the Past*. In *Trauma: Explorations in Memory*, edited by Cathy Caruth, 151–57. Baltimore: Johns Hopkins University Press, 1995.

———. "Parting Words: Trauma, Silence and Survival." *Cultural Values* 5, no.1 (2001): 7–27.

———, ed. *Trauma: Explorations in Memory*. Baltimore: Johns Hopkins University Press, 1995.

———. *Unclaimed Experience: Trauma, Narrative, and History*. Baltimore: Johns Hopkins University Press, 1996.

Cheyette, Bryan, ed. *Between "Race" and Culture: Representations of "the Jew" in English and American Literature*. Stanford, CA: Stanford University Press, 1996.

Chodorow, Nancy. *Feminism and Psychoanalytic Theory*. New Haven, CT: Yale University Press, 1989.

Cole, Tim. *Selling the Holocaust: From Auschwitz to Schindler: How History is Bought, Packaged, and Sold*. New York: Routledge, 2000.

Collins, Robert A., and Howard D. Pearce, eds. *The Scope of the Fantastic—Culture, Biography, Themes, Children's Literature*. Westport, CT: Greenwood, 1985.

Cook, Méira. "At the Membrane of Language and Silence: Metaphor and Memory in *Fugitive Pieces*." *Canadian Literature* 164 (2000): 12–33.

Criglington, Meredith. "The City as a Site of Counter-Memory in Anne Michaels's *Fugitive Pieces* and Michael Ondaatje's *In the Skin of a Lion*." *Essays in Canadian Writing* 81 (2004): 129–51.

Danieli, Yael, ed. *International Handbook of Multigenerational Legacies of Trauma*. New York: Plenum, 1998.

Dawidowicz, Lucy. *The War Against the Jews, 1933–1945*. New York: Holt, Rinehart and Winston, 1975.

Des Pres, Terrence. "Holocaust *Laughter?*" In *Writing and the Holocaust*, edited by Berel Lang, 216–33. New York: Holmes and Meier, 1988.

Doherty, Thomas. "Art Spiegelman's *Maus*: Graphic Art and the Holocaust." *American Literature* 68, no.1 (1996): 69–84.

Dwork, Deborah. *Children with a Star: Jewish Youth in Nazi Europe*. New Haven, CT: Yale University Press, 1991.

Eakin, Paul John. *How Our Lives Become Stories: Making Selves*. Ithaca, NY: Cornell University Press, 1999.

Egan, Susanna. *Mirror Talk: Genres of Crisis in Contemporary Autobiography*. Chapel Hill: University of North Carolina Press, 1999.

Ewert, Jeanne C. "Reading Visual Narrative: Art Spiegelman's *Maus*." *Narrative* 8, no.1 (2000): 87–103.

Faye, Esther. "Missing the 'Real' Trace of Trauma: How the Second Generation Remember the Holocaust." *American Imago: Studies in Psychoanalysis and Culture* 58, no. 2 (2001): 525–44.

Feinstein, Stephen C. "Mediums of Memory: Artistic Responses of the Second Generation." In *Breaking Crystal: History and Memory after Auschwitz*, edited by Efraim Sicher, 201–51. Urbana: University of Illinois Press, 1998.

Felman, Shoshana. "The Return of the Voice: Claude Lanzmann's *Shoah*." In *Testimony: Crises of Witnessing in Literature, Psychoanalysis, and History*, by Shoshana Felman and Dori Laub, 204–83. New York: Routledge, 1992.

Felman, Shoshana, and Dori Laub. *Testimony: Crises of Witnessing in Literature, Psychoanalysis, and History*. New York: Routledge, 1992.

Fine, Ellen S. "Transmission of Memory: The Post-Holocaust Generation in the Diaspora." In *Breaking Crystal: History and Memory after Auschwitz*, edited by Efraim Sicher, 185–200. Urbana: University of Illinois Press, 1998.

Finkelstein, Norman. *The Holocaust Industry*. London: Verso, 2000.

Finkielkraut, Alain. *The Imaginary Jew*. Translated by Kevin O'Neill and David Suchoff. Lincoln: University of Nebraska Press, 1994.

Flanzbaum, Hilene, ed. *The Americanization of the Holocaust*. Baltimore: Johns Hopkins University Press, 1999.

———. "Introduction: The Americanization of the Holocaust." In *The Americanization of the Holocaust*, edited by Hilene Flanzbaum, 1–17. Baltimore: Johns Hopkins University Press, 1999.

Fresco, Nadine. "Remembering the Unknown." *International Review of Psychoanalysis* 11 (1984): 417–27.

Freud, Sigmund. "Beyond the Pleasure Principle." In *The Essentials of Psychoanalysis*, selected by Anna Freud, translated by James Strachey, 218–68. London: Penguin, 1986.

———. "Family Romances." In *The Penguin Freud Library*. Vol. 7, *On Sexuality: Three Essays on the Theory of Sexuality and Other Works*, translated and edited by James Strachey, 219–25. London: Penguin, 1977.

———. *Moses and Monotheism*. In *The Penguin Freud Library*. Vol. 13, *The Origins of Religion*, edited by Albert Dickson and translated and edited by James Strachey, 237–86. London: Penguin, 1990.

———. "Mourning and Melancholia." In *The Standard Edition of the Complete Psychological Works of Sigmund Freud*. Vol. 14, *On the History of the Psycho-Analytic Movement, Papers on Metapsychology, and Other Works*, edited and translated by James Strachey, 237–60. London: Hogarth, 1962.

———. "A Note Upon the 'Mystic Writing-Pad.'" In *The Standard Edition of the Complete Psychological Works of Sigmund Freud*. Vol. 19, *The Ego and the Id and Other Works*, edited and translated by James Strachey, 225–32. London: Hogarth, 1961.

———. "Remembering, Repeating and Working-Through." In *The Standard Edition of the Complete Psychological Works of Sigmund Freud*. Vol. 12, *The Case of Schreber, Papers on Technique, and Other Works*, edited and translated by James Strachey, 145–56. London: Hogarth, 1962.

———. "The Uncanny." In *The Standard Edition of the Complete Psychological Works of Sigmund Freud*. Vol. 17, *An Infantile Neurosis and Other Works*, edited and translated by James Strachey, 219–52. London: Hogarth, 1955.

Frey, Hugo, and Benjamin Noys. "History in the Graphic Novel." *Rethinking History* 6, no. 3 (2002): 255–59.

Friedlander, Saul. *Nazi Germany and the Jews: Volume 1: The Years of Persecution, 1933–1939*. London: Weidenfeld and Nicolson, 1997.

Friedman, Michelle A. "The Labor of Remembrance." In *Mapping Jewish Identities*, edited by Laurence J. Silberstein, 97–121. New York: New York University Press, 2000.

Furman, Andrew. "Inheriting the Holocaust: Jewish American Fiction and the Double Bind of the Second-Generation Survivor." *The Americanization of the Holocaust*, edited by Hilene Flanzbaum, 83–101. Baltimore: Johns Hopkins University Press, 1999.

Gathercole, Peter, and David Lowenthal, eds. *The Politics of the Past*. London: Routledge, 1990.

Geis, Deborah R. *Considering* Maus: *Approaches to Art Spiegelman's "Survivor's Tale" of the Holocaust*. Tuscaloosa: University of Alabama Press, 2003.

Gelley, Ora. "Critical Response I: A Response to Dominick LaCapra's 'Lanzmann's *Shoah*.'" *Critical Inquiry* 24 (1988): 830–32.

Gilbert, Martin. *The Holocaust: The Jewish Tragedy*. London: Fontana, 1997.

Gilman, Sander L., and Jack Zipes, eds. *Yale Companion to Jewish Writing and Thought in German Culture, 1096–1996.* New Haven, CT: Yale University Press, 1997.

Ginzberg, Louis, ed. *Legends of the Jews.* 7 vols. Philadelphia: Jewish Publication Society of America, 1954.

Goertz, Karein. "Transgenerational Representation of the Holocaust: From Memory to 'Post-Memory.'" *World Literature Today* 72, no. 1 (1998): 33–38.

Goldman, Anne E. "Is That What She Said?: The Politics of Collaborative Autobiography." *Cultural Critique* 25 (1993): 177–204.

Gomel, Elana. "Aliens Among Us: Fascism and Narrativity." *Journal of Narrative Theory* 30, no. 1 (2000): 127–62.

Greenspan, Henry. "Lives as Texts: Symptoms as Modes of Recounting in the Life Histories of Holocaust Survivors." In *Storied Lives: The Cultural Politics of Self-Understanding,* edited by George C. Rosenwald and Richard L. Ochberg, 145–64. New Haven, CT: Yale University Press, 1992.

Grimwood, Marita. "Postmemorial Positions: Reading and Writing after the Holocaust in Anne Michaels's *Fugitive Pieces.*" *Canadian Jewish Studies / Études juives canadiennes* 11 (2003): 111–30.

Grubrich-Simitis, Ilse. "From Concretism to Metaphor: Thoughts on Some Theoretical and Technical Aspects of the Psychoanalytic Work with Children of Holocaust Survivors." *Psychoanalytic Study of the Child* 39 (1984): 301–19.

Gubar, Susan. "Empathic Identification in Anne Michaels's *Fugitive Pieces*: Masculinity and Poetry after Auschwitz." *Signs* 28, no. 1 (2002): 249–76.

Hansen, Miriam Bratu. "*Schindler's List* is not *Shoah*: The Second Commandment, Popular Modernism, and Public Memory." *Critical Enquiry* 22, no. 2 (1996): 292–312.

Harrison, Keith. "Telling the Untellable: Spiegelman's *Maus.*" *Rendezvous* 34, no. 1 (1999): 59–73.

Hart, Alexander. *Writing the Diaspora: A Bibliography and Critical Commentary on Post-Shoah English Language Jewish Fiction.* PhD diss., University of British Columbia, 1996.

Hass, Aaron. *In the Shadow of the Holocaust: The Second Generation.* Cambridge: Cambridge University Press, 1996.

Herzog, James. "World Beyond Metaphor: Thoughts on the Transmission of Trauma." In *Generations of the Holocaust,* edited by M. S. Bergmann, and M. E. Jucovy, 103–20. New York: Basic Books, 1982.

Higonnet, Anne. *Pictures of Innocence: The History and Crisis of Ideal Childhood.* London: Thames and Hudson, 1998.

Hillger, Annick. "'Afterbirth of Earth': Messianic Materialism in Anne Michaels' *Fugitive Pieces.*" *Canadian Literature* 60 (1999): 28–45.

Hirsch, Marianne, ed., *The Familial Gaze.* Hanover, NH: University Press of New England, 1999.

———. *Family Frames: Photography, Narrative and Postmemory.* Cambridge, MA: Harvard University Press, 1997.

———. "Projected Memory: Holocaust Photographs in Personal and Public Fantasy." In *Acts of Memory: Cultural Recall in the Present*, edited by Mieke Bal, Jonathan Crewe, and Leo Spitzer, 3–23. Hanover, NH: University Press of New England, 1999.

———. "Surviving Images: Holocaust Photographs and the Work of Postmemory." In *Visual Culture and the Holocaust*, edited by Barbie Zelizer, 215–46. London: Athlone, 2001.

Horowitz, Sara R. "Auto/biography and Fiction after Auschwitz: Probing the Boundaries of Second-Generation Aesthetics." In *Breaking Crystal: History and Memory after Auschwitz*, edited by Efraim Sicher, 276–94. Urbana: University of Illinois Press, 1998.

———. *Voicing the Void: Muteness and Memory in Holocaust Fiction*. Albany: State University of New York, 1997.

Hungerford, Amy. "Surviving Rego Park: Holocaust Theory from Art Spiegelman to Berel Lang." In *The Americanization of the Holocaust*, edited by Hilene Flanzbaum, 102–24. Baltimore: Johns Hopkins University Press, 1999.

Hutcheon, Linda. "Literature Meets History: Counter-Discursive 'Comix.'" *Anglia Zeitschrift für Englische Philologie* 117, no. 1 (1999): 4–14.

Huyssen, Andreas. "Of Mice and Mimesis: Reading Spiegelman with Adorno." In *Visual Culture and the Holocaust*, edited by Barbie Zelizer, 28–42. London: Athlone, 2001.

Iadonisi, Rick. "Bleeding History and Owning His [Father's] Story: *Maus* and Collaborative Autobiography." *CEA Critic* 57, no. 1 (1994): 41–56.

Jackson, Rosemary. *Fantasy: The Literature of Subversion*. London: Routledge, 1991.

Jankélévitch, Vladimir. "Should We Pardon Them?" Translated by Ann Hobart. *Critical Inquiry* 22 (1996): 552–72.

Jardine, Lisa. "Pieces of Mind." *Times* metro section, December 2–January 2, 1998.

Jewish Encyclopedia, The. Vols. 1–124. Edited by Isidore Singer. New York: Funk and Wagnalls, 1901–1906.

Kadar, Marlene, Linda Warley, Jeanne Perreault, and Susanna Egan, eds. *Tracing the Autobiographical*. Waterloo, ON: Wilfrid Laurier University Press, 2005.

Kaplan, Alice Yaeger. "Thewelweit and Spiegelman: Of Men and Mice." In *Discussions in Contemporary Culture 4: Remaking History*, edited by Barbara Kruger and Phil Mariani, 150–72. Seattle: Bay Press, 1989.

Kaufman, Eleanor. "Falling From the Sky: Trauma in Perec's *W* and Caruth's *Unclaimed Experience*." *Diacritics* 28, no. 4 (1988): 44–53.

Kellerman, Natan P. F. "Psychopathology in Children of Holocaust Survivors: A Review of the Research Literature." *Israeli Journal of Psychiatry and Related Sciences* 38, no. 1 (2001): 36–46.

Kertzer, Adrienne. "Circular Journeys and Glass Bridges: The Geography of Postmemory." In *Tracing the Autobiographical*, edited by Marlene Kadar, Linda Warley, Jeanne Perreault, and Susanna Egan, 205–21. Waterloo, ON: Wilfrid Laurier University Press, 2005.

———. "*Fugitive Pieces*: Listening as a Holocaust Survivor's Child." *English Studies in Canada* 26, no. 2 (2000): 193–217.

Kessel, Barbara. *Suddenly Jewish: Jews Raised as Gentiles Discover their Jewish Roots.* Hanover, NH: Brandeis University Press, 2000.

King, Nicola. *Memory, Narrative, Identity: Remembering the Self.* Edinburgh: Edinburgh University Press, 2000.

———. "'We Come After': Remembering the Holocaust." In *Literature and the Contemporary: Fictions and Theories of the Present*, edited by Roger Luckhurst and Peter Marks, 94–108. Harlow, England: Longman, 1999.

Koch, Gertrud. "'Against All Odds' or the Will to Survive: Moral Conclusions from Narrative Closure." *History and Memory* 9 (1997): 393–408.

Kremer, S. Lillian. *Witness Through the Imagination: Jewish American Holocaust Literature.* Detroit: Wayne State University Press, 1989.

Kruger, Barbara, and Phil Mariani, eds. *Discussions in Contemporary Culture 4: Remaking History.* Seattle: Bay Press, 1989.

LaCapra, Dominick. "Critical Response II: Equivocations of Autonomous Art." *Critical Enquiry* 24 (1988): 832–36.

———. *History and Memory after Auschwitz.* Ithaca, NY: Cornell University Press, 1998.

———. "Lanzmann's *Shoah*: 'Here There Is No Why.'" *Critical Enquiry* 24 (1988): 231–69.

———. *Representing the Holocaust: History, Theory, Trauma.* Ithaca, NY: Cornell University Press, 1994.

———. *Writing History, Writing Trauma.* Baltimore: Johns Hopkins University Press, 2001.

Lang, Berel. *Holocaust Representation: Art within the Limits of History and Ethics.* Baltimore: The Johns Hopkins University Press, 2000.

———, ed. *Writing and the Holocaust.* New York: Holmes and Meier, 1988.

Langer, Lawrence L. *Admitting the Holocaust: Collected Essays.* Oxford: Oxford University Press, 1995.

———. *Holocaust Testimonies: The Ruins of Memory.* New Haven, CT: Yale University Press, 1991.

———. *Preempting the Holocaust.* New Haven, CT: Yale University Press, 1998.

———. *Versions of Survival: The Holocaust and the Human Spirit.* Albany: State University of New York Press, 1982.

Laplanche, J., and J.-B. Pontalis. *The Language of Psycho-Analysis.* Translated by Donald Nicholson-Smith. London: Hogarth, 1973.

Lappin, Elena. "The Man with Two Heads." *Granta* 66 (1999): 7–65.

Laub, Dori. "Bearing Witness or the Vicissitudes of Listening." In *Testimony: Crises of Witnessing in Literature, Psychoanalysis, and History*, by Shoshana Felman and Dori Laub, 75–92. New York: Routledge, 1992.

———. "An Event without a Witness: Truth, Testimony and Survival." In *Testimony: Crises of Witnessing in Literature, Psychoanalysis, and History*, by Shoshana Felman and Dori Laub, 75–92. New York: Routledge, 1992.

Lehmann, Sophia. "'And Here [Their] Troubles Began': The Legacy of the Holocaust in the Writing of Cynthia Ozick, Art Spiegelman, and Philip Roth." *Clio* 28, no. 1 (1998): 29–52.

Lerner, Michael, ed. *Best Contemporary Jewish Writing*. San Francisco: Jossey-Bass, 2001.

Levine, Michael G. "Necessary Stains: Art Spiegelman's *Maus* and the Bleeding of History." In *Considering* Maus: *Approaches to Art Spiegelman's "Survivor's Tale" of the Holocaust,* by Deborah R. Geis, 63–104. Tuscaloosa: University of Alabama Press, 2003.

Leys, Ruth. *Trauma: A Genealogy*. London: University of Chicago Press, 2000.

Lipstadt, Deborah. *Denying the Holocaust: The Growing Assault on Truth and Memory*. New York: Free Press, 1993.

Lubow, Arthur. "Crawling into the Brain of Art Spiegelman." *Graphis* 315 (1998): 40–49.

Luckhurst, Roger, and Peter Marks, eds. *Literature and the Contemporary: Fictions and Theories of the Present*. Harlow: Longman, 1999.

Ma, Sheng-mei. "*The Great Dictator* and *Maus*: 'The Comical' before and after the Holocaust." *Proteus* 12 (1995): 47–50.

———. "Mourning with the (as a) Jew: Metaphor, Ethnicity, and the Holocaust in Art Spiegelman's *Maus*." *Studies in American Jewish Literature* 16 (1997): 115–29.

Mandel, Naomi. "Rethinking 'After Auschwitz': Against a Rhetoric of the Unspeakable in Holocaust Writing." *boundary 2* 28 (2001): 203–28.

Marcus, Laura. *Auto/biographical Discourses: Theory, Criticism, Practice*. Manchester: Manchester University Press, 1994.

Mazower, Mark. *Inside Hitler's Greece: The Experience of Occupation, 1941–44*. New Haven, CT: Yale University Press, 1993.

McCann, W. J. "'Volk und Germanentum': The Presentation of the Past in Nazi Germany." In *The Politics of the Past*, edited by Peter Gathercole and David Lowenthal, 74–88. London: Routledge, 1994.

McGlothlin, Erin. *Holocaust Literature of the Second Generation: Legacies of Survival and Perpetration*. Rochester, NY: Camden House, 2006.

Michaels, Walter Benn. "'You Who Never Was There': Slavery and the New Historicism—Deconstruction and the Holocaust." In *The Americanization of the Holocaust*, edited by Hilene Flanzbaum, 181–97. Baltimore: Johns Hopkins University Press, 1999.

Mikics, David. "Underground Comics and Survival Tales: *Maus* in Context." In *Considering* Maus: *Approaches to Art Spiegelman's "Survivor's Tale" of the Holocaust*, by Deborah R. Geis, 15–25. Tuscaloosa: University of Alabama Press, 2003.

Miller, Nancy K. "Cartoons of the Self: Portrait of the Artist as a Young Murderer: Art Spiegelman's *Maus*." *M/E/A/N/I/N/G* 12 (1992): 43–54.

———. "Representing Others: Gender and the Subjects of Autobiography." *differences* 6 (1994): 1–27.

Mintz, Alan. *Popular Culture and the Shaping of Holocaust Memory in America*. Seattle: University of Washington Press, 2001.

Morahg, Gilead. "Breaking Silence: Israel's Fantastic Fiction of the Holocaust." In *The Boom in Contemporary Israeli Fiction*, edited by Alan Mintz, 143–83. Hanover, NH: University Press of New England, 1997.

———. "Israel's New Literature of the Holocaust: The Case of David Grossman's *See Under: Love.*" *Modern Fiction Studies* 45 (1999): 457–79.

Muller, Gilbert H. *New Strangers in Paradise: The Immigrant Experience and Contemporary American Fiction.* Lexington: University Press of Kentucky, 1999.

Neuman, Shirley, ed. *Autobiography and Questions of Gender.* London: Frank Cass, 1991.

New Fontana Dictionary of Modern Thought, The. Edited by Alan Bullock and Stephen Trombley. London: HarperCollins, 1999.

New Standard Jewish Encyclopedia, The. Edited by Geoffrey Wigoder. New York: Facts on File, 1992.

Nicholls, Peter. "The Belated Postmodern: History, Phantoms, and Toni Morrison." In *Psychoanalytic Criticism: A Reader,* edited by Sue Vice, 50–74. Cambridge: Polity Press, 1996.

Nora, Pierre. "Between Memory and History: *Les lieux de mémoire.*" *Representations* 26 (1989): 7–25.

Novick, Peter. *The Holocaust in American Life.* New York: Mariner, 2000.

Orvell, Miles. "Writing Posthistorically: Krazy Kat, *Maus,* and the Contemporary Fiction Cartoon." *American Literary History* 4 (1992): 110–28.

Ozick, Cynthia. "The Rights of History and the Rights of Imagination." *Commentary* 107 (1999): 22–27.

Parry, Ann. "'. . . to give. . . death a place': Rejecting the 'Ineffability' of the Holocaust: The Work of Gillian Rose and Anne Michaels." *Canadian Literature* 160 (1999): 28–45.

Patterson, David. *Sun Turned to Darkness: Memory and Recovery in the Holocaust Memoir.* Syracuse, NY: Syracuse University Press, 1998.

Raczymow, Henri. "Memory Shot through with Holes." *Yale French Studies* 85, *Discourses of Jewish Identity in Twentieth-Century France,* edited by Alan Astro (1994): 98–105.

Ramadanovic, Petar. "When '*To Die in Freedom*' Is Written in English." *Diacritics* 28 (1998): 54–67.

Ramras-Rauch, Gila. "The Holocaust and the Fantastic: A Negative Revelation?" In *The Scope of the Fantastic—Culture, Biography, Themes, Children's Literature,* edited by Robert A. Collins and Howard D. Pearce, 33–42. Westport, CT: Greenwood, 1985.

Rapaport, Herman. "Archive Trauma." *Diacritics* 28 (1998): 68–81.

Ravvin, Norman. *A House of Words: Jewish Writing, Identity and Memory.* Québec City: McGill and Queen's University Press, 1997.

Reizbaum, Marilyn. "Surviving on Cat and *Maus*: Art Spiegelman's Holocaust Tale." In *Mapping Jewish Identities,* edited by Laurence J. Silberstein, 122–44. New York: New York University Press, 2000.

Rimmon-Kenan, Shlomith. *Narrative Fiction: Contemporary Poetics.* London: Methuen, 1983.

Rose, Jacqueline. *The Haunting of Sylvia Plath.* London: Virago, 1992.

Rosen, Alan. "The Language of Survival: English as Metaphor in Spiegelman's *Maus.*" *Prooftexts* 15 (1995): 249–62.

Rosen, Norma. "Poetry after Auschwitz." *Partisan Review* 65 (1998): 313–17.

Rosenberg, Pnina. "*Mickey Mouse in Gurs*—Humour, Irony and Criticism in Works of Art Produced in the Gurs Internment Camp." *Rethinking History* 6 (2002): 273–92.

Rosenwald, George C., and Richard L. Ochberg, eds. *Storied Lives: The Cultural Politics of Self-Understanding.* New Haven, CT: Yale University Press, 1992.

Rosten, Leo. *The Joys of Yiddish.* London: Penguin, 1971.

Rothberg, Michael. *Traumatic Realism: The Demands of Holocaust Representation.* Minneapolis: University of Minneapolis Press, 2000.

———. "'We Were Talking Jewish': Art Spiegelman's *Maus* as Holocaust Production." *Contemporary Literature* 35 (1994): 661–87.

Rowland-Klein, Dani, and Rosemary Dunlop. "The Transmission of Trauma across Generations: Identification with Parental Trauma in Children of Holocaust Survivors." *Australian and New Zealand Journal of Psychiatry* 31 (1997): 358–69.

Schama, Simon. *Landscape and Memory.* New York: Vintage, 1985.

Schaverien, Joy. "Inheritance: Jewish Identity and the Legacy of the Holocaust Mediated Through Art Psychotherapy Groups." *British Journal of Psychotherapy* 15 (1998): 65–79.

Schwarz, Daniel. *Imagining the Holocaust.* New York: St. Martin's, 1999.

Segal, Lore. "Memory: The Problems of Imagining the Past." In *Writing and the Holocaust*, edited by Berel Lang, 58–65. New York: Holmes and Meier, 1988.

Seidler, Victor Jeleniewski. *Shadows of the Shoah: Jewish Identity and Belonging.* Oxford: Berg, 2000.

Sicher, Efraim, ed. *Breaking Crystal: History and Memory after Auschwitz.* Urbana: University of Illinois Press, 1998.

———. "The Burden of Memory: The Writing of the Post-Holocaust Generation." In *Breaking Crystal: History and Memory after Auschwitz*, edited by Efraim Sicher, 19–88. Urbana: University of Illinois Press, 1998.

———. "The Future of the Past: Countermemory and Postmemory in Contemporary American Post-Holocaust Narratives." *History and Memory* 12, no. 2 (2000): 56–91.

———. "The Holocaust in the Postmodernist Era." In *Breaking Crystal: History and Memory after Auschwitz*, edited by Efraim Sicher, 297–328. Urbana: University of Illinois Press, 1998.

———. Introduction to *Breaking Crystal: History and Memory after Auschwitz*, edited by Efraim Sicher, 1–16. Urbana: University of Illinois Press, 1998.

Silberstein, Laurence J., ed. *Mapping Jewish Identities.* New York: New York University Press, 2000.

Solms, Wilhelm. "On the Demonising of Jews and Gypsies in Fairy Tales." In *Sinti and Roma: Gypsies in German-Speaking Society and Literature*, edited by Susan Tebbut, 91–106. New York: Berghahn, 1998.

Solokoff, Naomi B. *Imagining the Child in Modern Jewish Fiction.* Baltimore: Johns Hopkins University Press, 1992.

Sontag, Susan. *Illness as Metaphor* and *Aids and Its Metaphors.* London: Penguin, 1991.

Sorcher, Nechama, and Lisa J. Cohen. "Trauma in Children of Holocaust Survivors: Transgenerational Effects." *American Journal of Orthopsychiatry* 67 (1997): 493–500.

Spiegelman, Art. *Art Spiegelman: Comix, Essays, Graphics and Scraps. From* Maus *to* Now *to* Maus *to* Now. Rome: Sellerio Editore—La Centrale dell'Arte, 1999.

———. "Little Orphan Annie's Eyeballs." In *Art Spiegelman: Comix, Essays, Graphics and Scraps. From* Maus *to* Now *to* Maus *to* Now, 17–18. Rome: Sellerio Editore—La Centrale dell'Arte, 1999.

———. "Looney Tunes, Zionism and the Jewish Question." In *Art Spiegelman: Comix, Essays, Graphics and Scraps. From* Maus *to* Now *to* Maus *to* Now, 14–16. Rome: Sellerio Editore—La Centrale dell'Arte, 1999.

Stadden, Pamela. "Narrative Techniques and Holocaust Literature: Joseph Skibell's *A Blessing on the Moon.*" *Studies in American Jewish Literature* 24 (2005): 153–57.

Steedman, Carolyn. *Landscape for a Good Woman: A Story of Two Lives.* London: Virago, 1986.

Steiner, George. *In Bluebeard's Castle: Some Notes towards the Re-definition of Culture.* London: Faber and Faber, 1974.

———. "A Kind of Survivor." In *Language and Silence,* by George Steiner, 164–79. London: Faber and Faber, 1985.

———. *Language and Silence.* London: Faber and Faber, 1985.

———. "A Season in Hell." In *In Bluebeard's Castle: Some Notes towards the Re-definition of Culture,* by George Steiner, 31–48. London: Faber and Faber, 1974.

Stewart, Victoria. *Women's Autobiography: War and Trauma.* Basingstoke, England: Palgrave Macmillan, 2003.

Tabachnik, S. E. "Of *Maus* and Memory: The Structure of Art Spiegelman's Graphic Novel of the Holocaust." *Word and Image* 9 (1993): 154–62.

Tal, Kalì. *Words of Hurt: Reading the Literatures of Trauma.* Cambridge: Cambridge University Press, 1996.

Tanner, Laura. *Intimate Violence: Reading Rape and Torture in Twentieth Century Fiction.* Bloomington: Indiana University Press, 1994.

Tebbut, Susan, ed. *Sinti and Roma: Gypsies in German-Speaking Society and Literature.* New York: Berghahn, 1998.

Thomas, Laurence Mordekhai. "Suffering as a Moral Beacon: Blacks and Jews." In *The Americanization of the Holocaust,* edited by Hilene Flanzbaum, 198–210. Baltimore: Johns Hopkins University Press, 1999.

Todorov, Tzvetan. *Introduction à la littérature fantastique.* Paris: Seuil, 1970.

Van der Kolk, Bessel A., and Onno Van der Hart. "The Intrusive Past: The Inflexibility of Memory and the Engraving of Trauma." In *Trauma: Explorations in Memory,* edited by Cathy Caruth, 158–82. Baltimore: Johns Hopkins University Press, 1995.

Vice, Sue. *Holocaust Fiction.* London: Routledge, 2000.

———. *Psychoanalytic Criticism: A Reader.* Cambridge: Polity Press, 1996.

Wardi, Dina. *Memorial Candles.* London: Routledge, 1992.

Warner, Marina. *From the Beast to the Blonde: On Fairytales and their Tellers.* London: Chatto and Windus, 1994.

Wasserstein, Bernard. *Vanishing Diaspora: The Jews in Europe Since 1945.* London: Penguin, 1997.

Weissman, Gary. *Fantasies of Witnessing: Postwar Efforts to Experience the Holocaust.* Ithaca, NY: Cornell University Press, 2004.

Whitehead, Anne. "A Still, Small Voice: Letter-Writing, Testimony and the Project of Address in Etty Hillesum's *Letters from Westerbork*." *Cultural Values* 5 (2001): 79–96.

Wilner, Arlene Fish. "'Happy, Happy Ever After': Story and History in Art Spiegelman's *Maus*." In *Considering Maus: Approaches to Art Spiegelman's "Survivor's Tale" of the Holocaust,* by Deborah R. Geis, 105–21. Tuscaloosa: University of Alabama Press, 2003.

———. *Trauma Fiction.* Edinburgh: Edinburgh University Press, 2004.

Yablonka, Hanna. "The Formation of Holocaust Consciousness in the State of Israel: The Early Days." In *Breaking Crystal: History and Memory after Auschwitz,* edited by Efraim Sicher, 119–36. Urbana: University of Illinois Press, 1998.

Yaoz, Hanna. "Inherited Fear: Second-Generation Poets and Novelists in Israel." In *Breaking Crystal: History and Memory after Auschwitz,* edited by Efraim Sicher, 160–69. Urbana: University of Illinois Press, 1998.

Young, James E. *At Memory's Edge: After-Images of the Holocaust in Contemporary Art and Architecture.* New York: Yale University Press, 2000.

———. "The Holocaust as Vicarious Past: Art Spiegelman's *Maus* and the Afterimages of History." *Critical Inquiry* 24 (1998): 666–99.

———. *The Texture of Memory: Holocaust Memorials and Meaning.* New Haven, CT: Yale University Press, 1993.

———. *Writing and Rewriting the Holocaust: Narrative and the Consequences of Interpretation.* Bloomington: Indiana University Press, 1990.

Yudkin, Leon I. "Holocaust Trauma in the Second Generation: The Hebrew Fiction of David Grossman and Savyon Liebrecht." In *Breaking Crystal: History and Memory after Auschwitz,* edited by Efraim Sicher, 170–81. Urbana: University of Illinois Press, 1998.

Zelizer, Barbie, ed. *Visual Culture and the Holocaust.* London: Athlone, 2001.

Zinsser, William, ed. *Inventing the Truth: The Art and Craft of Memoir.* Boston: Houghton Mifflin, 1987.

Zipes, Jack. *Fairy Tales and the Art of Subversion: The Classical Genre for Children and the Process of Civilization.* New York: Routledge, 1991.

Zucotti, Susan. *The Italians and the Holocaust.* London: Peter Halban, 1987.

Index